1 Peter

A Collaborative Commentary

1 Peter

A Collaborative Commentary

Edited by
PETER R. RODGERS

RESOURCE *Publications* • Eugene, Oregon

1 PETER
A Collaborative Commentary

Copyright © 2017 Wipf and Stock Publishers. All rights reserved. Except for brief quotations in critical publications or reviews, no part of this book may be reproduced in any manner without prior written permission from the publisher. Write: Permissions, Wipf and Stock Publishers, 199 W. 8th Ave., Suite 3, Eugene, OR 97401.

Resource Publications
An Imprint of Wipf and Stock Publishers
199 W. 8th Ave., Suite 3
Eugene, OR 97401

www.wipfandstock.com

PAPERBACK ISBN: 978-1-5326-0598-7
HARDCOVER ISBN: 978-1-5326-0600-7
EBOOK ISBN: 978-1-5326-0599-4

Manufactured in the U.S.A.   09/07/17

Dedicated to all Christians throughout the world
Who suffer for the name of Christ

1 Peter 5:9

Contents

Contributors | ix
Preface | xi
Abbreviations | xiii

Introduction to the First Letter of Peter | 1
    By Peter R. Rodgers

1 Peter 1:1–2 | 12
    by Peter R. Rodgers

1 Peter 1:3–9 | 16
    by Joel Moody

1 Peter 1:10–12 | 25
    by Katherine Atkinson

1 Peter 1:13–21 | 31
    by Joseph Muradyan

1 Peter 1:22—2:3 | 43
    by Zach Mazotti

1 Peter 2:4–10 | 53
    by Max Botner and Peter R. Rodgers

1 Peter 2:11–17 | 62
    by William R. Simmons

1 Peter 2:18–25 | 70
    by Peter R. Rodgers

1 Peter 3:1–7 | 79
    by Brittany K. Hale

1 Peter 3:8–12 | 88
    By Janet C. Hanson

1 Peter 3:13–17 | 96
    by Amanda Van Vliet Snyder

1 Peter 3:18–22 | 104
   By Stephen R. Rodriguez

1 Peter 4:1–6 | 113
   by Corbett Cutts

1 Peter 4:7–11 | 122
   by Amanda Beuerman

1 Peter 4:12–19 | 128
   by Aubrey Freely

1 Peter 5:1–7 | 137
   by Brian Lucas

1 Peter 5:8–11 | 149
   by Keith Calara

1 Peter 5:12–14 | 157
   by Chris Maggitti

Excursus 1—The Text of 1 Peter | 165
   By Peter R. Rodgers and Stephen Rodriguez

Excursus 2—The Old Testament in 1 Peter | 168
   By Peter R. Rodgers and Richard Rohlfing

Holy and Royal Priesthood—
Interpretation of 1 Peter 2:5, 9 in Church History | 178
   By Greg Flagg

The Persecutions in 1 Peter | 184
   By Jonathan Elliott

Temple Imagery in 1 Peter | 190
   by Vince Conroy

Bibliography | 201
Index of Names | 211
Index of Scripture and Other Ancient Texts | 215

Contributors

Katherine Atkinson teaches at Bradshaw Christian Academy

Amanda Beuerman is a Campus Leader with Cru Ministries in Sacramento

Max Botner (PhD St. Andrew's University), Researcher and Lecturer in New Testament and Early Christianity at Goethe-Universität, Frankfurt am Main.

Keith Calara is Director of Youth and Family ministries, Napa Methodist Church

Vince Conroy is an MAT student at Fuller Theological Seminary

Corbett Cutts teaches at William Jessup University

Jonathan Elliott works with InterVarsity Christian Fellowship in Sacramento

Greg Flagg is Administrative Assistant at the Center for Bible Study, Sacramento.

Aubrey Freely teaches at William Jessup University

Brittany Hale is an MAT candidate at Fuller Theological Seminary

Janet Hanson teaches at William Jessup University

Brian Lucas teaches at William Jessup University

Chris Maggitti is a candidate for the ordained ministry in the Evangelical Presbyterian Church.

Zach Mazotti teaches at Woodland Christian Academy

Joel Moody is a student at Princeton Theological Seminary

Joseph Muradyan works for the California Department of Water Resources

Peter R. Rodgers is Vicar of St. Andrew's Episcopal Church, Antelope, California and Director of the Center for Bible Study

Stephen Rodriguez is Global Outreach Coordinator at River City Christian Church, Sacramento, California.

Richard Rohlfing is a PhD candidate at Durham University, England

Will Simmons works for the Environmental Protection Agency, California

Amanda VanVliet Snyder is campus Pastor at Alaska Christian College

Preface

This commentary began with a question. When my long-time friend N.T. Wright was lecturing in Sacramento, California in 2015 he asked me: "So when are you going to write your commentary on First Peter?" It was a fair question since he has known of my interest in this letter since our days as graduate students in Oxford in the mid-seventies. I had had no plans for such a commentary, but Tom's question changed that. However, since I was increasingly convinced that Peter collaborated with several people in writing the letter, I decided not to research and write it on my own. I recruited a number of my most promising students at Fuller Theological Seminary, Sacramento campus. Thus was born the idea of a collaborative commentary.

To the 20 contributors to this commentary I owe a great debt of thanks. They have been wonderful conversation partners in the study of the letter. But as the project progressed others wished to play a part. By the time I was ready to collect and edit the contributions a number of other students and colleagues volunteered to help in different ways. I wish to thank all those who participated in this editorial team. In addition to contributors Janet Hanson who assembled the bibliography, Joseph Muradyan who offered valuable formatting assistance, and Brian Lucas who read through the whole of the commentary twice, and offered encouragement at every stage of the project, I wish to record my thanks to the following: Elizabeth Crane, Kathleen Doty, Adriana Findlay, Trapper Garrett, Jim Shields and Jeremiah Wenneker. To the Seitz brothers I owe a special debt of gratitude: To Daniel for valuable comments on form and content, and to Darren for formatting all the Greek and Hebrew in the volume to conform to SBL font. I am also grateful to Patrick Oden, Jessica Rentz, and Amanda Yates Rodgers for compiling the indexes. Dr. David R. Vinson gave valuable advice regarding how research is conducted in the scientific community, and helped me to see how that model might be applied to Biblical studies. We are also grateful to Matthew Wimer and the editorial team at Wipf and Stock for their efficient and courteous work in seeing this commentary through the publication process. This has been a collaborative effort on a larger scale than I could have imagined when I began the project.

Halfway through this process Fuller Theological Seminary announced the closure of the Sacramento campus, where I had taught for thirteen years. Through Fuller Northern California I worked with a remarkable group of students, and a number of them contributed to this commentary. I am only sorry that I could not have included more of the excellent people who took my classes over the years. I hope that this commentary might provide a model for scholars to produce similar commentaries on other books of scripture. And I hope that this collaborative commentary on 1 Peter will stand as a monument to the scholarship and fellowship at Fuller Sacramento.

The Collaborators have agreed that any proceeds from the sale of the book should be donated to the Langham Foundation (formerly John Stott Ministries) to support theological education projects in the two-thirds world, where Christianity is growing but resources are scarce. In many of the places served by that ministry Christians are experiencing suffering for the name of Christ. It is to sisters and brothers throughout the world, who are being persecuted for their faith, that we dedicate this volume.

Peter R. Rodgers

Abbreviations

AB	Anchor Bible
ABD	Anchor Bible Dictionary
ACNT	Augsburg Commentary on the New Testament
ACC	Ancient Christian Commentary on Scripture New Testament
ANF	Ante-Nicene Fathers
ANTC	Abingdon New Testament Commentaries
BDAG	Bauer, Danker, Arndt, and Gingrich. *Greek-English Lexicon*, 2000
BDB	*The Brown, Driver, and Briggs Hebrew and English Lexicon.*
BECNT	Baker Exegetical Commentary on the New Testament
BTB	Biblical Theology Bulletin: Journal of Bible and Culture
BNTC	Black's New Testament Commentaries
BZ	Bibliche Zeitschrift
CE	Common Era
CEB	Common English Bible
CBQ	Catholic Biblical Quarterly
CNTUOT	Commentary on the New Testament Use of the Old Testament
CS 193	Crosby–Schøyen Coptic Codex 193
DLNT	Dictionary of the Later New Testament and its Developments
DOT	Dictionary of the Old Testament
DPL	Dictionary of Paul and His Letters
DSSE	Dead Sea Scrolls in English (Vermes)
DTIB	Dictionary for the Theological Interpretation of the Bible

EBR	Encyclopedia of the Bible and its Reception
ECM	*Editio Critica Maior*
EGGNT	Exegetical Guide to the Greek New Testament
ESV	English Standard Version
HALOT	The Hebrew and Aramaic Lexicon of the Old Testament
HRCS	Hatch and Redpath, Concordance to the Septuagint
ICC	International Critical Commentary
Int	Interpretation
IVPNTC	InterVarsity Press New Testament Commentary Series
JBL	Journal of Biblical Literature
JETS	*Journal of the Evangelical Theological Society*
JR	The Journal of Religion
JSNT*Sup*	Journal for the Study of the New Testament: Supplement Series
JTS	Journal of Theological Studies
KJV	King James Version
LCC	Library of Christian Classics
LCL	Loeb Classical Library
LNTS	The Library of New Testament Studies
LSJ	Liddell, H. G., R. Scott, H. S. Jones. *A Greek-English Lexicon*
LXX	Septuagint
MM	Moulton and Milligan, *Vocabulary of the Greek New Testament*
MSS	Manuscripts
MT	Masoretic Text
NA28	Nestle-Aland Greek New Testament, 28th edition
NABPR	National Association of Baptist Professors of Religion
NASB	New American Standard Bible
NCBC	New Century Bible Commentary
NE	Aristotle, *Nichomacian Ethics*
NETS	New English Translation of the Septuagint
Neot	Neotestamentica
NIBC	New Interrpreter Bible Commentary
NICNT	*New International Commentary on the New Testament*

NICOT	New International Commentary on the Old Testament
NIDNTTE	New International Dictionary of New Testament Theology and Exegesis
NIV	New International Version
NIVAC	NIV Application Commentary
NovT	Novum Testamentum
NovT*Sup*	Novum Testamentum Supplement
NRSV	New Revised Standard Version
NTS	New Testament Studies
OTP	Old Testament Pseudepigrapha (Charlesworth)
REB	Revised English Bible
RevExp	Review and Exposition
SBL	Society of Biblical Literature
SBLDS	Society of Biblical Literature Dissertation Series
SNTSMS	Society for New Testament Studies Monograph Series
SP	Sacra Pagina
TC	Textual Criticism
TCGNT	*Textual Commentary on the Greek New Testament, (2nd Ed, Metzger)*
TDNT	Theological Dictionary of the New Testament
THNTC	The Two Horizons New Testament Commentary
TNIVAC	The New International Version Application Commentary
TNTC	Tyndale New Testament Commentaries
WBC	Word Biblical Commentary
WUNT	Wissenschaftliche Untersuchungen Sum Neuen Testament
ZNW	Zeitschrift für die Neuetestamentliche Wissenschaft und die Kunde der älteren Kirche

Commentaries on 1 Peter, together with Dubis' *Handbook* and Forbes' *Exegetical Guide* are noted with last name and page number only in the footnotes.

Introduction to the First Letter of Peter
By Peter R. Rodgers

The First Letter of Peter has been treasured, preserved and handed on by Christians since the earliest days of the church. It purports to be a letter of the Apostle Peter to persecuted Christians in five provinces of Asia Minor. Despite its relative neglect, compared to the gospels and the writings of Paul, it is a succinct summary of Christian faith and life. Thus Martin Luther referred to the letter as "One of the noblest books of the New Testament," and ranked it on a level with Romans and John.[1] First Peter's theological depth, its vision of the suffering and glory of Christ, its practical encouragement to Christians under trial, and its extensive citation from the Old Testament: all these make it a letter worthy to be read, studied, memorized and lived out. Those of us collaborating in this commentary have been honored to live closely with this remarkable letter.

The introduction to a commentary customarily treats a number of issues in interpreting a scripture book. These include questions of authorship, date, recipients, occasion, sources, and major theological ideas. What follows is a review of these issues. For the final form of the introduction I take responsibility as editor. But from start to finish this commentary has been a collaborative effort, and it has been a privilege to think through comments of my collaborators, and at several points to moderate what I had written in light of new insights and fresh perspectives that they have contributed.

Author: The letter presents itself as written by the Apostle Peter, the chief spokesman for the Christians in the earliest days of the Church, and the one among Jesus' disciples whom he singled out as leader of the band. This view was commonly accepted throughout much of the church's history, but it has been challenged in modern times. Many commentators today place the letter in the latter decades of the first century.[2] J.H. Elliott, for

---

1. Jobes, 1.
2. Achetmeier, 43,

example, places the date of writing "sometime in the period between 73 and 92 CE."[3] Those who doubt that Peter was the author of the letter point to several factors in defense of their position:

1. The Greek of the letter is of too high a quality to have been written by a Galilean fisherman.
2. The thought and language is similar to that of Paul.
3. The pattern of ministry and church organization points to a later date than the middle of the first century CE.
4. The persecutions alluded to in the letter suggest a later date than the lifetime of the apostle Peter.

Each of these objections to Petrine authorship was ably addressed over a half century ago by A.F. Walls,[4] and we need not rehearse them here. Several major scholarly contributions in recent years have served to strengthen the picture of 1 Peter as a distinctive and independent letter, and also a work that could have been written in the middle of the first century.

J.H. Elliott has made a convincing case that 1 Peter is not dependent on Paul's thought and language. Commenting on 1 Peter's use of Isaiah 53 at the end of chapter 2, Elliott wrote, "In its fusion of biblical themes and motifs, kerygmatic formulas, and his extensive use of Isaiah 52–53 this passage illustrates both an independence from Pauline thought and a theological formulation that is as creative as it is singular in the NT."[5] The collaborators of this commentary join Elliott and a growing number of scholars who refuse to rob from Peter to pay Paul.

Karen Jobes addressed the issue of the level of Greek in 1 Peter. Admittedly, the Greek of 1 Peter is among the best in the NT from a stylistic point of view. Nevertheless, she notes that this argument against Peter as author is sometimes overblown. In the excursus of her 2005 commentary, Jobes demonstrates that the Greek of 1 Peter is not as good as that of Polybius or even Josephus, and argues that the author was not a native Greek speaker. When the quotations in 1 Peter (excluded from her study) are added, the syntax approaches that of LXX Suzanna, Esther and Daniel. Jobes' findings serve to offset any argument from the style of the letter when considering authorship.[6] When we add to these considerations the prospect of Peter's

---

3. Elliott, 138 note 47.
4. Stibbs and Walls, 18–64. See Marshall, 22, Robinson, *Redating*, 140–69.
5. Elliott, 504.
6. Jobes, 325–338. See also Achtemeier, 2.

INTRODUCTION TO THE FIRST LETTER OF PETER 3

collaboration with Silvanus and others (see below), the argument from the level of Greek style becomes irrelevant.

On the matter of style and rhetoric in 1 Peter, the recent contribution of Ben Witherington III is important. Building on the work of George A. Kennedy and Barth Campbell, Witherington has demonstrated that the rhetorical style of 1 Peter conforms to "deliberative rhetoric in an Asiatic mode."[7] This style is distinct from *koine* or Atticistic Greek in its special characteristics of repetition and ornamental language, and the "deliberative" quality refers to the aim of changing thought and behavior. Witherington notes that this style of rhetoric was very widely used in western Asia Minor in the first century. But for all the rhetorical artistry of the letter, Witherington does not hesitate to assert that Peter was the author, and that Silvanus (Silas) had a hand in both writing and delivery.[8]

In the late 1940's two important commentaries appeared offering widely divergent views of the authorship of 1 Peter. Selwyn argued strongly that Peter was the author, Beare strongly contended that he was not.[9] This led Stephen Neill to comment that 1 Peter was "the storm center of New Testament studies."[10] Since then both views have been argued by distinguished scholars.[11] The view taken here is that Peter was the author (with help from others). Collaborators on this commentary been encouraged, though not required, to follow this view.

However, to think of Peter as the author of the letter and Silvanus as offering secretarial help (and possibly serving as the letter carrier) misses the potential richness of what is stated in 5:12–13. There two other potential collaborators are mentioned. In 5:13 Peter mentions *Mark, my son*. In addition he mentions *the elect lady in Babylon*. Most commentators think this latter expression refers to the church (most likely in Rome). But some have taken it to refer to an individual.[12] Paul uses a similar cryptic mode of expression to commend a co-worker in 2 Cor 8:18. Perhaps here we have yet another collaborator in the writing of the letter. So while Peter is the author of record, we suggest that the letter is in fact the product of a team effort, in which each of the collaborators played a distinctive role. Thus it is all the

---

7. Witherington, 45, citing Kennedy, *New Testament Interpretation,* and Campbell, *Honor, Shame.*

8. Ibid. 246.

9. Selwyn, 1946, F.W. Beare, 1947

10. Neill, *Interpretation of the New Testament,* 343.

11. Eg.Jobes and Witheringtom in favor, Elliott and Feldmeier against petrine authorship.

12. J. Applegate, "The Co-Elect woman of 1 Peter," *NTS* 38(1992) 587–604.

more appropriate that this is the nature of this commentary on 1 Peter. A truly collaborative effort deserves a truly collaborative response.

Date: The date of the writing of 1 Peter is closely tied to the issue of authorship. If the letter was written after the middle of the sixties in the first century, it was clearly not written by the Apostle. It is commonly believed that Peter suffered a martyr's death when the Christians in Rome were blamed for the fire in the summer of 64 CE. Therefore those who wish to claim Peter as author, albeit in collaboration with others, must show that there is nothing in the letter that demands a date later than the apostle's lifetime. We do not find anything in the letter that demands a later dating. To the contrary, we believe the letter contains elements that suggest it is best placed in the time we are suggesting, i.e. 63–64 CE. Chief among these features is the "primitive and sectarian" use of scripture.[13]

Recipients: Patristic and Medieval commentators on 1 Peter were virtually unanimous in their conviction that 1 Peter was written by the apostle to Jews in the five provinces of Asia Minor. The outstanding dissenters were Jerome and Augustine, who believed that the letter was written to Gentiles. In modern times the situation is reversed. Most commentators believe that the letter was written to Gentile converts. They base this assertion on several expressions in the letter (1:14, *the passions of your former ignorance,* 1:18, *the futile ways inherited from your ancestors,* 2:9–10, *Once no people. etc,* 4:3–4, *doing what the Gentiles like to do*). Some also include 2:25 and 3:6 as pointing to a Gentile audience.[14] But three recent commentators (Jobes, Green and Witherington) all believe that the recipients of the letter were largely Jewish Christians, although they were joined by some of Gentile origin. Witherington's defense of the Jewish background of the recipients is especially compelling. He shows that Jews in that region were thoroughly Hellenized. This together with Jobes' assertion that the Emperor Claudius, who expelled the Jews from Rome in 49 CE, "established Roman cities in *all five* of the regions named in 1 Peter 1:1,"[15] has nudged us to adopt the working hypothesis that 1 Peter was written to Jewish converts to Christianity. Added to these arguments is the extensive use of the Old Testament in quotations, allusions, echoes, and narratives, which would not have been understood by an audience of largely Gentile background. Even J.H. Elliott, who strongly believes the recipients were mainly Gentile Christians, admits that there must have been some Jewish Christians among the recipients of

---

13. Sargent, *Written to Serve,* 143–46.
14. Davids, 8.
15. Jobes, 29.

the Letter.[16] These considerations taken together lead us to affirm the words of our collaborator, Joseph Muradyan, who states that the recipients were "Jewish until proven Gentile."[17]

Since the publication of J.H. Elliott's landmark study *A Home for the Homeless: A Sociological Exegesis of 1 Peter, Its Situation and Strategy* (1981), many studies have focused on the socio/cultural/religious situation of the addressees of the letter.[18] Scholarly debate continues as to whether the recipients were primarily Jewish or Gentile, urban or rural, and whether they possessed some, little or no disposable income. There is ongoing debate as to whether key terms in the letter like the οικ- word group or the word *grace* should be interpreted primarily in sociological or in theological terms. This commentary's collaborators are alert to the range of possibilities and hope with D. Horrell "that social analysis and theological interpretation can be mutually informative."[19]

The recent studies of Horrell and Williams have served to underline the complexity of the issue of the background of the writer and the recipients. Certain elements of the letter have led commentators to emphasize the strongly Jewish character of the epistle. Other aspects suggest a Gentile milieu, best seen against the background of Roman imperial claims, or Greek philosophy and rhetorical culture, or the popular mystery religions of the first century. It is better to accept all these influences, and to think of what I call "the four faces of Peter:"

1. A face toward Jerusalem: The Jewish cultural background.

2. A face toward Rome: The pervasive presence of the Roman empire.

3. A face toward Athens: The influence of Hellenistic culture and philosophy.

4. A face toward the east: The appeal of popular mystery cults.

While the first should take pride of place, all four must be constantly kept in mind, so that the complexity of the letter, of both its writers and recipients, can be properly appreciated.

Occasion: First Peter is a letter written to address a crisis: Christians were enduring suffering for the name of Christ. Earlier studies of the letter tended to find its setting in one of the "official" persecutions of the first and

---

16. Elliott, *Home for the Homeless*, 55–56.

17. See 31 Lightfoot, in his recently discovered and published commentary on 1 Peter believed the recipients were largely Gentile. 90.

18. See Horrell, *Becoming Christian*, 132–63. For a recent review.

19. Horrell, *Becoming Christian*. 132.

second centuries.[20] Of these, the three choices are the persecutions under Nero (64), Domitian (95), and the situation in Bythinia depicted by Pliny the younger (112). A more recent consensus among scholars is that the persecutions were of a more local and "unofficial" sort, and might be assigned to almost any date between 64 and 112 CE. The discussion has recently been advanced by Travis B. Williams, who has argued that "neither the 'official' persecution theory nor the 'unofficial' persecution theory adequately represents the persecutions depicted in the epistle."[21] The value of the discussions of both Williams and Witherington is that they attempt an in-depth study of the actual social, cultural, political, and religious situation on the ground in Asia Minor in the first century. After the fire in Rome in 64 CE, for which the Christians were blamed, it became a crime to be a Christian. The government did not seek Christians out but officials were expected to examine those who were formally accused of being Christian, and could punish or kill those who professed faith in Christ.

E. G. Selwyn, who believed that the persecutions in 1 Peter were primarily "unofficial," nonetheless states with confidence that the writing of 1 Peter may be dated between the death of James in 62 CE. and the Neronian persecution after the Roman fire in August of 64 CE. He stated, "We arrive at a period of a year or eighteen months which is in no way discordant with anything that we know of the movements of St. Peter, St. Mark or Silvanus."[22] But perhaps we can be even more precise. If the tone of the letter changes at 4:12 so that the persecutions which were a possibility in the first half now have become a present reality, it is entirely plausible to suggest that the letter was begun in the early summer of 64 CE, on the basis of fresh developments either in Asia Minor or in Rome, and was completed by the collaborators as the rumors began to spread that Christians had started the fire in Rome. This scenario is the working hypothesis of this commentary. The comments of various collaborators may tease out its strengths and weaknesses.

Sources: In thinking about the sources, literary and non-literary, that stand behind the letter chief among them is the Old Testament. The frequency of citation, the variety of application, the depth of exegetical insight displayed in the letter are all remarkable. Collaborators comment on the use of the OT as it appears throughout the letter, whether as quotation, allusion,

---

20. Williams, "Suffering from Critical Oversight," 275–92 gives a thorough review of the issue.
21. Williams, *Persecutions*, 335
22. Selwyn, 60.

echo or narrative. And an excursus has been devoted to the subject. It is clear that the grand narrative of scripture is the chief influence on 1 Peter.[23]

Some scholars have suggested that other sources have been influential in the shaping of the letter. F.L. Cross proposed a pascal liturgy.[24] Others have suggested that hymn fragments, or a baptismal homily form the basis of the letter.[25] Still others emphasize affinities with the Letters of Paul, other New Testament writers, or with Qumran, the Mystery Religions or writers of Greece and Rome. It is clear that Peter and his co-workers are working within and shaping a developing catechetical pattern which they share with other NT writers (especially Ephesians, Colossians, and James).[26] In the final analysis, what we have in 1 Peter is a genuine letter, drawing on a wide variety of sources, and making a number of stylistic and literary moves designed to transform the way of thinking and living (ἀναστροφή) of the Anatolian Christians it is addressing.

Text and Reception: Students of the text of 1 Peter are fortunate to have available the *Editio Critica Maior,* and also the 28th edition of Nestle-Aland, which has revised the text of the Catholic Epistles using the recently developed Coherance–Based Geneological Method. This method seeks to find the earliest recoverable text based on the existing manuscript tradition, which its practitioners refer to as the *initial text.* Whatever the strengths and weaknesses of the method, new material for fresh study of the text of 1 Peter has been offered in the nine changes from the 27th edition to the 28th.[27] At least one of these changes is very significant and controversial (4:16, the change from ονοματι (*name*) to the weakly-attested μερει (*matter*). The study of the text has also received stimulus from the recently-published papyrus P125 (POxy 4934).[28] This fragment contains part of chapters 1 and 2, and is of similar date to our other oldest manuscript, papyrus P72. This manuscript has several interesting readings, and is especially significant in joining P72 in reading the abbreviation XPC (for Christ) at 1 Peter 2:3. We follow Comfort in his assertion that this is the original reading in 1 Peter.[29] Another significant early manuscript of 1 Peter, perhaps the earliest of all, is the Crosby-SchØyens Coptic manuscript 193, dating perhaps from the

---

23. See Excursus 2, The Old Testament in 1 Peter, 168–77.
24. Cross, *Pascal Liturgy, passim*
25. For full discussion see Achtemeier, 9–23., S.C. Pearson, DLNT, 522–24.
26. Carrington, *Primitave Christian Catechism,* Selwyn, 363–466.
27. NA 28, 50–51*
28. Comfort, *A Commentary,* 90–91.
29. Ibid. 387. See 165.

mid-third century, and containing the whole letter, along with four other documents. This text deserves more attention than it has so far received.[30]

Reception history has become an important feature of biblical studies in recent years, and several of our collaborators have contributed to the multi-volume work, *The Encyclopedia of the Bible and its Reception* (EBR). We therefore include an essay by Greg Flagg that is devoted to the reception of the letter in the history of the church, focusing on priesthood and the interpretation of 2:5,9. Suffice it to say that the First Epistle of Peter was considered canonical scripture from as far back as we can trace the church's effort to determine such matters.

Biblical Narratives: The recent interest in the biblical narratives that undergird the NT writings has paid dividends for the study of 1 Peter. There are, of course, the obvious references to the biblical story (Sarah and Abraham 3:6, Noah and the flood, 3:20). But scholars have also detected features of the biblical story just beneath the surface of the text, and these have exercised a significant influence on the author and collaborators of 1 Peter. Note in particular the following:

Exodus: The story of the Exodus may be clearly recognized in 1 Peter 1:13–20 in the expressions "gird up the loins of your mind" (1:13) and ransom through "the precious blood of Christ like that of a lamb without blemish or spot" (1:19). Other echoes of Exodus have been found elsewhere in the letter, for example "the mighty hand of God" (5:6). The story of the Exodus seems to be shaping the thought of the letter throughout.[31] This will include not only the story of the Exodus and Passover, but also the wilderness wanderings and the journey toward the promised inheritance. The recent monograph of Kelly Liebengood, *The Eschatology of 1 Peter,* has not only demonstrated this point, but has also argued plausibly that Zechariah 9–14 has significantly influenced the thought of the letter, although this section is never quoted or alluded to for certain in 1 Peter.[32]

Exile: The exile and deportation to Babylon in the sixth century BCE has become an important focus of Biblical studies. The work of N.T. Wright,[33] among others, has brought this critical element of the narrative to the fore. Jews living in the first century imagined that they were still in some sense in exile. Christians spoke to this sense of ongoing exile, asserting that in the life, death and resurrection of Jesus the Messiah or Anointed one, the exile has come to an end. In his important and underappreciated monograph,

---

30. Horrell, *Becoming Christian,* 47–54.
31. Deterding, "Exodus Motifs," 58–67.
32. Liebengood, *Eschatology in 1 Peter.*
33. Wright, *The New Testament and the People of God,* 268–71.

Temple, Exile and Identity in 1 Peter, Andrew M. Mbuvi has built on the work of Wright and others in this connection.[34] He shows that the sense of ongoing exile and the longing for the restoration of Israel in the second temple period is a valuable background against which to read 1 Peter.[35]

Temple: Andrew Mbuvi makes an important contribution in his thorough study of the temple imagery in 1 Peter.[36] This insight into the letter is of sufficient importance that it merits a special excursus. In recent years the creative work on the temple in scripture has opened up many new avenues of interpretation. The work of G.K. Beale and others has established a strong link in ancient Israel (and the Ancient Near East) between Temple and Creation.[37] This link will be explored in the commentary,[38] and offers several collaborators new opportunities for fresh readings of problematic passages in the letter (especially 3:1–7, 4:17–19).

The Good Shepherd: The great biblical theme of God as the Good Shepherd is given special emphasis in 1 Peter.[39] It is mentioned at 2:25 and expounded in chapter 5, and echoes both the scriptural texts (Psalm 23, Ezekiel 34 etc) and the teaching of Jesus (Luke 15; John 10; John 21).

THEOLOGICAL HORIZONS OF 1 PETER:

This term is taken from Joel B.Green, who devotes almost half of his commentary on 1 Peter to engaging the theological horizons of the letter.[40] It reflects the growing interest in and the importance of the theological interpretation of scripture.[41] In the study of the theology of 1 Peter we find the following elements to be of special importance:

God: In 1 Peter God is *the God and Father of our Lord Jesus Christ* (1:3). He is a *faithful creator* (4:19), *the one who judges each person impartially* (1:17), and *the one who judges justly* (2:23). He is the *God of all grace* who *has called us to his eternal glory in Christ Jesus,* (5:10) and he himself will exalt those who humble themselves under his mighty hand (5:7). If God is the key theological term in Romans,[42] it is no less so in 1 Peter.

34. Mbuvi, *Temple, Exile and Identity,* 14–16.
35. Ibid. 10–46.
36. Ibid. 71–126. See Mbuvi's summary on 142.
37. Beale, *The Temple and the Church's Mission, passim.*
38. See especially the excursus by Conroy, 190–200.
39. See Bailey, *The Good Shepherd,* 250–70.
40. Green, 187–288.
41. For 1 Peter see Rodgers, "1 Peter, Book of" in DTIB, 581–83.
42. Fitzmyer, *Romans,* 104.

Jesus Christ: Jesus is the Messiah or the Anointed One, who was *destined before the foundation of the world, but was revealed at the end of the ages.* (1:20). He is the *living stone, rejected by mortals, yet chosen and precious in God's sight* (2:4), and we are *living stones* built into him as a *spiritual house* which is the new temple (2:5). He is the one who *bore our sins in his body on the tree* (2:24) and is the *example that we should follow in his steps.* (2:21). He has risen from the dead (1:3, 3:21), has *gone into heaven and is at the right hand of God* (3:22). He is therefore to be reverenced as Lord (3:15). His Spirit inspired the prophets (1:11) and he is to be revealed at the last time (1:13).

The Holy Spirit: God's Spirit inspired the prophets of old (1:10–12) and rests upon those who suffer for the name of Christ (4:14).

The Church: The word "church" (ἐκκλησία) is never used in 1 Peter, but the idea of the Christian household or family (οἶκος) is everywhere to be seen. J.H. Elliott has made a strong case that the οἶκ- word group in 1 Peter refers not to the temple but to the household.[43] We would argue that both images are in view in Peter's use of this rich word group. Christians are both God's royal priesthood and God's family (2:9).

The Christian Life: The Christians who seek to *live as servants of God* (2:16) can expect hostility from the world. They should not be surprised by the fiery trials that come upon them to test them (4:12). But Peter urges that their posture should be not one of withdrawal from the world, nor absorption into it, but rather being in but not of the world. Miroslav Volf characterizes this posture as "soft differences."[44] Their lives should display a conduct of doing good that distinguishes them from the world, commends them to those around them, and subverts the world order(2:12).[45]

Eschatology: *The end of all things is at hand* (4:7). This declaration sums up the eschatological focus of 1 Peter. The letter tells of a salvation *ready to be revealed at the last time* (1:5). This focus is on the revelation of Jesus Christ (1:13) the one who is the coming judge (2:12) and who will bestow on the faithful *an unfading crown of glory.* (5:4). So then, Christians can rejoice in suffering, confident that Christ's glory is soon to be revealed (4:13). This emphasis on the coming of Jesus Christ is a key feature of 1 Peter.[46]

---

43. Elliott, *Home for the Homeless*, 220–233, For critique see Mbuvi, *Temple, Exile and Identity,* 90.

44. Volf, "Soft Differences," passim.

45. Williams, *Good Works in 1 Peter.*

46. Selwyn, "Escatology in 1 Peter."

Honor and Shame: The Greco-Roman world in which Christianity first flourished was an honor/shame culture. Christians, often shamed for their profession of the name of Christ, are characterized as those who are "disgraced yet graced."[47]

Suffering and Glory: Many have observed that in 1 Peter there is a close connection between suffering and glory. The two terms are regularly found in close proximity. This is not unique to 1 Peter. In Luke 24 Jesus asks the Emmaus disciples, *Was it not necessary that the Messiah should suffer these things, and then enter into his glory?* (Luke 24:26). And Paul wrote that *the sufferings of this present time are not worth comparing with the glory about to be revealed to us* (Rom 8:18, see also 2 Cor 4:17). But this link of suffering and glory is especially prominent in 1 Peter. The classic commentator Robert Leighton referred to it as "the *via regia,* the royal way of suffering that leads to glory."[48] And if we inquire how Peter and the other NT writers discovered this theological insight, we will find a fruitful answer by considering the life, death and resurrection of Jesus, and the pattern that the prophets prophesied concerning this grace (1:10–12). This grace is discovered all the more not just as we study the scripture, but as we *follow in his steps.* (2:21).

+++

What we offer here is a commentary of 21 voices, in chorus of comments on the First Epistle of St. Peter. Each has offered comments based on close reading and engagement with other commentaries, ancient and modern. And each speaks with a distinctive voice, seeking to blend with other voices in this concert. We trust that you will find here much to encourage, to challenge and to stimulate your own close and deep reading of the text of 1 Peter, and that this will provide for you a greater desire and determination to follow in the steps of Christ.

---

47. Campbell, *Honor and Shame,* Elliott, "Disgraced yet Graced."
48. Leighton, *A Practical Commentary,* 425.

1 Peter 1:1–2
by Peter R. Rodgers

1:1

Peter, An apostle of Jesus Christ, to the exiles of the Dispersion in Pontus, Galatia, Cappadocia, Asia, and Bithynia.

Peter, an apostle of Jesus Christ. This letter presents itself as a letter from Peter, chief among the apostles appointed by Jesus, and lead spokesman in the early years of the Jerusalem church. While many scholars today regard the letter as pseudonymous, and believe it was the work of close associates of the apostle who wrote it in his name some time after his death,[1] others have continued to defend petrine authorship,[2] and this is the working hypothesis of this commentary, with the added proposal that Peter collaborated with those mentioned in 5:12–13.

The term *apostle*, refers to those who were chosen by Jesus, and were witnesses to his resurrection, and commissioned to spread his gospel to the ends of the earth (Acts 1:8). *Christ*, which is the English translation of the Greek Χριστοῦ, is not a surname for Jesus, as is commonly assumed, but designates him as God's Anointed One, the Messiah.

To the chosen exiles who are dispersed. These three words indicate the thoroughly Jewish character of the recipients of the letter. Each in turn draws deeply from Israel's scripture and story. The *elect* or *chosen* refers to God's election of Israel (see Isa 43:20, 1 Peter 2:9). *Exiles* evokes the story of the Babylonian captivity of God's people, which was considered by Jews

---

1. Achtemeier, 43, Elliott, 130, Horrell, *1 Peter,* 23.
2. Jobes, 5–19, Green, 10. Witherington, 38.

of the second temple period to be still ongoing,³ and by Christians to have ended in the death and Resurrection of Jesus. In 1 Peter the term is used both sociologically and theologically. *Dispersed* is a term used of Jews who by force or circumstances were living outside of the land of Israel.⁴ All three of these word underline the picture accepted in this commentary that the recipients of the letter were primarily Jewish Christians living in exile and dispersed in scattered communities in Asia Minor in the middle of the first century.

With the application of these words for Israel (and others, cf 2:9–10) to the church, does this mean that "the language and hence the reality of Israel *pass without remainder* into the language and hence the reality of the new people of God?"⁵ First Peter does not see the church (mostly Jewish, but fully including Gentiles) as superseding Israel but as the fulfillment of the ancient promise to Abraham that he would be the father of many nations (Gen 12:3, 17:5), and that in fulfillment of that promise God's salvation would reach to the ends of the earth (Isa 49:6, 1 Peter 5:9). See comments on 2:9–10.

In Pontus, Galatia, Cappadocia, Asia, and Bithynia. Jobes has noted that the Emperor Claudius had established Roman colonial cities in all five of the regions named in 1 Peter. She further suggests that the expulsion of the Jews by Claudius in 49 CE provides a likely background for the displaced Christians who would have known the Apostle Peter.⁶ Hort's proposal that the currier took the letter around to the churches in Asia Minor in clockwise fashion, in the order of appearance in the letter (beginning in Pontus and ending in Bithynia), has much to commend it.⁷

1:2

Who have been chosen and destined by God the Father and sanctified by the Spirit to be obedient to Jesus Christ and to be sprinkled with his blood. May grace and peace be yours in abundance.

The "Trinitarian" formulation in this sentence, like so many others in the New Testament (eg. Matthew 28:20, 2 Cor 13:13, etc.) bears witness to the

---

3. Wright, *Paul and the Faithfulness of God*, 139–63. Mbuvi, *Temple, Exile and Identity*, 28–33
4. Elliott, 313.
5. Achtemeier, 69, Horrell, *1 Peter*, 103.
6. Jobes, 28–41.
7. Hort, 157–84.

earliest Christian perception of God manifest as Father, Son and Holy Spirit. I once heard J.I Packer remark, "Nowhere is the word *trinity* used in the New Testament, but everywhere it is clamoring to be said."

The three prepositional phrases describing the Christians in Asia Minor further identify the chosen exiles of the dispersion in verse 1,[8] and the richness of these descriptions introduce themes that will be emphasized throughout the letter.

The Anatolian Christians were set aside in advance by God the Father. This foreordaining is the second item in the helpful timeline given by Boring in his valuable Appendix 1, "The Narrative World of 1 Peter."[9] This enables both the persecuted Christians of the first century and the readers of the twenty-first to see their lives from the larger narrative of what God is doing.

Through Sanctification of the spirit (or perhaps better *Spirit*). Holiness is at the heart of the message of 1 Peter (see 1:16). Careful study should be made of the early Christian Holiness code which Carrington proposed and Selwyn developed.[10] Holiness was essential to effective Christian living in Asia Minor in the mid-first century. It is equally essential for Christian living today.

Obedience and sprinkling are best taken together.[11] Goppelt noted a "conspicuous similarity" between 1 Pet 1:2 and the *Community Rule* at Qumran 1QS 3:6–8.[12] That text mentions both obedience and sprinkling. It is at least likely that both the Qumran sectaries and 1 Peter are participating in a rich exegetical tradition on Exodus 24, the confirmation of the covenant, in which people pledge obedience and are sprinkled. The reference to sprinkling may be yet another allusion to Isaiah 53, which is so formative for the letter. Interestingly, the MT of Isaiah 53:15 reads *So will he sprinkle many nations*.[13] The sprinkling of blood was connected with the sacrificial cult in Lev 5:9 and 15:16. Mbuvi connects this with the larger tabernacle/temple narrative in 1 Peter, an important interpretive key for understanding the epistle.[14]

May Grace and Peace be poured out lavishly on you! Peter follows a common convention in letter writing, but instead of the normal Greek

---

8. Grudem, 51, Beare, 75.

9. Boring, 183–201.

10. Carrington, *The Primitive Christian Catechism*, Selwyn, *The First Epistle of Peter*, 369–375.

11. Carson, CNTUOT, 1017.

12. Goppelt, 70–72.

13. Childs, *Isaiah*, 408, 412.

14. Mbuvi, *Temple, Exile and Identity in 1 Peter*, 140–42.

greeting ("many greetings," πλεῖστα χαίρειν) he uses words of greeting which are theologically freighted in biblical usage.[15]

---

15. Kelly, 45.

1 Peter 1:3–9
by Joel Moody

This introductory section "provides the foundation for *all* of the author's subsequent remarks."[1] Multiple liturgical portions are embedded in the passage, and while 1 Peter does not represent a paschal liturgy,[2] the evidence points toward Peter's language in 1:3–9 coming from an early Christian hymn or creed.[3] Similarities exist between 1 Peter's introduction and other epistles (James, Titus, and Ephesians). Yet since each epistle has an internal unity, it is likely that they all used similar source material, perhaps sharing a "common bedrock of traditional credal and catechetical material."[4] So although identifying which portions of this introduction came from early liturgies/creeds/hymns is difficult, based on the repetition of εἰς, the shared material with other epistles, and the poetry in this passage, it is clear that Peter structured this introduction around primitive Christian creeds, hymns, or liturgies.

1:3

Blessed be the God and Father of our Lord Jesus Christ! By his great mercy he has given us a new birth into a living hope through the resurrection of Jesus Christ from the dead.

Blessed be the God and Father of our Lord Jesus Christ! This same doxological phrase appears in two of Paul's letters (2 Cor 1:3, Eph 1:3). Therefore it is conceivable that this was a common greeting among believers, similar

---

1. Kendall, "Literary," 106 (emphasis original).
2. E.g. Perdelwitz, *Die Mysterienreligion*, 12–26; Cross, *1 Peter*; Beare, 6–9, 55.
3. E.g., Coutts, "Ephesians," 115–27; Mitton, "Relationship," 67–73.
4. Parsons, *Born Anew*, 316.

to Paul's *grace to you and peace* (χάρις ὑμῖν καὶ εἰρήνη). This opening hearkens back to an exclamation of praise found frequently in the LXX. Blessed (εὐλογητός) is used over seventy times in the LXX as a translation of ברוך,[5] and only sixteen times refers to someone other than God. All sixteen of those times, εὐλογητός refers to someone or something which has been blessed by God.[6] As Coutts argues, "εὐλογητός in the N.T. always occurs in stereotyped or quasi-liturgical contexts," similar to a modern-day quotation of Shakespeare.[7] Both Tite and Martin observe the liturgical language here as well.[8] To appeal to the past liturgy of the Jewish Christian addressees seems strategic on Peter's part.[9]

Theologically, Peter packs this statement with doctrine. While he directs the eulogy toward God, he also keeps *our Lord Jesus* in view, insisting that Jesus bears responsibility for the praise and blessing ascribed to God. This elevates Jesus, as God's Anointed One, to the level of winning praise and blessing on God's behalf, while also describing their relationship—as close as Father and Son. Furthermore, Peter names Jesus not simply as Lord, but as "*our* Lord"—God *pro nobis*. No wonder Peter blesses and praises this God!

By his great mercy he has given us a new birth into a living hope through the resurrection of Jesus Christ from the dead. Peter avoided the common term for rebirth (παλιγγενεσία) and has instead employed the term *born anew* (ἀναγεννάω) which was used infrequently in Hellenistic letters and then only in an improper and non-technical sense.[10] Earlier commentators used this "new birth" as evidence that the early church borrowed their theology from mystery religions.[11] However, Parsons demonstrates that such usage actually points to Peter's theological grounding in the LXX—through an understanding of the Psalms (particularly Ps 2:7), along with an understanding of γεννάω as "generate," Peter could have understood the work of Jesus as being to *regenerate* (ἀναγεννάω).[12] Moreover, it is possible that Peter has Jesus' conversation with Nicodemus (John 3) in view. There Jesus plays

---

5. Elliot, 330.
6. HRCS, 574.
7. Coutts, "Ephesians," 116.
8. Martin, *Metaphor*, 47–52; Tite, *Compositional Transitions*, 49–54.
9. Shimada, *Formulary Material*, 84–106, 139–98, 149–53.
10. Parsons, *Born Anew*, 80–81.
11. Perdelwitz, *Die Mysterienreligion*. See also Goppelt, 81–83; Kelly, 49–50; TDNT 1:673–75; NIDNTTE 1:563.
12. Parsons, *Born Anew*, 176–203, particularly 202.

on the double meaning of ἀναγεννάω as both "born again" and "born from above"

The Greek word, εἰς, translated *into*, might be rendered as "oriented toward" throughout this doxological section, to approximate better the liturgical aspect of Peter's thought in this introductory section. This first εἰς introduces the first of three markers of this new birth: living hope. *Living* is not a throwaway adjective. Any hope not completely dependent upon Jesus' resurrection is no *living* hope at all.[13] For this reason, Calvin wrote that "wherever this [Christian] faith is alive, it must have along with it the hope of eternal salvation as its inseparable companion."[14] Similarly, Jürgen Moltmann suggests that when living hope is absent, "[d]espondency and despair are sin, indeed, they are the origin of all sins."[15]

This hope is founded not upon naïveté—far from it! Rather, Christian hope, living through Jesus' resurrection from the dead, carries a profound understanding of the world's brokenness. Implicit in this hope is the world's rejection of its Lord and Savior, so any hope based upon the Crucified One can never remain ignorant of sin. Because Jesus faced a world of sinners, died for us, and lived in spite of death, our hope lives based upon his resurrection. Christian hope is not hope placed in human institutions, but is strictly "from above," placed in God, through Jesus, in the power of the Spirit. Put simply, "Christian hope is thoroughly Christocentric."[16]

1:4

and into an inheritance that is imperishable, undefiled, and unfading, kept in heaven for you,

An inheritance is the second mark of the new birth believers have in Jesus. Because "scholars are in general agreement that St. Peter's understanding of this inheritance awaiting the Christian is derived from the religious faith and experience of Israel,"[17] the LXX helps in understanding this inheritance. The LXX uses the κληρο- family of words (κληρονομεῖν, κληρονομία, and κλῆρος) to render forms of יָרַשׁ, "take possession, inherit" (especially land),[18]

---

13. Parsons, *Born Anew*, 173.
14. Calvin, *Institutes*, 3.2.42.
15. Moltmann, *Theology*, 121.
16. Kendall, "I Peter," 69.
17. Parsons, *Born Anew*, 102.
18. *BDB*, 439.

נָחַל "take possession, inherit" (especially land),[19] and גּוֹרָל, "lot for dividing land."[20] While κληρο- words sometimes translate other words, they nearly always refer to land.[21]

This understanding of *inheritance* has a particular poignancy for Peter's audience: Jewish Christians, yearning for God to bring them out of exile, back to the Promised Land. These Jewish Christians placed their hope in an inheritance before, of land, nation, and culture. It all perished, was defiled, or faded. Peter's triple modification of the inheritance uses alliterative α-privitives—considered "sophisticated Greek style."[22] This points both to the weightiness of this promise and to an underlying liturgical/poetic/hymnic tradition.

The triple description is rhetorical, but also hints at the threefold office of Jesus. According to Calvin, the *prophetic* office keeps the expectation of God's work from fading,[23] the *kingly* office refers to Jesus' eternal (imperishable) kingdom,[24] and the *priestly* office requires an undefiled sacrifice to reconcile humanity to God.[25] Furthermore, the marks of the new birth also map to these three offices: hope is prophetic, inheritance is kingly, and salvation is priestly.

Peter's use of the divine passive of *kept* (τηρέω) offers a strong guarantee that this inheritance will be kept safe. This verb can also refer to guarding a prisoner or a building.[26] Although rendered as a passive, there is nothing passive about how God guards this inheritance promised to Christians.

1:5

who are being protected by the power of God through faith for a salvation ready to be revealed in the last time.

who are being protected by the power of God, through faith. Similarly to how God guards (τηρέω) Christians' inheritance, God also protects (φρουρέω) Christians.[27] However, an inheritance cannot choose to stand up and walk

---

19. Ibid., 635.
20. Ibid., 174.
21. *HRCS*, 768–70; *TDNT* 3:769–76
22. Goppelt, 86.
23. Calvin, *Institutes*, 2.15.1–2.
24. Ibid., 2.15.3–5.
25. Ibid., 2.15.6.
26. BDAG, 1002.
27. Grudem, 58.

away from the one guarding it; the guard need only watch for thieves and robbers who would take it away. Christians, on the other hand, can walk away. Despite this agency, God takes responsibility for guarding and protecting both the inheritance and the Christian.[28]

for a salvation, ready to be revealed in the last time. A split emerges here between commentators who understand εἰς σωτηρίαν to modify ἀναγεννήσας in 1:3 and those who understand εἰς σωτηρίαν to modify τοὺς φρουρουμένους or διὰ πίστεως earlier in 1:5. While decent grammatical arguments exist for both positions, du Toit shows decisively that grouping εἰς σωτηρίαν with ἀναγεννήσας is more likely.[29]

Salvation "involves more than escaping hell and going to heaven when we die. . .It is so to come within the sphere of God's delivering grace that we are set free from that which has robbed our existence of its meaning."[30] Theologically, salvation has always led toward the goal of becoming more like the Savior, and just as Jesus was *born again* (ἀναγεννάω!) from the grave, so too are Christians *born again* to become like God's Anointed One. Yet this steady transformation of being formed more and more like Jesus is only fully revealed in *the last time,* as Paul suggests: *For now we see in a mirror, dimly, but then we will see face to face* (1 Cor 13:12).

Moreover, each mark of the new birth—hope, an inheritance, and salvation— has a *present* and an *eschatological* component.[31] God has not yet completed the work of the new birth. As Miller claims, "beginning and process are not the whole story. There is also consummation, an end."[32] The *last time* includes the wedding banquet of the Lamb, where God completes the work of the new birth by "making all things new" (Rev 21:5). In this season, the hope, inheritance, and salvation of God's people will be revealed fully.

1:6

In this you rejoice. even if now for a little while you have had to suffer various trials,

In this you rejoice, Here Peter pivots from the thanksgiving section into the reality of suffering Peter's audience knows. Despite this phrase's brevity (three words in Greek) it has generated some contention.

28. John 10:28.
29. du Toit, "Discourse Analysis," 59–65.
30. Miller, "Deliverance," 414.
31. Parsons, *Born Anew*, 79–123.
32. Miller, "Deliverance," 421.

Although there are a number of ways to translate ἐν ᾧ ἀγαλλιᾶσθε, one fact is clear: throughout this introductory blessing, Peter has maintained one foot in the present reality and one foot in the eschatological future. Changing his rhetorical strategy at this point would feel odd.[33] For this reason, ἐν ᾧ ἀγαλλιᾶσθε is best understood as a pastoral exhortation. Peter is emphatic that those who are rejoicing should continue rejoicing (since all Christians ought to rejoice because of God's work), and all *will* rejoice at the consummation of God's work.

Even if now for a little while you have had to suffer various trials, is an odd way to follow *In this you rejoice*. However, it demonstrates that Christians (in particular, Peter's audience) do not rejoice oblivious to suffering, but instead rejoice fully cognizant of suffering, "confident that their present suffering must be followed by future glory."[34] It seems unlikely that Peter wants them to take joy in their suffering. Their joy resides in what God has done.[35] Although it is true that "they suffer because that is what happens to Christians,"[36] Peter notes that they did not seek this suffering. Rather, he argues that it was necessary.

When Christianity becomes a shield from lament, sadness, and grief, it has lost the thread of the gospel message. Perhaps some Christians, when confronted with suffering, immediately begin to *rejoice, be glad, and shout for joy* (1 Pet 4:13). Yet for many, the joy that comes from suffering can only be found after lamentation and anguish. Scripture itself notes this pattern, particularly through the examples of David (Psalm 55), Jeremiah (Lamentations), and Jesus himself (Luke 22:41–44). The gospel, far from shielding Christians from the pain of suffering, allows them to feel it more acutely. Christians know what life ought to look like, and therefore they have a keener sense of the disconnect between *what is* and *what should be*. Grief is an appropriate response to Christian suffering.

However, "suffering must not obscure the immense present privilege of the Christian."[37] Christians' living hope spans past, present, and future. After all, *God works all things together for good for those who love him* (Rom 8:28). So while lamentation remains necessary, Christians must ultimately confess the greatness of God's faithfulness, even through the darkest night.

---

33. Feldmeier, 80.
34. Kendall, "1 Peter," 70. See Introduction, 11.
35. Contra Nauck, "Freude," 68–80.
36. Hill, "On Suffering," 185.
37. Filson, "Partakers," 405.

The word Peter uses for *various* (ποικίλος) also means *many-colored*.[38] and refers to the variety of trials Christians can expect to face. Interestingly, the one other time Peter uses this word is in reference to God's grace (4:10).[39] This sums up his theology of joy and suffering: suffering exists, and Christians are subjected to many varieties. Yet God's grace exists, too, and Christians can rely on its many varieties over and against their suffering.

1:7

so that the genuineness of your faith—being more precious than gold that, though perishable, is tested by fire—may be found to result in praise and glory and honor when Jesus Christ is revealed.

Peter returns in 1:7 to speaking about reasons for joy. While some analyses focus on the metallurgy aspect of this passage, such an interpretation remains incomplete. This passage (coupled with 1:6) resembles Jas 1:2–4, suggesting a shared tradition. Several sources have been proposed for such a tradition, including Greco-Roman extrabiblical writings, wisdom literature (both apocryphal and non-apocryphal), and Old Testament prophecy.[40]

Although parallels exist between 1 Pet 1:6–7, Wis 3:4–6, and Sir 2:1–6, Liebengood vigorously defends Zech 13:7–9 as Peter's primary source for depicting trials Christian must undergo.[41] Peter may intend to reference all three, perhaps to subvert expectations in Wisdom and Sirach. In both Wisdom and Sirach, those who survive God's testing have proven their worthiness, while in 1 Peter, the worthiness of those tested by God is never doubted. For Peter, the faith was never in question; therefore, it need not be discovered or proven, only shown.[42]

Peter moves back to doxology in 1:7b. All of this, beginning with the new birth in 1:3, comes via the revelation of Jesus. But to whom does it come? And why *praise and glory and honor*? This series of ascriptions appears nowhere else in Scripture, so why does Peter use these specific nouns?

First the subject. Ultimately, as seen elsewhere in Scripture (e.g., Rev 7:12), God is sole and final recipient of praise, glory, and honor. Although all of these may be directed toward Christians, the one who boasts must boast in the Lord (1 Cor 1:31; 2 Cor 10:17). Therefore, if Christians find

---

38. BDAG, 842.
39. Jobes, 94. See on 4:10, 126.
40. Liebengood, *Eschatology*, 107–29.
41. Ibid., 110–16, 130–34, 153–55.
42. Contra Martin, *Metaphor*, 64–67.

themselves the objects of praise, glory, and honor—even from God—they must ascribe it to God, lest they have reason to boast other than in the Lord. So God, in Jesus, is the subject of praise and glory and honor.

Second, why praise and glory and honor? Peter has a fondness for triads.[43] Just as he groups the three α-primitives in 1:4 and gives three marks of the new birth in 1:3–5, so here Peter names three attributes resulting from Christians' genuine faith. While they fail to fit the threefold office of Jesus as well as the other triads in this passage, they are all qualities Christians ascribe to God presently, and will ascribe more fully to God in eschatological future.

1:8

Although you have not seen him, you love him; and even though you do not see him now, you believe in him and rejoice with an indescribable and glorious joy,

This verse shows the rhythm of Peter's writing. The negative participles in each line (οὐκ ἰδόντες and μὴ ὁρῶντες) both have a similar field of meaning and similar sound. Such a rhythm and rhyme suggests that Peter is quoting liturgy/poetry/hymnody. Whether intended or not, Peter uses similar vocabulary and structure to John 20:29, where Jesus speaks with Thomas (μακάριοι οἱ μὴ ἰδόντες καὶ πιστεύσαντες). If intentional, perhaps Peter means to apply Jesus' blessing to Thomas to his audience as well. The other message Peter communicates in this doxology is that "[f]aith substitutes for seeing."[44]

and rejoice with an indescribable and glorious joy, gives the result of their belief: indescribable and glorious joy. The word rendered *indescribable* (ἀνεκλαλήτῳ) appears nowhere else in the NT. Literally, its component parts mean "an inability to speak out." This current and future joy in which Christians participate nourishes their living hope.

Scholars differ on the meaning of *rejoice* (ἀγαλλιᾶσθε)—whether it has in view the present or the future. To locate the joy of Christians strictly in the future, when Jesus is fully revealed, misses the magnificent promise to Christians now. Even without seeing God's Son in the flesh, believing in him and loving him is possible. Christians can grasp onto a hope that lives because Jesus lives, and therefore can have joy in the present. This is not some unreasonable, future joy, but *realistically* inexpressible, because of the Christians' *present* belief. That the Anointed One of God made his dwelling

---

43. Elliott "Salutation," 417.
44. Thurén, *Argument*, 101.

among humankind ought to bring Christians great joy. Naturally, the full consummation of this joy takes place in the eschatological future. But placing Christian joy *completely* in the future misses the work Jesus is currently doing in the world and in Christians. Such joy, although partially located in the complete revelation of God in the future, *must* burst forth into the present.

1:9

for you are receiving the outcome of your faith, the salvation of your souls.

The word *outcome* (τέλος) can mean "goal" or "end," but can also connote "the final end to which things are driving."[45] All of these translations work for Peter's thought. Because Peter shows concern not only for how God will work in the eschatological future, but also how God is working in the present, he likely intends both the final end of faith as well as the present goal of faith when he uses τέλος.

The phrase σωτηρία ψυχῶν is most frequently rendered *the salvation of your souls*. Yet "human salvation" might be more accurate.[46] Dautzenberg establishes that ψυχή often translates the Hebrew נֶפֶשׁ, which has an "earthier" meaning than ψυχή usually has. It refers to the "body" or "human life" more often than to some sort of metaphysical "soul";[47] therefore, while "souls" *can* translate ψυχή, it fails to suffice in this context.[48]

So why not use Dautzenberg's translation, "your sure salvation"? "Human salvation" underscores the communal nature of faith. Faith does not concern itself strictly with the salvation of one particular community, but with the salvation of "every nation, from all tribes and peoples and languages" (Rev 7:9). While Dautzenberg's translation is *technically* correct, the dangerous undercurrent of individualism in American Protestantism has led Christians to understand faith individualistically. Dautzenberg's translation is preferable, with a focus broader than individual salvation.

---

45. BDAG, 998–99.
46. Dautzenberg, "Σωτηρία ψυχῶν," 275–76.
47. BDB, 659–61.
48. See also Green, 27.

1 Peter 1:10–12
by Katherine Atkinson

As Peter continues on in these next three verses, which comprise the end of one sentence that began in v. 3 in Greek, he concludes his opening exhortation by linking his message with that of the past prophets, while also highlighting what a privileged time his audience is living in. As he concludes his opening section, Peter also offers a glimpse of his hermeneutical principle for understanding and applying Scripture. After doing this, Peter is ready to move forward with his theological paraenesis, elaborating on themes he has already mentioned in his entire opening exhortation and weaving in Scripture throughout his writing.

1:10

Concerning this salvation, the prophets who prophesied of the grace that was to be yours made careful search and inquiry,

In verse 10, Peter writes *Concerning this salvation*. The phrase links and transitions Peter's thoughts from the previous pericope to the present section. The salvation that Peter has just been describing, as something yet to be revealed (1.5), and as the outcome of believers' faith (1.9), is the precise subject matter about which the prophets were earnestly interested.

A variety of views have been offered, providing a range of options of who these prophets might be. Selwyn argued that Peter is referring to New Testament Christian prophets,[1] while Michaels suggests that since *prophets* (προφῆται) lacks a definite article, Peter's audience has the freedom to determine which prophets fit this description in verses 10–12.[2] More convincing-

---

1. Selwyn, 259–68.
2. Michaels, 40.

ly, Jobes recognizes that since these prophets are speaking of the sufferings of the Messiah (verse 11) long before the Messiah experienced them, Peter must have in mind Old Testament prophets.[3] For example, Peter interprets the prophet Isaiah's words from chapter 53 throughout this epistle to be about the sufferings of Jesus Christ. Peter does this especially in 2:21–25.

Thus, it was Old Testament prophets who prophesied of the grace that has come to them.[4] It was these prophets who *made careful search and inquiry* (ἐξεζήτησαν καὶ ἐξηραύνησαν). These verbs together emphasize just how earnestly and intently the prophets sought out the meaning of their message. In Daniel, the discerners engage in this same careful searching (Dan 9:3), and as Witherington III points out, the prophets had personal relationships with the Lord such that there was dialogue back and forth as the prophets sought out the meaning of their prophecies.[5]

1:11

inquiring about the person or time that the Spirit of Christ within them indicated when it testified in advance to the sufferings destined for Christ and the subsequent glory.

That these two verbs in verse 10 complement one another is reflected in the fact they are amplified[6] by the first word of verse 11, *inquiring* (ἐραυνῶντες). Here Peter goes on to describe what the prophets were inquiring after, but there is exegetical debate over the interpretation of *about the person or time* (εἰς τίνα ἢ ποῖον καιρόν). F. F. Bruce interprets τίνα as a masculine singular interrogative pronoun, rendering a reading *what person or time* the prophets inquired about.[7] Kilpatrick observes that τίνα is more often used as a pronoun, also rendering a reading of *to whom or what sort of time* the prophecies pointed to.[8] Prophets were often most concerned about when their prophecies would come to pass.[9] Green objects to this by reminding readers that relying on only OT and Jewish usage here is incomplete because Peter is actually trying to show his audience how to read the Scriptures through the lens of Christ; Green thus believes the prophets are inquiring

---

3. For the full argument for her position, see Jobes, 98–100.
4. For further comments on the nuances of "grace," see 2:19.
5. Witherington III, 83.
6. Dubis, 18.
7. F.F. Bruce, *Biblical Exegesis in the Qumran Texts*, 67. Michaels, 41.
8. Kilpatrick, *NovT* 28, 91–92.
9. Jobes, 102, Michaels, 41.

about what the person will be like.[10] However, Jobes offers another possibility. She observes that τίνα could also be parsed as a neuter plural accusative interrogative pronoun, offering the translation *what circumstances or what the time would be like*.[11] Michaels and Jobes together highlight that Peter is not referring to Christ in this expression, but rather that the prophets inquired earnestly about what the *kairos* time would be like, when and what it would be like when that eschatological season of the fulfillment of God's promises would occur.[12]

The prophets inquired into this as the *Spirit of Christ* (πνεῦμα Χριστοῦ) within them testified to them. The phrase *Spirit of Christ* is used only here and in Rom 8.9, which states *and if anyone does not have the Spirit of Christ, they do not belong to Christ*, although the NT also contains expressions such as *the Spirit of Jesus Christ* (Phil 1:19) and *the Spirit of Jesus* (Acts 16:7). In 1 Peter, it is likely overstepping Peter's intention to take this phrase as a proof for Christ's preexistence. Rather, Peter is likely referring to the Spirit, or Holy Spirit, anticipating the Christian doctrine of the Trinity.[13] Yet, it is interesting to note Peter's Christological emphasis within verses 10-12, for it is the Spirit of Christ which foretold the sufferings and glories (note the plural of both here) destined for Christ (suffering and glory often appear together in 1 Peter, eg. 4:14, 5:1, and in the NT Lk 24, Rom 8, 2 Cor). In a new full-length study of this passage, and the use of Scripture in 1 Peter, Benjamin Sargent argues that the sole reference of the prophetic proclamation was to serve the Anatolian recipients of the letter. Sargent views verses 10-11 as Peter's foundation for understanding Scripture's function as "a proclamation of the suffering and glories of Christ, in advance, through the Prophets whose words had no meaning other than to refer to this future."[14] While Peter certainly has a Christocentric view of Scripture, Sargent's argument seems unfairly to ignore the original purpose of the prophecies. Peter may have recognized the role of Scripture for each generation, for surely the prophets' message wasn't useless for the exiles.

Testified in advance (προμαρτυρόμενον), which BDAG offers translations of "bear witness to beforehand, predict,"[15] is used only once in the New Testament and is not found in the LXX or classical Greek. Most commenta-

---

10. Green, 21–22.

11. Jobes, 103

12. For a more complete and compiled explanation of the various arguments, see Jobes 101–103. Dubis, 19. Michaels, 42–3.

13. Witherington III, 84.

14. Sargent, *Witten to Serve*, 48. See Rodgers/Rohlfing 168–77

15. BDAG, 872.

tors do not make much of this occurrence, but Peter's use of the word here may indicate just how unique the Spirit's work is in foretelling.

Once again at this juncture though, one must be aware of the difficulty in translating another phrase, *the sufferings destined for Christ* (τὰ εἰς Χριςτὸν παθήματα). As indicated above, Jobes believes that this phrase refers to the sufferings of Christ.[16] Others have translated this passage such that the Spirit testified to the sufferings experienced by Christians, sufferings on behalf of Christ, or even the sufferings that indicate the return of Christ.[17] Both interpretations accord with teaching in the letter and elsewhere in the New Testament. Throughout the New Testament, Christians can expect to face suffering on account of following Christ's way (Mt 5:11), and they can also expect suffering to accompany the end times (Mt 24:9-13). However, Jobes' argument based on the syntax of this expression throughout the New Testament indicates that hers is the likely reading.[18] Peter here has in mind the sufferings and subsequent glories of Christ. Here is the first time that Peter makes the close connection between suffering and glory, but he will address this theme later in the letter (4:14). Notice in general that the New Testament is clear about suffering and glory going together (Luke 24:26, Rom 8:17). Later in the epistle Peter makes the connection between the sufferings of Christ and the sufferings of believers (2:21, 4:1, 4:12-14, 5:9). Peter certainly knows all of these sufferings firsthand, having watched Christ endure sufferings and then having endured suffering himself. For now, Peter's audience can trust Peter's experience and take comfort knowing that though Christ suffered many things from his time in ministry through to his crucifixion and death, Christ also experienced the accompanying glories of resurrection, ascension, and sending the Holy Spirit upon his people.

1:12

> It was revealed to them that they were serving not themselves but you, in regard to the things that have now been announced to you through those who brought you good news by the Holy Spirit sent from heaven—things into which angels long to look!

Through their inquiry, the prophets learned that they were serving not themselves, but the current Christians Peter is writing to in regard to the good news that these Christians have heard (verse 12). The same Spirit that

---

16. Jobes, 100. For her full explanation and argument, see 98-100.
17. Selwyn, 136.
18. Jobes, 99.

spoke to the prophets has sent messengers to bring the good news currently to Christians. Peter is acknowledging continuity of the Spirit's work from the Old Testament through to his current context. Peter's assertion that the prophets served this later generation is actually a contribution that he distinctively makes to one's understanding of the role and purpose of Old Testament prophecy, with Sargent going so far as to assert that Peter views the prophets' work as only for this later generation.[19] While this view may be taking Peter's hermeneutics to the extreme, Sargent's view is helpful for reminding readers that Peter sees salvation and history as oriented around Christ.

The things which the evangelists have preached are things which even angels desire to look upon! Throughout the Bible, one learns that humans enjoy a special status that angels do not (Psa 8.5). Here, the point is elaborated upon that angels do not even know all the mysteries of the prophetic message or of salvation. *To look* (παρακύψαι) carries with it the image of "stretching to look through a window," offering a picture of the heavenly host peering down through the windows of heaven to catch a glimpse of God's great works.[20] Often *long* (ἐπιθυμοῦσιν) is used to indicate evil desire,[21] as is the case two verses later in 1.14. However, here there is no such connotation of the angels nor of evil inent on their part. Instead, Peter is making the point that what his audience knows of the sufferings, glories, and salvation of Christ is an incredibly privileged experience. The prophets inquired purposely into this knowledge and the angels long to understand it. However it is Christians who actually get to experience and know much more fully the good news of God.

At this point in the letter, Peter turns toward instruction for Christian living. He has spoken highly of salvation and of the Christians' privileged status to know God's work. Peter has hopefully sufficiently established rapport with his audience such that they will be ready to hear his words of instruction in regard to impending suffering.[22] His readers are experiencing trials and persecution of various kinds. They are in need of encouragement to understand how to live in this world and why they are experiencing the suffering that they are facing. In verses 10–12, Peter places his audience squarely within the tradition of God's people. The Spirit, at work in the past, revealed to the prophets in part what Peter's audience has heard in full. Sufferings were not the end of Christ's story, so Peter's Christians can expect

---

19. Sargent, *Written to Serve*, 30.
20. Dubis, 22.
21. *TDNT* II, 170.
22. Witherington III, 75.

that it will not be the end of theirs either. Though their current sufferings are difficult, these Christians still have knowledge and experience of which the prophets, and even angels, would be envious.

1 Peter 1:13–21
by Joseph Muradyan

1:13

Therefore prepare your minds for action; discipline yourselves; set all your hope on the grace that Jesus Christ will bring you when he is revealed.

Peter begins this section with an inferential conjunction *therefore/for this reason* (διό) to link what came before with what will follow.[1] Before arriving at *therefore*, Peter greets the sojourners (mostly of Jewish origin: the audience is Jewish until proven Gentile) within Asia Minor (verse 1–2), recalls the Father's mercy towards them and their new birth through the resurrection of Jesus (verse 3), reminds them of their inheritance (verse 4) and their faithfulness, love, and joy through trials (verses 6–8), their salvation (verse 9), and the good news of Messiah announced to them through the preachers inspired by the Holy Spirit (verses 10–12).

Prepare your minds for action. Peter links the aorist middle participle of the verb *to gird up* (ἀναζώννυμι) with *loins* (ὀσφῦς) to form a Semitic idiom to describe "the act of tucking up a long robe into a belt, allowing the legs more freedom of movement."[2] The contemporary equivalent would be: "roll up your shirt sleeves."[3] Similar phrases are used by: Moses (Exod 12:11); Elijah (1 Kings 18:46); Elisha (2 Kings 4:29; 9:1); God (Jer 1:17); and Jesus (Luke 12:35–36).

---

1. Jobes, 109
2. Jobes, 111
3. Jobes, 111

The *mind* (διάνοια) signifies something other than intellectual life divorced from conduct.[4] It encompasses "faculty of thinking, comprehending, and reasoning"[5] as well as "disposition, objective, purpose, and plan," all shaped by the story one chooses to embrace concerning God, humanity, and creation. Peter intends for the story of God's faithfulness towards Israel to transform their thinking. To live in accordance with their new birth, the old garments must be brought into order. Just as the chaos of creation in Genesis 1 was reordered, so their old life of chaos must be brought into the holy-ordering influence and sphere of the Spirit.

Discipline yourselves. In the NT, the verb *be sober* (νήφοντες), here a present active participle translated as "being sober-minded" (continually), describes "self-controlled and attentive behavior,"[6] and "restraint and moderation which avoids excess in passion, rashness, or confusion."[7] Sober-mindedness facilitates prayer and sober judgment of oneself (4:7) and alerts against the schemes of the Devil (5:8).[8]

Set all your hope. The adverb *fully/entirely/undividedly* (τελείως)[9] can modify either the participle preceding it ("being fully sober-minded")[10] or the imperative following it ("fully set your hope").[11] When hope is placed fully in the coming revelation of Jesus, then no confidence is placed "in the things that society trains us to put our hope in, such as status, education, money, and so on."[12]

The aorist imperative of the verb *to hope* (ἐλπίζω) translates into *set your hope*.[13] Hope in the NT looks back to God's faithful actions in the past (Exodus from Egyptian slavery, return from Babylonian exile, and new birth in the resurrection of Jesus from the dead) so that one can stand in the present and look towards the future of God with confidence.[14] Because the Messiah lives, the believer's hope lives (verse 3) and directs its gaze towards God (verse 21; 3:5).

---

4. Jobes, 111
5. BDAG, 234–35.
6. Forbes, 37
7. Jobes, 111
8. Jobes, 111
9. Goppelt, 107
10. Forbes, 37
11. Jobes, 109; Dubis, 23
12. Jobes, 110
13. Forbes, 5, 37.
14. Jobes, 109

On the grace that Jesus Christ will bring you when he is revealed. Peter uses the present passive participle of *to bring* (φέρω) to elucidate the unfolding nature of grace "being brought" both presently and at a definite future time when Messiah returns. Hope stands on grace (with respect to a foundation)[15] and moves towards grace (oriented towards a goal).[16]

The noun *grace/favor* (χάρις) plays a prominent role in the letter (cf. 1:2, 10, 13; 2:19–20; 3:7; 4:10; 5:5, 10, 12). Peter may be echoing Psalm 33:18 or 147:11: "in those who hope in his steadfast love." The Hebrew word for *steadfast love* is (חֶסֶד: *hesed*), which the LXX generally translates with the Greek *mercy* (ἔλεος). Considering the wide spectrum of meanings for *steadfast love* (kindness, goodness, favor, grace, mercy, and faithfulness)[17] Peter may be alluding to or echoing God's *steadfast love* towards Israel.

Peter uses the noun *revelation/disclosure* (ἀποκάλυψις).[18] Since the context of other passages where Peter uses ἀποκάλυψις implies future tense (cf. 1:5, 7; 4:13; 5:1; except for 1:12, where a revelation occurred in the past), we can safely infer that 1:13 also implies a future revealing of the Messiah.[19]

1:14

Like obedient children, do not be conformed to the desires that you formerly had in ignorance.

Like obedient children. Throughout the letter, Peter uses familial language[20] to admonish his recipients to view themselves—and live their lives—according to their identity *like/as* (ὡς) *obedient* (ὑπακοή) *children* (τέκνον). The phrase "obedient children" or "children of obedience" functions as a Semitism,[21] with three interpretive possibilities: (1) "children who are heirs of obedience"[22] (inheritors of Christ's/Abraham's obedience); (2) "children whose chief characteristic is obedience"; or, (3) "children born for obedience."[23]

---

15. Achtemeier, 119
16. Dubis, 24; Goppelt, 105
17. BDB, 338–39.
18. BDAG, 112
19. Dubis, 24
20. Green, 33–34
21. Selwyn, 140
22. Selwyn, 140–41.
23. Achtemeier, 119

Do not be conformed. The present passive/middle participle of *be conformed* (συσχηματίζω: "to form according to a pattern or mold; model after")[24] is used only one other time in the NT (Rom. 12:2). The negative command here anticipates the positive command ("be holy") in verse 15. Similarly in Leviticus 18, God prohibits Israel from modeling themselves after the patterns of the surrounding nations, and then instructs them in Leviticus 19 how to live holy lives.[25]

To the desires that you formerly had in ignorance. Peter contrasts their *previous/former* (πρότερος) way of life with the new life they have in Jesus. When one comes to Messiah, the past is not erased or instantly healed. Rather, the new creation life unfolds over time, transforming us little by little (in conversation with our embodied historical past) until Messiah returns to transform us completely.

In Scripture, *ignorance* (ἄγνοια: unawareness, lack of discernment)[26] describes either Gentiles who do not know God or both Jews and Gentiles who fail to know the God revealed to them through Jesus.[27] When they lived *in ignorance*, they were enslaved and led astray by it.[28]

What did *ignorance* lead to in former times? Peter points to *desire* (ἐπιθυμία: longing, insatiable craving, lust). *Desire* appears in much ancient literature with negative connotations, addressing all manner of self-seeking.[29] However, when used positively, it simply denotes "impulses."[30]

1:15

Instead, as he who called you is holy, be holy yourselves in all your conduct;

Instead, as he who called you is holy. The adversative conjunction *instead* (ἀλλά: but, instead, rather, yet) contrasts the preceding clause with the following clause's positive call to holiness.[31] Two interpretive options exist: (1) "he who called you is holy;" and, (2) "the Holy One who called you."[32] The

---

24. BDAG, 979
25. Goppelt, 109; Selwyn, 141
26. BDAG, 13
27. Green, 38
28. Forbes, 38
29. Green, 38;
30. Micaels, 57;
31. Achtemeier, 120
32. Dubis, 26;

title "Holy One" is used elsewhere in Scripture (Is. 40.25; Mark 1:24; 1 John 2:20). The aorist active participle of the verb *to call* (καλέω) recalls God's call of Abraham from his father's home and Israel out of Egypt into the wilderness (Hos 11:1).

Be holy yourselves in all your conduct. Peter exhorts the recipients with the intensive pronoun of *you* (αὐτός: you yourselves). The Holy One's influence extends into *all* areas of life. As Green remarks, "holiness extends indeed into the nooks and crannies of life."[33]

Peter uses the imperative of the verb *to be* (γίνομαι). What does it mean "to become" holy? They have been sanctified in the Spirit (1:2) and are called a holy priesthood (2:5) and nation (2:9). Green puts it like this: "Holiness is a gift, grounded in relationship with God, before it is command."[34] Leonhard Goppelt explains that becoming holy involves appropriating "the sanctification that has [already] been encountered."[35]

The noun *conduct* (ἀναστροφή) displays a broad semantic range: "a turning upside down, a turning back, inversion, repetition in rhetoric, delay, dwelling, mode of life."[36]

1:16

for it is written, "You shall be holy, for I am holy."

For it is written. The conjunction *for* (διότι) introduces Scriptural citations (cf. 1:16, 24 and 2:6).[37] The story of God and Israel found in Scriptures remains the story that will shape their own stories, albeit now read through the life of Messiah.

You shall be holy, for I am holy. Peter quotes Lev 19:2 LXX verbatim,[38] though this phrase is found throughout Leviticus and Numbers numerous times with slight variations. By quoting Leviticus, Peter does not require them to adhere to the ancient customs and rituals prescribed for Israel. Instead, they would express their holiness in ways "appropriate to their own historical moment."[39]

---

33. Green, 44
34. Green, 44
35. Goppelt, 110
36. Silva, NIDNTTE, 289; See notes on verse 17 for verb form.
37. Achtemeier, 122
38. Jobes, 114
39. Jobes, 115

1: 17

If you invoke as Father the one who judges all people impartially according to their deeds, live in reverent fear during the time of your exile.

If you invoke as Father. In Greek, verses 17 to 21 form one long sentence.[40] The conjunction *if* (εἰ) is not a condition ("if you call upon") but rather an inference ("since you call upon").[41] Peter places *father* (πατήρ) at the front of the clause for emphasis[42] so that what follows is seen through the lens of the merciful father (verse 3). The filial relationship exemplified between the Father and Jesus is the model that Peter desires the recipients to bring to mind and imitate as children.[43] The verb *to call* (ἐπικαλέω) in the middle voice refers to "calling upon or invoking a deity in prayer."[44] This usage is common in the LXX (Ps 88:27; Jer 3:19) and NT (Acts 7:59; 1 Cor 1:2; Gal 4:6).[45] Jesus also called God "Father" (Matt 6:9; Luke 22:42).

The one who judges all people impartially. The present active participle of the verb *to judge* (κρίνω: to judge, prefer, consider, look upon, decide)[46] translates as: "one who judges." The adverb *impartial* (ἀπροσωπολήμπτως) is a Hebrew idiom meaning "to receive the face" or "to show favor."[47] As the impartial judge, the Father is not influenced or manipulated by worldly standards of status, rank, or privilege.

According to their deeds. The Father places *work* (ἔργον: work, deed, matter, action)[48] as the basis for judgement. What qualifies as *work*? The noun implies a "collective singular…referring to all of one's thoughts and actions."[49] A person's "character and allegiance" manifests through practice.[50] Scripture supports judgement according to *works* (Cf. Eccl 12:14; Ps 58:11; Rom 2:9–10, 2 Cor 4:5).

---

40. Jobes, 115
41. Achtemeier, 124
42. Dubis, 29
43. Green, 23–24
44. Dubis, 30
45. Selwyn, 142–43.
46. BDAG, 567-8
47. Green, 44;
48. BDAG, 390-1
49. Dubis, 30
50. Green, 44

Live in reverent fear during the time of your exile. Fear (φόβος), placed in front of the clause for emphasis,[51] and generally translated as fear, terror, or trembling, in this context allows for: reverence, respect, awe, or wonder.[52] Fear is not a response to a perception of God as threatening or vengeful, but to his character as merciful Father (verse 3) (Exod 34:6–8; Ps 130:4; Jer 33:9).

The meaning of *sojourning* (παροικία) is contested, with various definitions: exile, sojourning, pilgrimage; temporary residence without full citizenship rights; or, an in-between legal status.[53] Green asserts that in Second Temple Judaism, *sojourning* functioned as a "metaphor for exile life."[54] But are the recipients of Peter's letter suffering because of their sin?[55] Israel was exiled to the land of the Assyrians and Babylonians because of their sin. Abraham, Isaac, Jacob, and Moses (and the children of Israel in Egypt), however, were sojourners waiting for the promises of God—*not exiles because of sin.*[56]

Peter uses the passive imperative of the verb *to conduct* (ἀναστρέφω). It had a spectrum of meanings: "to go, dwell, settle somewhere; to move about in public, conduct oneself."[57] Note the relationship between the noun *sojourner* and the verb *to conduct*: both touch on the idea of "dwelling" or "settling," both carry an ethical flavor, and both imply transience as pilgrims. In the LXX, the two Hebrew words rendered in Greek for *to conduct* are *to return* (שׁוּב) and *to walk* (הָלַךְ).[58] In later Jewish writings, *to walk* gained a figurative sense denoting "a way of life or behavior."[59] In Peter, the noun αναστροφή is used 6 times (1:15, 18; 2:12; 3:1–2, 16), and the verb once (1:17).[60] Peter R. Rodgers, however, puts forth a most potent definition for *to conduct*: "a habit of mind leading to habit of life."[61]

---

51. Dubis, 30
52. Achtemeier, 125, Rodgers, EBR 8, 1025.
53. Forbes, 42
54. Green, 43;
55. Leibengood, 148; Liebengood does not think they were experiencing exilic suffering.
56. Abraham (Gen 22:4); Jacob (Gen 47:9); the Psalmist (Psa 39:12); David and Israel (1 Chron 29:15; Acts 10:34).
57. Silva, NIDNTTE, 289
58. Silva, 289
59. Silva, 289
60. Silva, 290
61. Rodgers; Lectures on 1 Peter(unpublished) 2015.

1:18

You know that you were ransomed from the futile ways inherited from your ancestors, not with perishable things like silver or gold.

With the participle form of the verb *to know* (εἰδότες) in the emphatic position, Peter presents the "motivational ground" for the preceding exhortation.[62] *Corruptible* (φθαρτός), rarely used in the LXX, can mean: subject to decay, perishable, transient, or corruptible.[63] Compare *corruptible* goods from their former life with their new life (1:4, 1:23). *Silver* (ἀργύριον) and *gold* (χρυσίον) fall under the broader category of transient or corruptible things.[64] In LXX, they are associated with idolatry.[65]

Peter uses the aorist passive of the verb *to redeem* (λυτρόω), affirming "God as the actor" who redeems.[66] In the Greco-Roman world, it referred to the ransom of prisoners of war or manumission of slaves.[67] In the LXX, it was used for: property redemption (Lev 25); retribution for crimes (Exod 21:30); ransom for firstborns (Exod 13:12–13); the "atonement price" (Exod 30:12–16); and deliverance from slavery or exile without price (Exod 6:6; Isa 44:22–23).[68] It appears in NT three times: Jesus as redeemer (Luke 24:21) and Jesus as the redemption/ransom (1 Cor 1:30; Mark 10:45). Jobes suggests that Peter echoes and conflates Isa. 52:3 and Ps 34:22.[69]

Futile (μάταιος) can also mean: worthless or foolish.[70] Peter appraises the conduct *handed down from the fathers* (πατροπαράδοτος) of the recipients negatively. In the Greco-Roman world, to break from one's ancestral customs was an invitation for the gods to take vengeance.[71] Peter knows Israel's history of falling into idolatry—and knows that his (mostly Jewish) audience knows—and reminds them to not be like their forefathers who developed a habit of falling into idolatry (Ps 78:8). Peter honored most aspects of his Jewish inheritance, yet he rejected the *futile and idolatrous* aspects of those very same inherited ways.

---

62. Dubis, 31
63. Forbes, 43
64. Dubis, 32
65. Achtemeier, 128.
66. Achemeier, 127
67. Achtemeier, 127
68. Achtemeier, 127
69. Jobes, 117
70. Forbes, 43
71. Green, 38

1:19

but with the precious blood of Christ, like that of a lamb without defect or blemish.

But with the precious blood. God ransoms with the *blood* (αἷμα) of Messiah, not silver or gold; the blood is *precious* (τίμιος: honorable, precious, highly respected, or valued).[72] In 1 Pet 1:2, the sprinkling of the blood of Jesus echoes Moses's sprinkling of the blood of the covenant on the people of Israel and Torah (Exodus 24). The author of Hebrews highlights the importance of blood for forgiveness of trespasses and in mediating the covenants, both the one Moses inaugurated (9:18–20) and the one Jesus inaugurated (9:15). The blood of Jesus redeems Israel from transgressions made under the first covenant and restores the people of God (Israel) through Jesus's new (renewed) covenant, thus making it possible for non-Jews to reconcile with God and join the covenant family of God.

Of Christ, like that of a lamb without defect or blemish. Peter likens Messiah (Χριστός) to a sacrificial *lamb* (ἀμνός) *without blemish* (ἄμωμος: without defect; in the moral sense, it means without fault, and thus, blameless)[73] and *without spot* (ἄσπιλος: "being of highest quality and without defect, spotless...being of untainted character, pure, without fault").[74] The lamb brings to mind Israel's Passover tradition (Exod 12:5), sacrificial cult, and John the Baptist's testimony.[75] The image of a lamb without blemish or spot ought to move the faithful to imitate the life of Messiah.

1:20

He was destined before the foundation of the world, but was revealed at the end of the ages for your sake.

He was destined before the foundation of the world. Peter begins the clause with the perfect passive participle of the verb *to foreknow* (προγινώσκω), which translates into: "having been foreknown/chosen/destined."[76] By linking Jesus's sacrificial death with God's eternal plan, Peter takes the work of Christ out of the realm of accident and into the realm of God's sovereign

---

72. Forbes, 43
73. BDAG, 56
74. BDAG, 144
75. Green, 41
76. Dubis, 33

will.⁷⁷ Jesus's sacrificial death was foreknown *before* (πρό) the *foundation* (καταβολή: foundation, beginning)⁷⁸ of the *world* (κόσμος: world, earth, universe, humanity").⁷⁹ Similar phrases are used several times in the NT (Matt 13:35; John 17:24; Eph 1:4; Heb 9:26; Rev 13:8).

Yet having been manifested. Peter contrasts the preceding clause with the passive participle of the verb *to manifest* (φανερόω), translated in the passive as *having been manifested*, highlighting "God as the active agent."⁸⁰ BDAG defines it as: "to cause to become visible or known; reveal, expose publically, or disclose."⁸¹

But was revealed at the end of the ages for your sake. Jesus's manifestation in these *last* (ἔσχατος) *times* (χρόνος) points principally to his incarnation (Heb 1:2 and 9:26).⁸² Similar phrases can be found in the NT (Acts 2:17; Heb 1:2; Jas 5:3; and 2 Pet 3:3). In Jewish apocalyptic literature, the "end of ages" denoted the expected time of suffering of the saints and the resurrection of the dead, which would mark the restoration of Israel.⁸³

The preposition *for* (διά) is used in two ways: "because of you"⁸⁴ or "for your benefit." This phrase, placed in the emphatic position, shows that "the community of the faithful"⁸⁵ was the focus of human history, placed at the center of God's plan for redemption.⁸⁶

1:21

> Through him you have come to trust in God, who raised him from the dead and gave him glory, so that your faith and hope are set on God.

Through him you have come to trust in God. The substantive verbal adjective *to believe* (πιστεύω)⁸⁷ has either an active sense ("the believing/trusting

---

77. Achemeier, 131
78. BDAG, 515
79. BDAG, 561-2
80. Dubis, 34
81. BDAG, 1048
82. Selwyn, 146
83. Green, 39
84. Forbes, 45
85. Green, 37
86. Achtemeier, 132

87. Bates, *Salvation by Allegiance Alone*, 82–83. Bates argues that the *pist*-root words in Paul's letters (but not limited to Paul) are best translated using the concept

ones in God") or passive sense ("the faithful/trustworthy to God").[88] Dubis,[89] Forbes,[90] and others[91] take the active sense as the correct translation.[92] Achtemeier and others note a significant textual variant: instead of the substantival adjective (manuscripts: A, B, Vulgate, and few others), some manuscripts (P72, C, P, Ψ, X and many minuscules) have the present active participle of *to believe*,[93] which would change the phrase to "believing/trusting in God."

Who raised him from the dead and gave him glory. Using the article *who* (τὸν), Peter connects "God" with both active participle verbs: *having raised up* (ἐγείροντα) from the dead and *having given* (δίδωμι) him glory, thus emphasizing God's action. In the NT, the confession that God raised Messiah *from* (ἐκ) *the dead* (νεκρός) is common.[94] Resurrection and exaltation (glorification) of Messiah are linked (cf. 3:21). Note, also, that "the dead" is plural; thus, from all those who have died, God raised up and gave glory only to Messiah.[95]

The recipients will share in the Messiah's *glory* (δόξα) just as they share in his suffering (1:7, 11; 4:13–14; 5:1–4, 10). Selwyn suggests a possible connection to Isa 52:13, where the suffering servant of Deutero-Isaiah "shall be high and lifted up, and shall be exalted."[96]

So that your faith and hope are set on God. The particle *that* (ὥστε) functions in two ways: the recipients "faith and hope" can be seen either as God's *reason for/intended result* or *the actual result* of the preceding clause: raising Jesus from the dead and giving him glory.[97] Faith and hope are linked together and directed toward God.[98]

---

of *allegiance*, which "welds mental agreement, professed fealty, and embodied loyalty." Jesus was raised from among the dead ones and given glory—he was exalted and enthroned as king at the Father's side (1 Pet 1:21; 3:21–22). Because Christ is "the enthroned divine-human king," he must be given allegiance (faithfulness, loyalty, or fidelity are also appropriate words).

88. Forbes, 45
89. Dubis, 34
90. Forbes, 45
91. Achtemeier, 132
92. Dubis, 34
93. Achtemeier, 123
94. Achtemeier, 132
95. Dubis, 7
96. Selwyn, 147
97. Forbes, 45
98. Dubis, 35

In God (εἰς θεός) brackets this verse as well as verses 3 through 21,[99] thereby highlighting the letters theocentric emphasis.[100] Thus, our hope is not directed towards the present world realities (or for a better world)[101] but rather towards God and his resurrection future.

---

99. Forbes, 46
100. Forbes, 45
101. Goppelt, 121

1 Peter 1:22–2:3
by Zach Mazotti

1 Peter 1:2–2:3 communicates the shape of the new life in Christ through examining both its challenges (1:22b–2:1) and its benefits (1:23–5, 2:2–3). For Christian living, deliverance is the beginning of new life (being "rebegotten"). What follows are moral and ethical grounds to abide by. Previously Peter had established two key imperatives—*hope fully* in 1:13 and *be holy* in 1:15.[1] In 1:22–2:3, Peter unpacks two more commands: *love one another* (1:22) and *long for/crave* (2:2).[2] Thus, Peter's language moves from right relation to God to right relation within the Christian community.

1:22

Now that you have purified your souls by your obedience to the truth, so that you have genuine mutual love, love one another deeply from the heart.

The Greek ἡγνικότες is a perfect participle, "having purified/sanctified," which demonstrates a present state growing out of a prior action.[3] The entire being, or *soul* (Τὰς ψυχὰς), has been purified and is being purified in those who are obedient to the truth.[4] Peter has proclaimed the word of God (1:12), and his audience has found themselves cleansed by their reception and fidelity to the Christian message.[5] Through their purification, the people of God are being built into a spiritual home (2:5) that has been cer-

---

1. Jobes, 122.
2. Jobes, 122.
3. Achtemeier, 136.
4. Dubis, 36.
5. Forbes, 48.

emonially cleansed by the Holy Spirit for those who are adopted into God's family (2:9-10), through the sprinkling of blood (1:2).⁶

The significance of this cleansing can hardly go unnoticed. The Roman Empire considered Christians as atheists who must be exposed and arrested. However, as promised by God, the soul is purified by receiving the gift of the Holy Spirit, enabling Christians to find a trustworthy home in the family of God. With the indwelling of the Holy Spirit, one is made ready and able to live faithfully against the forces of a powerful empire.

So that you have genuine mutual love, love one another deeply from the heart. What then are Christians to do now that they have purified their souls in obedience to the truth? How might their entry into the family of God be sustained when times get tough, as the letter makes clear that they will? Purification through obedience makes the next step of the Christian life possible: Christians are to love one another deeply from the heart.⁷ Since Christians have been adopted and indwelt by the Holy Spirit, they must practice the defining quality of their new, eternal life: *love one another*.⁸ This love is no fleeting emotion, it is *from a good heart* (ἐκ καθαρᾶς καρδίας), a heart that has already been purified and made obedient to the truth. It is a love that is *brotherly* (φιλαδελφίαν) and *constant* (ἐκτενῶς; or "fervent/sincere." See Romans 12:9-10). Sincere love is unfailing and reminds us of God's love exemplified by Jesus who suffered, died, and rose from the grave (1:3). Fervent (ἐκτενῶς) love has substance, vigor, constancy, and is the exact kind of love that can withstand the turbulent milieu Christians found themselves in during the 1st century.

In his commentary on 1 Peter, E.A. Maycock wrote that love belongs to the will.⁹ Like prayer (Acts 12:5), love is both demanding and powerful. Karen Jobes reasons, "The goal of God's redemptive purposes in this life is to restore right relationships, first between persons and God, but between people as well."¹⁰ Love is the external marker of the Christian family as made possible by Jesus' death and resurrection. He is the sustainer and builder of communities that can withstand trials and tribulations. Christians are made ready for the fiery trial (4:12) when they love one another constantly from their purified, Spirit-led hearts.¹¹

---

6. Hort, 87. Also, see excursus on Temple images in 1 Peter. 190-200.
7. Achtemeier, 137.
8. Jobes, 125.
9. Maycock,, *A Letter of Wise Counsel*, 45.
10. Jobes, *Letters to the Church*, 350.
11. See Rodgers, "Love: New Testament" EBR. Forthcoming.

1:23

You have been born anew, not of perishable but of imperishable seed through the living and enduring word of God.

Αναγεγεννημένοι, meaning "rebegotten" (instead of "rebirth")[12], is the gift of God's divine activity as the basis, along with purification, for why Christians should love one another.[13] As Jesus declared, *you must be born again*, Christians should praise God because he has brought them new life, a life in the Spirit—a life that is not perishable, but imperishable (1:4).

Further, "rebegotten" Christians are given this gift through God's *seed* (σπορᾶς), which has generated spiritual life through the message of the gospel, *the living and enduring word of God* (διὰ λόγου ζῶντος θεοῦ καὶ μένοντος). While there is uncertainty regarding the meaning of *living and enduring* (ζῶντος καὶ μένοντος) whether this refers to God or the word, many commentators agree that these modifiers describe God's word, even though they are also true of God.[14] Those who enter God's family through faith are conceived by the seed of God's word. God promises to sustain and empower them through all things.

1:24

For, "All flesh is like grass and all its glory like the flower of grass. The grass withers, and the flower falls."

Peter turns his attention to second Isaiah, a passage that proclaims, *Comfort, O comfort my people, says your God*. Like Isaiah 40, Peter also addresses an exiled audience and offers them hope based upon God's prior action and Jesus' glorious resurrection. There is an empire that encompasses Christ's family that Christians have just been "rebegotten" into. This empire stirs in Peter's memory, reminding him of Israel's misfortune in the 6th century BCE. The message to those in Babylon is the same message Peter wants to give to 1st century Christians: *The grass withers, and the flower falls*.[15] The Greek *falls* (ἐξέπεσεν) reminds listeners of falling off by natural processes.[16] As the seasons pass, the grass will wither and the flower will fade; both will

---

12. In agreement with Achtemeier, 138. See comments on 1:3.
13. Dubis, 38.
14. See discussion in Dubis, 38.
15. See Mbuvi, *Temple, Exile and Identity*, 36.
16. Dubis, 40.

be no more. So then, what comfort is Peter offering to his audience? In the same way Israel was delivered from exile in Babylon, so too will God deliver his people from the Roman Empire—a promise already enacted in the life, death, and resurrection of Jesus Christ (2:24–25). Using Isaiah 40, Peter communicates comfort by declaring that the empire has no lasting potential. As Jobes notes in her pioneering work on 1 Peter, the same God who delivered the people from exile will also deliver the Christians of Asia Minor from their exile.[17]

In view of God's past (Egypt and Babylon) and present (Jesus' victory) actions, there remains too much hope to fold now. Peter calls his people to love because it is God's way. It is worth becoming a community sustained by God's love during this harsh season—*the grass withers, and the flower falls*. The "glitter" and "pomp" of the Roman Empire is as a blade of grass compared to the life-giving, life-sustaining power of God's promises.[18]

"Comfort, O comfort my people," says your God.

1:25

"But the word of the Lord endures forever." That word is the good news that was announced to you.

Any proclamation that the Roman Empire or any other "fleshly" entity will fall is automatically contrasted with the word of the Lord that endures forever. Already spoken of by the prophets (1:10–12), all creation is transient as compared to the permanence of God's *word* (ῥῆμα). But what exactly is this *good news that was announced to you* (εὐαγγελισθὲν εἰς ὑμᾶς)? It is both God's self-disclosure in scripture and his creative power to restore all things.[19]

The phrase *word of the Lord* (ῥῆμα κυρίου) is surprising because we often expect to see the widely known λόγος (seen as recently as 1:23). Generally, ῥῆμα refers to specific utterances and λόγος refers to the overall message.[20] It is likely Peter uses ῥῆμα simply from its place in Isaiah 40, so there should be little concern about *word* here, as *the word of God* refers to scripture and the creative work of God either way. What is more interesting than *word* is the switch from *God* (θεοῦ) to *Lord* (κυρίου) since Peter regularly

---

17. Jobes, 129.
18. Achetemeier, 142.
19. Maycock, 46. Selwyn, 152. Goppelt, 127. Hort, 93. Hillyer, 55.
20. Forbes 52.

uses κυρίου to identify Jesus throughout his letter.[21] The significance of this usage is immense. If the utterances of God endure forever, then that which Jesus spoke will also be enduring. By announcing that God's promises have always been effective, from the exodus to the release from exile, Peter confirms that the afflicted church will be sustained by a God whose promises endure forever.

Not only will this creative and powerful God sustain his promises through his enduring word, but he will also invite a family of Spirit-led participants to join him in restoration through preaching this same word. Thus, Christians are invited to join in the celebration and preaching of God's fulfilled and future promises.[22] Having been purified (1:22), Christians will put on constant love for one another, a love made possible through the power of God's word (1:23). In doing so, they will participate as a glorified and eternal offspring "rebegotten" from God's living and enduring seed (1:24). Unlike all other beings, powers, and institutions, the speech and promises of God are going to endure (1:25). They are going to withstand all things. They are going to experience restoration. They are going to do so because of Jesus who was destined before the foundation of the world to rise and restore God's people to God (1:20–21). The question that remains is whether the church can possibly maintain her purity, her call to love, and keep in step with the good news that was announced and must be preached by God's people (1:25b).

2:1

Rid yourselves, therefore, of all malice, and all guile, insincerity, envy, and all slander.

The greatest danger to living a regenerate, Spirit-led life, that is made possible through being purified and made new by the living and enduring word of God, is to counteract that process of restoration with divisive and polluting habits—habits that promise to stunt the growth process or completely dissolve one's new life in God. According to Peter, these habits destroy community. If love is to be constant (1:23), then *evil* (κακία) habits must be replaced with good habits that preserve unceasing, familial love.[23] To continue these damaging practices is to serve the self and to benefit the self

---

21. Achtemeier, 141. 1:3, 2:13, 3:15.

22. James 1 (1:18 in particular) follows a similar structure. Deliverance is followed by the call to hear and do the word.

23. Green, 52. Cf. James 3:6.

while disparaging the neighbor. It is these attitudes and actions that make a community built on love impossible.[24]

In order to establish a community that can withstand trials, "rebegotten" Christians are to practice the Christian holiness code.[25] To withstand trials and to most properly put on love, Christians must *therefore, put aside* (ἀποθέμενοι οὖν) everything that inhibits love.[26] Reminiscent of baptism, but not necessarily referring to it, Christians are to rid, discard, renounce, or willfully cut themselves off from these habits.[27] They are to put away and replace these habits with both of Peter's key imperatives in this section: *love one another* (1:22) and *long for/crave* (2:2). The Christian life is not just an invitation to be a part of God's family; it is a call to live according to the new family in word and deed, namely through love. In this way theology and ethics are inseparable for 1 Peter. All Christians, whether converts or ongoing, are to remedy social alienation with love and ceasing of destructive habits.[28]

2:2

Like newborn infants, long for the pure, spiritual milk, so that by it you may grow into salvation—

In the face of persecution comparable to Egypt and Babylon, Christians need more than to "put on" love and "put off" destructive habits: they need to feast on the grace of Jesus Christ. Peter does not use infants (βρέφη) to communicate to brand new converts who are on their way to maturity (like Heb 5:12 and 1 Cor 3:2). Instead of displaying the immaturity of a child, Christians are to mimic the longing of a child for nourishment.[29] Incessantly and eagerly *crave* (ἐπιποθήσατε) *pure, spiritual milk*. Yearn for God's provision with the same single-mindedness with which an infant yearns for the milk that alone will nourish.[30]

---

24. Achtemeier, 145.

25. Put off (2:1), put on (1:22, 2:2), submit, watch and pray, and stand and resist. See Selwyn, 370, and Philip Carrington's *The Primitive Christian Catechism*.

26. Dubis, 43.

27. Hillyer, 56. Witherington, 111. Elliot, 80. Maycock, 47. Jobes, *Letters to the Church*, 235.

28. Witherington, 111.

29. Green, 53. Achtemeier, 146. Jobes, 131. Dubis, 43. Forbes, 56.

30. Achtemeier, 145.

While many take *pure, spiritual milk* (λογικὸν ἄδολον γάλα) to refer to *the living and enduring word of God*,[31] it seems more proper to include all graces, whether sacrament, scripture, fellowship, love—indeed, all that Christ offers us is his milk that we are to long for.[32] It is sensible to suggest that *milk* (γάλα) refers to the word of God, the good news that has been announced (1:25). However Jobes gives two substantial reasons why the case is not closed yet. First, *spiritual* (λογικὸν) does not need to relate to *word* (λόγος). If we look at Romans 12:2, we see this same word, *this is your spiritual* (λογικὸν) *act of worship*. The word might better be translated as "reasonable" or "compatible."[33] Christians are to long for a substance that is compatible with the Christian life, a substance that will allow them to live properly following the work of the mighty hand of God (5:6).[34] Thus, seeing how "put off" language is always followed by "put on" language, the milk Christians are to crave is the precise substance that will help them live properly in their new reality.[35] The milk of God is the rational choice for any Christian who wants to endure fiery trials (4:12). Incidentally, there is no need to mention mystery cults as many commentators have shown that Peter does not rely on those traditions.[36]

Second, in Peter's use of Psalm 34 (Psalm 33 LXX) in 2:3, we are reminded of David's context as one who was in danger, under pagan rulers, and living the life of a wanderer.[37] The passage makes no mention of the word of God. Had Peter wanted to use a passage to describe the "word" alone, he could have used Psalm 119:103, *How sweet are your words to my taste, sweeter than honey to my mouth!* Therefore, we are invited to imagine our longing for milk as a desire for preaching, the sacraments, friendship, testimony, forgiveness, and celebration: Christ's *pure/non-diluted* (ἄδολον) goodness is accessible in a variety of ways! Christians should crave this nourishment!

So that by it you may grow into salvation. To long for pure, spiritual milk is to crave the way of living that is most suitable for Christians at any time. It is an invitation to be sustained by a holy and nurturing God who

---

31. From 1:22. Green, 53. Achetemeier, 147. Dubis, 44. Silva, 539. Moulton, 2:377–79.

32. Jobes' article "Got Milk?" most clearly takes this position. Also Forbes, 57. Best, 98.

33. Jobes, 134. Forbes, 57.

34. Forbes, 59.

35. Jobes, "Got Milk?" 124.

36. Thanks to the work of Selwyn, 154 and Buchsel, TDNT I, 673–75. Goppelt, 130, Jobes, 141.

37. Jobes, "Got Milk?" 124.

has promised to provide for his people through the Holy Spirit, through the love and victory of Jesus Christ, and through establishing his kingdom even now, and allowing communion of himself to all who believe, follow and crave Jesus Christ. As a "rebegotten" family, God's people are given yet another grace: their journey toward being fully restored, a journey that requires constant love (1:22) and putting away of destructive habits (2:1), will be supported by the nourishment of God until the day of salvation. God has promised to partner with all who would entrust their lives to his good news—this is the team effort required to accomplish salvation.[38] As E. G. Selwyn puts it, "sanctification is not only effected by the Holy Spirit, but is consummated in obedience."[39]

In alluding to the milk and honey of the Promised Land (Exodus 33:3), Peter offers a guide for how one might walk into salvation. In again making sure to connect theology and ethics, Peter has no sense that God delivering his people decisively through the blood of Jesus will signal an end to living rightly in the eyes of God. Once ushered into the family of God, Christians are to long for the precise nourishment that will insure their growth into salvation. If they do not crave and feed on Christ's grace, it will be impossible to live as enlightened partakers of the Holy Spirit who can survive testing, tribulation, and the powers of the world. Like a blade of grass (1:24), they are doomed to fall away without the sustaining milk of God, which is available in many forms.[40] Long to experience the Lord himself, and you will grow up into salvation because, "God delivers from affliction anyone who perseveres with God to the end."[41]

Finally, this discussion reminds us of Paul's words on flesh and Spirit in Romans 8:5–9. Christians who resist the milk of God "cannot please God," because as they resist the Spirit, they resist the way of God—the way of Christian living—thus compromising their growth into salvation. Christians who do not long for and receive milk are Christians who are prone to fall away from God's nourishment and reclaim their life in the flesh.

---

38. Donelson, 57.
39. Selwyn, 149.
40. Selwyn, 156.
41. Goppelt, 132.

2:3

if indeed you have tasted that the Lord is good.

Better translated as, "since you have tasted,"[42] Christians have experienced something that those in the past could only anticipate but not fully understand (1:10–12).[43] Here Peter uses Psalm 34 (Psalm 33 LXX) to bolster his argument for why Christians should crave pure, spiritual milk. It is because they have experienced new life in Christ, a life that demands an adoption of attitudes and behaviors. Christians must crave the Lord and shed vices in order to grow up into salvation.[44] In order for Christians to become the people God will ultimately deliver in the future, they must partner with him in an ethical transformation that incorporates them into a new family with its distinctive practices.[45] In this sense, God both conceives and sustains the "rebegotten" life, the life of love that Christians are to enact.[46] Furthermore, Peter's words support the hypothesized context that these are not necessarily newly converted Christians; rather it is that all Christians have tasted and should go on craving the goodness of God.

None of this should be confused with earning salvation. While Peter is not one to clearly articulate the relationship between theology and ethics, he does allow for "growth into salvation" as a process begun and sustained by the Spirit of God in partnership with the believer. As Jobes summarizes the believers' part in this work, "instinctively, eagerly, incessantly crave the grace of God."[47]

Finally, there is an important textual variant in this verse. The word for *goodness/kindness* (χρηστὸς) looks and sounds similar to *Christ* (χριστὸς). As a result, tradition has passed down this text as both, "the Lord is good," and "Christ is Lord."[48] Both renderings ring true. It is through the goodness and kindness of Jesus that tasting went from a solely eschatological hope to a fundamental reality. It is because Christ is Lord that these same realities are true. Both renderings are valid and important in studying 1 Peter. What is critical is that Christ himself has not only been seen, heard, and touched,

---

42. Jobes, 139. Dubis, 44.
43. Green, 50.
44. Jobes, 140.
45. Jobes, 140.
46. Jobes, 140.
47. Jobes, 142.
48. Dubis, 45. Jobes, 136. Feldmeier, 131. See Excursus, "The Text of 1 Peter," 165. Note that Comfort, *A Commentary on the Manuscripts and Text,* 387, takes Lord to be the original reading.

but he has been tasted. God's precepts, God's way of living, and God's restoration have been offered through his very Son who has taken on flesh, offered himself, and conceived a brand-new way of living as a member of the household of God. We must be purified by him and crave him, that by doing so, we might love one another and grow up into salvation. There are many good reasons do this, since we have already tasted that Christ is a good and kind Lord. Unlike Caesar or any other god who hopes to lay claim to our lives, we must entrust ourselves to the good Lord who cares for us (5:7).

1 Peter 2:4–10

by Max Botner (4–6) and Peter R. Rodgers (7–10)

2:4

Come to him, a living stone, though rejected by mortals yet chosen and precious in God's sight, and *as [you] draw near to him*.[1]

This clause alludes to Ps 33:6 LXX: *Draw near to him* (προσέλθατε πρὸς αὐτόν) *And be enlightened and your faces shall never be put to shame*.[2] The plausibility of such an allusion is enhanced by (a) the citation of Ps 33:9 LXX in the previous verse (1 Pet 2:3), (b) Peter's extensive citation of Ps 33:13–16 LXX in 3:10–12, and (c) thematic correspondence between the epistle and the general tenor of the psalm, in which the righteous holy ones are instructed to live out their lives in the fear of the Lord by doing good and shunning evil as they await the time of their vindication (cf. Ps 33:23 LXX). The psalmist's hope is, for Peter, a *"living* hope" (1:3) precisely because the resurrection of God's "servant" Jesus (2:21–25) guarantees that God will do the same for all his "servants" (cf. 2:17, 25; 5:4).

The allusion to Ps 34(33):6 enhances an important christological point for the apostle: *Christ is to be identified with the Lord* (ὁ κύριος) of the psalm (ὅν stands in for αὐτόν [Ps 33:6 LXX], whose immediate antecedent in the psalm is τὸν κύριον [Ps 33:5 LXX]). Peter's identification of Christ with "the Lord" of Ps 34(33) draws his audience into a profound theological

---

1. Taking προσερχόμενοι as a circumstantial participle with indicative rather than imperatival force (based on reading οἰκοδομεῖσθε in verse 5 as an indicative); so also Michaels, 97; Achtemeier, 153; Elliott, 409; Donelson, 60; *pace* Goppelt, 134; Senior, 53.

2. Many recognize the continuing allusion to Ps 34(33); see, e.g., Hort, 104; Selwyn, 157; Snodgrass, "I Peter II.1–10," 102–3; Jobes, 145.

53

mystery: Christ followers draw near to the "Lord" as they approach θεός through χριστός by the πνεῦμα. Those who have "tasted" the Lord's goodness (χρηστός) in Christ (χριστός) are invited to draw near to the one true God in continuous worship.³

a living stone. The previous clause also serves as an intertextual hinge between Ps 34(33) and Peter's stone *testimonia* (1 Pet 2:6-8), so that the referent of the relative pronoun ὅν (Christ) is both "the Lord" (ὁ κύριος) of Ps 34(33) and the "stone" (λίθος) of Isa 8:14, Isa 28:16, and Ps 118(117):22.⁴ The stone is "living" (ζῶντα) because God has raised Jesus to imperishable life and exalted him to his right hand in the heavens (1 Pet 1:3-7, 21; 2:5; 3:18, 22).

rejected by humans. The perfect participle ἀποδεδοκιμασμένον anticipates the citation of Ps 118(117):22 in 2:7. The perfect tense draws out the ongoing significance of Christ's rejection and its implications for his followers.⁵ Peter generalizes the agency of Christ's rejection to humanity at large (ὑπὸ ἀνθρώπων) to accentuate that Christ (and thus implicitly, Christ followers) must endure rejection from all people, not simply the Judean leaders (cf. Mark 12:10 pars.; Acts 4:11).⁶

yet chosen [and] precious in God's sight. The adversative particle δέ contrasts the stone's rejection "by humanity" with his acceptance *in God's sight* (παρὰ θεῷ). Peter's description of the stone as *elect* (ἐκλεκτόν) and *precious* (ἔντιμον) grounds the community's election (2:9; cf. 1:1-2) in Christ's election in anticipation of the citation of Isa 28:16 in 2:6.⁷

---

3. In light of v. 5, it may be significant that προσεχρέσθαι can connote approaching YHWH *in order to present sacrifice* (cf. Lev 9:5, 7, 8; 21:17, 18, 21, 23; Num 16:40; Ezek 44:16).

4. Snodgrass ("I Peter II.1–10," 103) suggests that the description of "the Lord" (ὁ κύριος) as a "stone" (λίθος) in Isa 8:12-14 facilitated the link between Christ "the Lord" in Ps 34(33). Later in the letter Peter explicitly identifies Christ as "the Lord" (ὁ κύριος) in Isa 8:13 (cf. 1 Pet 3:15).

5. Achtemeier, 154.

6. Note the use of Ps 118(117) to contrast human and divine insight is also attested in the first passion prediction in Mark 8:31-33.

7. See Elliott, *The Elect and the Holy*, esp. 141-145.

2:5

like living stones, let yourselves be built into a spiritual house, to be a holy priesthood, to offer spiritual sacrifices acceptable to God through Jesus Christ.

you yourself also, as living stones, are being built.[8] The syntax of this clause emphasizes Christ followers' participation in Christ's resurrection life (cf. 1:3-5, 23-25; 2:3): just as Christ is a "living stone" (verse 4), so too they are "*as* living stones." The adverbial particle ὡς indicates that their status as those who will attain resurrection life in the future is derived from the present reality of Christ's resurrection and the ongoing work of the Spirit (a point also suggested by the present passive indicative verb οἰκοδομεῖσθε).[9]

Elliott may be correct to take οἰκοδομεῖσθε as a divine passive,[10] but the verb may also evoke scriptural traditions in which David's son would "build" (οἰκοδομέω) a "house" (οἶκος) for God:

> And it will be if your days are fulfilled and you lie down with your ancestors that *I will raise up your offspring* (ἀναστήσω τὸ σπέρμα σου) after you who shall be from your loins, and I will prepare his kingdom; *he shall build me a house for my name* (αὐτὸς οἰκοδομήσει μοι οἶκον τῷ ὀνόματί μου), and I will restore his throne forever. I will be his father, and he will be my son . . . (1 Sam 7:12-14 LXX; cf. 1 Chr 17:11-13).[11]

A retrospective reading of 2 Sam 7:12-14 would suggested that, now that God has *raised* (ἀνίστημι) Christ from the dead and enthroned him at his right hand (cf. 1 Pet 3:22), David's greater son builds a "house" for his Father by sending the Spirit upon communities of Christ followers (cf. 1 Pet 4:14; Mark 1:8 pars.; Acts 2:1-4). Such a retrospective reading receives plausibility in light of the immediate description of the community as a "spiritual house."

---

8. Reading οἰκοδομεῖσθε as a passive indicative rather than as a middle imperative; see n. 1, above.

9. Achtemeier, 155.

10. Elliott, 413.

11. Cf. Pss. Sol. 17; 4Q174 I, 1-13; Rom 1:3-4. By and large, the notion that David's son would build the temple is not reactivated until the destruction of the temple in 70 CE (e.g., Tg. Isa.; Tg. Zech.; see Ådna, *Jesu Stellung zum Tempel*, 25-89). Nonetheless, it is likely that some early Christians read 2 Sam 7:12-14 retrospectively as a prophecy about Christ's "building" a messianic Spirit-filled community.

a spiritual house.[12] Peter's description of the community as a *spiritual house* evokes the biblical metaphor of the tabernacle/temple as a "house" for Israel's God (cf. Mark 11:17 pars.; Acts 7:47, 49). Scholars have naturally been taken by the linguistic similarities between Peter's description of communities of Christ followers as a *spiritual house* and the self-descriptions of the Qumran sectarians as "a holy house for Israel" (בית קדוש לישׂראל; 1QS VIII 5) and "a sanctuary of men/Adam" (מקדשׁ אדם; 4Q174 I, 6). This language is often misinterpreted, however, to suggest that the Qumran sectarians identified "a group of men with the true temple,"[13] an interpretative move which is then used to bolster the conclusion that Peter and the sectarians are "products of a common Jewish mindset that had lost confidence in the physical temple as the abode of God and had sought an alternative."[14] In point of fact, the sectarians' response to their perceived defilement of the Second Temple was highly provisional; and all indications are that they longed for the day when proper sacrifice would resume in a future temple in Jerusalem.[15]

Peter's point does not appear to be that Christ followers have replaced the Jerusalem temple as such, but that they have gained access to God's heavenly throne/mercy seat through Christ. The apostle's logic, in our view, is quite close to that of the writer of Hebrews:

> Therefore, brothers and sisters, holy partners in a heavenly calling, consider that Jesus, the apostle and high priest of our confession, was faithful to the one who appointed him, just as Moses also 'was faithful in all his house.' Yet Jesus is worthy of more glory than Moses, just as the builder of a house has more honor than the house itself. (For every house is built by someone, but the builder of all things is God). Now Moses was faithful in all God's house as a servant, to testify to the things that would be spoken later. *Christ, however, was faithful over his house as a son* (Χριστὸς δὲ ὡς υἱὸς ἐπὶ τὸν οἶκον αὐτοῦ); *and we are his house* (οὗ οἶκός ἐσμεν ἡμεῖς) if we hold firm the confidence and the pride that belong to hope (Heb 3:1-6).

The writer's employment of the "house" metaphor, as Harold Attridge notes, presents the new covenant community as a "sacral community over

---

12. We read the nominative phrase in apposition with the subject of the previous clause.

13. Gärtner, *Temple*, 47.

14. Mbuvi, *Temple*, 93; see also Best, "I Peter II 4-10," 284; Snodgrass, "Formation," 104; Goppelt, 141; Boring 101; Senior, 59; Elliott, 415.

15. See Schiffman, *Gemeinde*, 267-84, esp. 280; Klawans, *Purity*, 145-174, esp. 162-68.

which Christ presides as the 'great High Priest.'"[16] Likewise, for Peter, the temple-esque nature of communities of Christ followers derives from Christ's priestly ministry at the right hand of God.[17]

to be a holy priesthood. The prepositional phrase indicates the *purpose* for which the community has been constituted. The phrase ἱεράτευμα ἅγιον draws on YHWH's charge to the people of Israel in Exod 19:6, "but you shall be for me a royal *priesthood* (βασίλειον ἱεράτευμα) and a *holy* nation (ἔθνος ἅγιον)" (cf. 2:9).[18]

to offer spiritual sacrifices to God through Jesus Christ. The infinitive purpose clause specifies the nature of the new covenant community's priestly ministry. Leviticus makes it clear that sacrifices are only "acceptable" (δεκτός; cf. Lev 1:3–4; 17:4) when worshippers present the prescribed offering to the priest at the entrance of the tent of meeting. That is, sacrifices which are "acceptable" (δεκτός/εὐπρόσδεκτος) are only those that are offered "to God" (τῷ θεῷ) through the agency of the (high) priest. This is precisely what the writer of Hebrews intends when he exhorts his audience: "*Through him [Jesus], therefore let us continually offer a sacrifice of praise to God* (Δι' αὐτοῦ [οὖν] ἀναφέρωμεν θυσίαν αἰνέσεως διὰ παντὸς τῷ θεῷ; Heb 13:15). Like Peter, the writer of Hebrews envisages communities of worshippers offering sacrifice (ἀναφέρειν + θυσία) to God (τῷ θεῷ) through Jesus (δι' αὐτοῦ). Since the writer of Hebrews manifestly understands the prepositional phrase δι' αὐτοῦ to signify priestly activity, it is highly plausible, a fortiori, that Peter understands the prepositional phrase διὰ Ἰησοῦ Χριστοῦ along similar lines.[19]

Peter's logic is thoroughly Pentateuchal: Israel's God redeems a people and makes covenant with them so that he might take up residence in their midst (cf. Exod 25–40; Lev; for Peter, this happens through Christ's death, resurrection, and ascension (cf. 3:18–22). The ascension, in particular, marks the point at which Christ takes up his priestly reign at the right hand of God (cf. 3:22), ensuring that Spirit-filled communities of Christ followers have access to the divine throne/mercy seat. Peter does not delimit the precise nature of the "spiritual sacrifices" Christ followers offer to God through Jesus Christ (cf. 4Q174 I, 7; 11Q17 IX, 4–5; T. Lev. 3:6; Rom

---

16. Attridge, *Hebrews* 111.

17. *Pace* Elliott (416–18) it is unnecessary to dichotomize "temple" and "royal residence," particularly if that "royal residence" is the "house" of the deity (so rightly Jobes, 150).

18. Elliott, 416.

19. *Pace* Elliott (421), who contends that, "[i]n 1 Peter, Christ is nowhere depicted as a priest."

12:1; Heb 13:15).[20] The point, rather, seems to be a vocational call to *imitatio Christi*—to entrusting one's life, in the midst of suffering, to the living God in the hope that God will grant Christ followers the same imperishable *life* that he has granted his Messiah (cf. 1:3–5).[21]

2:6

For it stands in scripture: "See, I am laying in Zion a stone, a cornerstone chosen and precious; and whoever believes in him will not be put to shame."

for it is contained in Scripture. This clause grounds the previous claim Peter has made about the identity of Christ and his addressees in the Scriptures. The so-called "stone *testimonia*" testifies to the Christ event and the subsequent (re-)constitution of the people of God. This collocation of "stone" texts (Isa 28:16; Ps 118[117]:22; Isa 8:4) forms part of a common early Christian exegetical tradition (cf. Rom 9:33; Barn. 6:2, 4).[22]

*"See, I lay a stone in Zion, a chosen and precious cornerstone, and the one who **trusts in** him will never be put to shame."* The final clause of this citation of Isa 28:16 agrees verbatim with our best LXX MSS, including the prepositional phrase ἐπ' αὐτῷ and the verb καταισχύνειν (cf. Rom 9:33).[23] There are, however, some significant differences between 1 Peter and LXX MSS: the first clause of 1 Pet 2:6 (a) lacks the first person pronoun (ἐγώ), (b) uses a different verb (τίθημι instead of ἐμβάλλω) and tense (present instead of future), (c) lacks the prepositional phrase εἰς τὰ θεμέλια, (d) lacks the adjective πολυτελῆ, and (e) presents the adjectives ἀκρογωνιαῖον and ἐκλεκτὸν in a different order. The data thus prohibits firm judgment concerning Peter's *Vorlage*.

Some suggest that Isa 28:16 constitutes a pre-Christian "messianic" source text.[24] But this is far from certain. First, the addition of the preposi-

---

20. So rightly Best, I Peter II 4–10," 287.

21. McKelvey, *New Temple*, 130.

22. See Dodd, *According*, 41–43; Fitzmyer, *Essays*, 85; Moyise, "1 Peter," 178–81. For a counterargument that the "stone" *testimonia* bears witness to an early written collection of scriptures, see Albl, *'And Scripture Cannot be Broken.'*

23. ἐπ' αὐτῷ is absent in B. MT reads the final clause as: יחיש לא המאמיןQIsab XI, 1; 3 may agree with MT, although it is difficult to tell on account of a lacuna prior to the characters חיש (see ed. Ulrich, 501). Tg. Isa. 28:16 includes the object of belief/trust in the plural: "who believe *in these things* [באלין]."

24. E.g., Snodgrass, "I Peter II. 1–10," 100; Elliott, 424; Jobes, 147; Carson, "1 Peter," 1025.

tional phrase ἐπ' αὐτῷ tells us nothing about the Greek translator's intention. Second, while the observation that the targumist interprets the stone as a "king" (מלך) is illuminating, it does not provide secure evidence for a Second Temple messianic interpretation of Isa 28:16. Third, the clearest extant Second Temple interpretation of Isa 28:16 equates the "stone" with an elect community (1QS VIII, 7–8). To be sure, none of these points obviate the *possibility* that some Second Temple Jews read Isa 28:16 messianically; rather, they suggest that we ought to exercise greater caution in our judgments concerning "pre-Christian" interpretations of this text.

Peter's reuse of Isa 28:16 presupposes that Christ is the elect "cornerstone." He applies his conviction that the Spirit of Christ spoke through Isaiah about the events of Christ's rejection and vindication (cf. 1:10–12) to YHWH's announcement through the prophet that he is setting a "cornerstone" in Zion. This oracle is both a word of hope to those who will trust in the elect stone and a word of judgment against the leaders of YHWH's people, those who have made "a covenant with Hades" (Isa 28:15). For Peter, this oracle divides humanity into two groups: (1) those who trust in the one whom God has vindicated from the dead and thus will not be put to shame, and (2) those who reject him and thus remain in a "covenant" with death.

2:7

To you then who believe, he is precious; but for those who do not believe, "The stone that the builders rejected has become the very head of the corner,"

To you then who believe, he is precious. Peter emphasizes that the audience (ὑμῖν) is a part of the former group—those who trust in the "stone." They share God's judgment in ascribing "honor" (ἡ τιμή) to the rejected and crucified Messiah.

But for those who do not believe, "The stone that the builders rejected has become the cornerstone." Whether *the head of the corner* (κεφαλὴν γωνίας) refers to the cornerstone or the copestone (scholars disagree) the force is the same: this is the stone on which all else depends. Psalm 118 was among the most important *testimonia* for the NT writers[25] Peter adds Psa 118:22 to those he shares with Paul (Rom 9:32–33). These stone texts were probably taken from a collection of messianic *testimonia* similar to those found at Qumran (4Q174, 4Q175).[26] Peter and Paul worked independently, each

25. Dodd, *According to the Scriptures*, 35–6.
26. DSSE, 525–8.

demonstrating exegetical sophistication and in each case working with coworkers in a school of exegesis.[27] Jobes notes that Psalm 118 (like Psalm 34) was sung by Levites during the Passover when the lambs were slaughtered.[28]

2:8

and "a stone that makes them stumble, a rock that makes them fall." They stumbled because they disobey the word, as they were destined to do.

The third stone text is from Isaiah 8:14, which Peter quotes in a form closer to MT than to LXX.[29] Although the use of this text in 1 Peter concerns primarily judgment for unbelief (as with verse 7), the competent reader of the letter will recall the full echo of Isa 8:14, with the words of Isaiah's oracle, *If you trust in him*,[30] and will discern that the ultimate purpose of God is not disbelief, stumbling and falling, but belief and salvation.

2:9

But you are a chosen race, a royal priesthood, a holy notion, God's own people, in order that you may proclaim the mighty acts of him who called you out of darkness into his marvelous light.

With a rich combination of OT allusions Peter brings to a glorious climax the first section of his epistle. The texts in verses 9–10 are: Exodus 19:6, Isa 43:20–21 and Hos 1:9; 2:23. These verses are not normally considered a hymn,[31] but their musical quality is obvious both in Greek[32] and in English.[33] The term *Royal Priesthood* has been much discussed,[34] and probably should be taken as two substantives.[35] Christians' calling as kings and priests (cf.

---

27. See Introduction, 3–4.
28. Jobes, 53.
29. Marcar, "The Quotations of Isaiah in 1 Peter." 20.
30. NETS Isa 8:14.
31. Peason, "Hymns, Songs," DLNT, 522-4.
32. Rodgers, 1 Peter 2:9-10, Jonny Rodgers, Cindertalk, forthcoming on youtube (forthcoming in 2017).
33. The achingly beautiful Anthem by Samuel S. Wesley, "Blessed be the God and Father."
34. See Excursus by Flagg, 178–83.
35. Elliott, 406 "a royal residence, a priestly community," But the context calls for

Rev.1:6) echoes Exodus 19:6. This dual calling looks back to God's creation ordinance in which man and woman were called to rule and worship.[36] This kingly and priestly calling is an inheritance restored by the Resurrection of Jesus Christ, (1:4) and re-constitutes men and women in Christ as *co-heirs of the grace of life* (3:7).

2:10

Once you were not a people, but now you are God's people; once you had not received mercy, but now you have received mercy.

Most commentators take these words from Hosea as written to Gentile converts, with the consequence that the blessings formerly belonging to Israel have now been transferred to the church: a supersessionist, or replacement theology.[37] But if the letter is written primarily to Jewish Christians in Asia Minor,[38] then the words of Hosea, originally spoken to Jews, are not quoted in disregard of the context, and are entirely appropriate here.[39]

---

both corporate and individual application of the phrase. See *NovT* XLVI, 294.
36. Beale, *The Temple and the Church's Mission*, 83–4.
37. Beare, 107, Achtemeier, 69.
38. see introduction 4–5.
39. Witherington, 121.

1 Peter 2:11–17
by William R. Simmons

2:11

Beloved, I urge you as aliens and exiles to abstain from the desires of the flesh that wage war against the soul.

A term of direct address, *Beloved* (ἀγαπητοί) demonstrates the high esteem in which the author holds his recipients: they are dearly loved by the author, by fellow Christians, and, most importantly, by God.[1] When read alongside 2:9-10, ἀγαπητοί encapsulates a new reality in which the transformative love of God is fully realized in the people of God. From this perspective the author addresses his recipients as ἀγαπητοί, the *Beloved*.

Furthermore, Michaels notes how in the closing of the letter the author characterizes the entirety of what he has written as an "appeal."[2] Given that the exhortation immediately follows the direct address and that the author characterizes the entire epistle as an "appeal," it would seem that παρακαλῶ should be read with a degree of urgency.

Regarding *as aliens and exiles*, a variety of different approaches are taken by scholars when handling this phrase.[3] One of its challenges is deciding whether the language is intended to be interpreted figuratively or concretely. As Jobes notes, there are some instances in which *as* is intended to be read figuratively (comparatively) while there are other instances in

---

1. Goppelt, 155.
2. Michaels, 115–116.
3. See Selwyn, 169; Michaels, 116; Goppelt, 156; Achtemeier, 174; Elliot, 457; and T. Williams, *Good Works in 1 Peter*, 49.

which it is intended to be read concretely (causally).[4] However, the *as* in verse 11 is preceded by six instances of figurative uses[5] and is followed by six instances of concrete uses.[6] Because of its precarious placement, the exegete, as Jobes states, must make a decision. However, characterizing the interpretation as an exegetical decision between figurative and concrete language creates a false dichotomy. Perhaps the nuance of this phrase allows for multiple interpretations.

Both Psalm 39:13[7] and Genesis 23:4 appear to provide the foundation of the phrase *aliens and exiles*. Given that Psalm 39 speaks of suffering in a general sense,[8] it would seem that Genesis 23:4, a portrait of personal suffering, is more likely the source for the Petrine phrase. While Abraham mourns the bitter loss of Sarah, his wife, he refers to himself as "a stranger and an alien,"[9] a reference to earlier events in which God calls him to leave his ancestral land for a promised land. At the time of Sarah's death, Abraham is in the promised land,[10] but the land is not yet his. Abraham's loss is exacerbated by his inability to provide Sarah a proper burial because his social, political, geographical, and theological situation renders him "a stranger and an exile."[11] Because of his obedience to God, Abraham suffers in a foreign land while awaiting the fulfillment of God's promises. It seems that Abraham's plea[12] reverberates through the Petrine phrase in 2:11. Furthermore, it seems that the author portrays the recipients of his letter as a people of anticipation who, in spite of personal suffering, faithfully await the visitation of justice and the fulfillment of God's promises.[13] While beyond the scope of this project, the connection between Genesis 23:4 and 1 Peter 2:11 deserves more attention than has been previously paid to it.

---

4. Jobes, 168.

5. 1:14, 19, 24 (2); 2:2, 5.

6. 2:12, 13, 14, 16 (3).

7. 38:13 in LXX.

8. Mays, 165: "But the suffering is portrayed less as a case of personal and social affliction (contrast Psalm 38) and more as a matter of the general human predicament of transience and futility."

9. Genesis 23:4 NRSV. Unless otherwise noted, biblical references will be from the NRSV.

10. Genesis 23:2.

11. Genesis 23:4 LXX.

12. Genesis 23:4 LXX.

13. I was first alerted to this thematic concept by Steve Graham's "Aliens and Strangers in the World" article appearing in the 69th issue of the online publication *Reality Magazine* (http://www.reality.org.nz/article.php?ID=473).

The infinitive phrase *to abstain from fleshly desires which wage war against the soul* describes the need to distance oneself from fleshly desires,[14] but it does not describe a dualistic conflict. The struggle is not between the flesh and the soul, but is between desires and the soul. As Moulton and Milligan explain, there is a vast difference between something exhibiting the nature and/or characteristics of the flesh (*carnalis*) and something being composed of actual flesh (*carneus*).[15] In this case, the desires exhibit the characteristics of the flesh (*carnalis*) and threaten one's call to good and honorable living:[16] "Peter urges on his readers a clean moral break with the 'natural impulses' of their past (cf. ἐπιθυμίαι in 1:14; 4:2), impulses belonging to the 'darkness' out of which they have been called (cf. 2:9)."[17] These desires campaign to conquer one's existence and, therefore, the author beseeches his recipients to distance themselves from these lesser desires.

2:12

> Conduct yourselves honorably among the Gentiles, so that, though they malign you as evildoers, they may see your honorable deeds and glorify God when he comes to judge.

When faced with conflict, the Beloved are to respond honorably. Lacking specificity, the nature of conflict seems of little importance to either the Beloved or the author.[18] Instead the focus seems to be upon the Beloved's responses to antagonism, whether internal (2:11) or external (2:12), in light of a future hope possible only through the *true grace of God*.[19] This hope is couched within the phrase *when he comes to judge*.[20] Read alongside 1:5,

---

14. This reinforces the earlier directive in 1:15–16, that is to remain holy, and the language in 2:5 and 2:9.

15. MM, 569.

16. Goppelt n. 13, 157: "It is not the opposition of σάρξ and ψυχή, as in the struggle between 'flesh' and 'thought' (νοῦς) in Rom. 7:14ff., between 'flesh' and 'the (Holy) Spirit' (πνεῦμα) in Gal. 5:17, or even between the bodily and the intellectual side of humankind in Greek-Hellenistic philosophy (e.g., Plutarch, *Moralia* 101B [LCL II, 99]). It is noteworthy that the Qumran documents speak only of a battle of the various spirits of the flesh, never of a battle between flesh and spirit (*TDNT* VII, 114)." See also Selwyn 169–170.

17. Michaels, 116.

18. For a more in depth study of the potential conflicts, see Williams, *Persecution*.

19. 5:12.

20. 2:12; see Achtemeier 178 n.82 for eschatological emphasis of phrase. For theological implications of this expression, see Hays, *Echoes of Scripture in the Gospels*, 257–58.

7, and 13, the image that emerges is of an apocalyptic event: the advent of God where salvation and grace are revealed in and through Jesus resulting in the rendering of tribute (i.e., praise, glory, and honor) unto him.[21] The future will bring with it salvation and, presumably, the end of all conflict, injustice, and suffering. Until that day, such things are part of the Beloved's daily existence. How then should they respond? Faced with conflict, the Beloved are not to respond with evil (e.g., 1 Peter 2:1 and 3:9), but instead are to respond by maintaining honorable conduct. This exhortation seems to echo the *verba Christi* found in Matthew 5:38–48[22] and in Matthew 5:16: *In the same way, let your light shine before others, so that they may see your good works and give glory to your Father in heaven.* Verse 12 ends with a memorable scene: on the day of judgement Gentiles are glorifying God. The author, however, stops short of describing what happens to the Gentiles after they glorify God. Perhaps all one can do is wrestle with the final image: the Gentiles glorifying God.[23]

2:13–14

> For the Lord's sake accept the authority of every human institution, whether of the emperor as supreme, or of governors, as sent by him to punish those who do wrong and to praise those who do right.

Verses 13 and 14 continue the navigation theme in regards to living under power and authority. Employing a *via negativa* approach, aspects of what this passage is and is not become clear. First, this passage is neither evidence of nor argument for the divine establishment of the Roman Empire and its emperors.[24] Second, this passage does not mythologize, deify, or divinize the emperor. Rather, the text emphasizes the humanity of the emperor: "One must therefore pay attention to the deliberate limitations placed here on the status of civil government: the emperor is a 'human creature' [ἀνθρωπίνῃ κτίσει] to whom subordination is due as an example of general subordination on the part of Christians within civil society. That point is reinforced in

---

21. 1:5, 7, 13; contra Isaiah 10:3–4. See also Jeremiah 6:15.

22. 1 Peter 2:12 seems to share similarities with the omission in Matthew 5:44. However, the good works are not done to the Gentiles but instead the Gentiles benefit from the good works.

23. Isaiah 43 and 56.

24. Achtemeier, 180 n. 10. The similarities between 2:13–17 and Romans 13:1–7 do not equate to an agreement. See also Achtemeier, 180–182.

the final verse [of the *inclusio*], where honoring the emperor (τὸν βασιλέα τιμᾶτε) follows advice for a similar honoring of all people (πάντας τιμᾶτε)."[25] This point is all the more salient given the geographical and social situation of the recipients. If readers accept that the recipients of this letter included the regions listed in 1:1, then this means that the recipients were surrounded by the imperial cults, cults numbering "about 180 communities throughout Asia Minor. These communities range from small villages up to cities, with a concentration in a few places (Aphrodisias, Ephesus, Mytilene, Pergamum and Stratonicea)."[26] The evidence for Price's estimations comes from a variety of sources throughout Asia Minor, such as "nonliterary material, numismatics, and inscriptions."[27] Furthermore, as Friesen insists, one should not refer to the imperial cult, but rather to the imperial cults.[28] To render it in the singular would be to treat it as if it were a monolithic cult, which it was not, and would ignore the fact that "the imperial cult was intertwined with local religious divinities and observances."[29] Given that the author of 1 Peter insists upon the humanity of the emperor while writing to recipients who are surrounded by imperial cults, such a statement would have rung loudly in the ears of the intended audience.

Third, this passage is not a call for revolution. To cite the text concerning the humanity of the emperor as evidence for Christian resistance would be overreaching. Reading this as a subtle, or not so subtle, call for resistance would undermine the function of the emperor and his governors as agents out of whom justice flows. Furthermore, there is no explicit evidence found within 1 Peter to indicate a call for resistance. While at the very least one might expect a retelling of Jesus' death by Roman crucifixion to take on a more resistant tone, like that in 4 Maccabees,[30] the author only addresses this topic euphemistically citing either Christ's suffering or suffering in the flesh. The closest statement to an explicit reference is 2:24, in which Christ

---

25. Achtemeier, 180.

26. Price, *Rituals and Power*, 4–5.

27. W. Carter, "Roman Imperial Power," 140.in Brodd and Reed, *Rome and Religion*

28. S. Friesen, "Normal Religion, or, Words Fail Us," in Brodd and Reed, *Rome and Religion*, 24.

29. W. Carter, "Roman Imperial Power," 140.

30. "On this anniversary it is fitting for me to praise for their virtues those who, with their mother, died for the sake of nobility and goodness, but I would also call them blessed for the honor in which they are held. All people, even their torturers, marveled at their courage and endurance, and they became the cause of the downfall of tyranny over their nation. By their endurance they conquered the tyrant, and thus their native land was purified through them." 4 Maccabees 1:10–11.

bears the sins of humanity upon the ξύλον.³¹ If this were a call for Christians to resist the Roman Empire, using σταυρός (Philippians 2:8), rather than the less precise ξύλον,³² would have made far more sense. Given this, the emphasis in verses 13–14 is about navigating the relationship between the Christian and those in power and authority over the Christian.

2:15

For it is God's will that by doing right you should silence the ignorance of the foolish.

Once again there is an emphasis upon *doing right* in plain view of antagonists. Verse 15 differs from verse 12 in that the agencies involved in the exoneration of the Beloved are human rather than divine. The governors have the ability to differentiate that which is good from that which is not good. However, the author does not seem to argue that human agencies always perform their functions. While divine, the will of God is juxtaposed alongside the ignorance of the foolish people as if to underscore that human will often competes with God's will. But as long as human agents perform their functions and carry out their duties,³³ the Beloved have hope not only in the future but also in the present.³⁴

2:16

As servants of God, live as free people, yet do not use your freedom as a pretext for evil.

Here the author encourages the Beloved to live as "free people" and as "servants [slaves] of God." What may seem contradictory may actually be explained by an "old Greek custom":³⁵

31. NRSV: "cross"; KJV: "tree."

32. The use of ξύλον seems to hint at a different intention altogether; one that draws from a similar source in the tradition of Deut. 21:23 as used in Gal. 3:13.

33. Selwyn notes: "We have first a reason given (ὅτι) for the moral function of civil government, and then a restatement of this reason in narrower terms, drawing out the implications of the general principle" (Selwyn, 173).

34. Daniel 6:22 and Isaiah 52:13–15. Also, φιμοῦν could share a relationship to Matthew 22:34 in which the Pharisees learned that Jesus had silenced (ἐφίμωσεν) the Sadducees.

35. Deissmann, *Light from the Ancient East*, 322. It is, according to Selwyn, also possible to relate this to the *verbum Christi* in Matthew 17:26 in which Jesus and Peter

> Among the various ways in which the manumission of a slave could take place by ancient law we find the solemn rite of fictitious purchase of the slave by some divinity. The owner comes with the slave to the temple, sells him there to the god, and receives the purchase money from the temple treasury, the slave having previously paid it in there out of his savings. The slave is now the property of the god...he is a completely free man.[36]

This ancient custom describes a cultic practice whereby a person transitions from slave to free person. The significance of this custom should not be lost. In 1 Peter 1:18–19, the author seemingly alludes to this custom: "You know that you were ransomed... not with perishable things like silver or gold, but with the precious blood of Christ."[37] The author reminds the Beloved that while they are free people they still remain slaves of God and as such their behavior should reflect their new state of being. Furthermore, the Beloved are typecast as people set free yet still under systemic authority (e.g., slaves under their masters; wives under their husbands; husbands under religious rituals; all under the emperor and his imperial system; but ultimately freed/ransomed people under the sacral ownership of God). In addition to positively affecting relationships with Gentiles, perhaps this is why it was necessary for the author to include "as he who called you is holy, be holy yourselves in all your conduct" in 1:15. It is also possible, as Deissmann notes, that maintaining a certain level of conduct was an appropriate response of former slaves who had become free people. Citing a letter written during the reign of Caesar Augustus, Deissmann states, "It is a remarkable letter, extremely valuable for the N.T., and was written by a freedman apparently to his patron: 'as a slave for (the sake of) freedom desires to please (his lord), so have I also, desiring thy friendship, kept myself blameless.'"[38]

2:17

Honor everyone. Love the family of believers. Fear God. Honor the emperor.

This rather terse phrasing of verse 17 leaves little open to interpretation. However, it provides contrasting elements and a descriptive structure that

---

discuss the Temple tax. See Selwyn, 174.

36. Deissmann, *Light from the Ancient East*, 322.

37. The purchasing deity in this case is God and the currency is the blood of Jesus Christ.

38. Deissmann, *Light from the Ancient East*, 324 n. 5.

reinforces the necessity to navigate wisely power, authority, and culture. When divided into sections, honor and love are the first elements contrasted. Given the exhortation in verse 12, it would seem that the use of all people refers to Gentiles and/or anyone not initiated into the family of Christ-followers. Similarly, fear and honor are the second elements to be contrasted. The emperor, just as all other people, is to be honored, but God alone is to be feared.[39] The contrasting elements appear to be grouped intentionally to highlight certain aspects of the position and/or relationship. For example, the imperatives to honor and to love are both positive commands. However, the command to love implies a greater degree of relational involvement than does the command to honor. The command to love the body of believers is not as difficult as the command to love enemies.[40] Additionally, the juxtaposition of God and the emperor highlights two positions of great authority and power. Yet, only one is to be feared. Is this another allusion to *verba Christi*?[41] It seems that part of the logic of 1 Peter is to identify and contextualize positions of power, authority, and status in order to properly negotiate such complex relationships[42]. Verse 17 is not arguing for retreat from or even outright defiance of such positions, but is arguing for engagement at all levels. As for the structure of this verse, it seems to flow from external to internal to external. Is it possible that this simple structure reinforces the perception of alienation and exile, being surround by those outside the body of believers, in 1 Peter 2:12? Mirroring Matthew 5:48, the response in 1 Peter is: "Instead, as he who called you is holy, be holy yourselves in all your conduct; for it is written, 'You shall be holy, for I am holy,'"[43] and "Honor everyone." Love the family of believers. Fear God. Honor the emperor."[44] Such exhortations, in addition to the submission imperative, may sound restrictive, but they are not. In fact, the ability to adhere to such things is only afforded to the truly free: "The Christian's submission to the civil power is the act of a free [person]."[45] As free people and slaves of God, the power to choose how to respond to conflict, suffering, injustice, and power ultimately rests with the Beloved.

---

39. Achtemeier, 188.
40. Matthew 5:46–48.
41. Matthew 10:28.
42. Williams, *Good Works*, 25; see also 22 and 186 n.5.
43. 1 Peter 1:15–16.
44. 1 Peter 2:17.
45. Selwyn, 174.

1 Peter 2:18–25
by Peter R. Rodgers

2:18

Slaves, accept the authority of your masters with all deference, not only those who are kind and gentle but also those who are harsh.

Household Servants. The first specific group to be addressed by Peter in the "household codes" is the slaves, or more precisely *household servants*. The word used here is not the usual word used for slaves (δοῦλος) but a term designating domestic workers. A third of the population in the Greco-Roman world was in slavery, and slaves were not considered moral free agents. It is the more remarkable that Peter (and other New Testament writers) address them directly, according them a dignity and honor that was not known in their cultural setting.[1] The word Peter used for *slaves* (Οἱ οἰκέται) may reflect the fact that in Asia Minor most of the slaves were household servants.[2] But the more likely reason that this particular word was used here was that it was regularly used in Deuteronomy (5:15, 6:21, 15:15, 15:17, 16:12, 24:18, 24:20, 24:22) to remind the Israelites that they were a slave (οἰκέτης) in Egypt, and that God delivered them, and therefore they should show kindness to slaves and the marginalized. Thus the whole story of the Exodus from Egypt, which we have seen to influence this letter already, is brought to mind by this one word, and prepares the way for Peter's presentation of the new Exodus in the death of Christ (2:24) and the kind of life that issues from it.

---

1. Jobes, 185.
2. Elliott, 514.

Submit yourselves. Most commentators interpret this middle present participle as having imperatival force.[3] This call to submit, much misunderstood and resisted today, is the middle directive of the five-fold catechetical pattern discerned by Carrington[4] and thoroughly investigated by Selwyn.[5] As a participial imperative here, and in 3:1, the word offers a more supple form of command for Christians to live out their life in "soft difference" from the surrounding culture.[6] Its theological importance can be seen in that the same word is used in 3:22 to affirm that in Jesus' resurrection and ascension, angels, authorities and powers are subject to him. Although this passage seems problematic in that it appears to uphold the institution of slavery (and has been shamefully used in the past to justify the practice), yet the fact that slaves here are addressed as moral agents must, in the end, "trigger the unraveling of the institution of slavery."[7]

with all reverence. Literally this reads "with all fear," but given the command to fear God in relation to their attitude toward other social relations, that sense of awe, respect and reverence should be taken here[8] The fear of God is especially prominent in 1 Peter (1:17, 2:17, 2:18, 3:2)[9] This fear of God has a special place in social ethics, since it "places ethics into the realm of the Creator's sovereign rule over history."[10]

to your masters. The Greek word used here, from which we get the English term *despot*, refers to the owner of the house, and of the slaves as his chattel or property. It is important to note that this word is used in address to God twice in the NT (Luke 2:29, Acts 4:24). This usage may also be found in the LXX (eg. Job 5:8) and is sometimes used in Josephus where the MT has *YHWH* (J.W. 7.8.6).[11] The term is also used of Christ in Jude 4, Rev 6:10 and 2 Peter 2:1. Could it be that Peter has consciously chosen this term to keep the theological focus on God as sovereign creator and ruler, so that, in relations with earthly masters, slaves remain 'conscious of God?'

Not only to the good and gentle. Gentle (ἐπιεικής) is used of Christ in 2 Cor 10:1 (see also Phil 4:5). Christ and Christians are willing to forego retaliation when threatened. Martin especially notes 1 Pet 2:18 in this

---

3. On participial imperative see Dubis, 25–26.
4. Carrington, *Catechism, passim.*
5. Selwyn, 363–466.
6. Volf, "Soft Differences."
7. Green, 79.
8. Feldmeier, 170.
9. Rodgers, *EBR* 8, 1025.
10. Goppelt, 195.
11. Fitzmyer, *The Acts of the Apostles*, 307.

connection. In Phil 2:5–11 Christ's obedience and his not insisting on his rights become the center of gravity.[12] Indeed, Aristotle noted this word as indicating a willingness to forgo one's rights, and so to be content with less than one's due.[13] Within this short verse, several ordinary words have theological connotation due to their use elsewhere in the LXX or the NT, and help to prepare for the main theme of the section: Jesus' non-retaliation, and trust in God.

But also to the overbearing. Literally this word means "crooked." The word is used of Israel as a crooked and perverse nation in LXX Deut 32:5, Psa 77:8. See also Is. 40:4 and 42:16. Once again the language of Israel's storied past is drawn into the open and fronted to tell the story of the people of God, a story whose contours will be shaped in this passage by the Christological application of the Suffering Servant of Isaiah 53.

2:19

For it is a credit to you if, being aware of God, you endure pain while suffering unjustly.

This is commendable. Grace (χάρις), one of the key theological words in the NT (though not so in the LXX) is used here in the non-theological sense, and is often translated "commendable" (NIV,CEB) or "it is a credit." (NRSV). Its use at the end of vs. 20 provides an *inclusio*[14] for the intervening phrases. We also note that this word occurs twice in a passage that applies other terms in the ordinary sense (οικέται, επιιεκής, σκολιοῖς), terms used theologically in the LXX and elsewhere in the NT. This ordinary use of otherwise theological terms hints at the rich theological discussion that is to follow in verses 21–25.[15]

If being conscious of God. The word "conscious" translates the Greek συνείδησιν, which normally means conscience in the NT, and indeed in 1 Peter 3:16, 21. There are two senses of the word: "knowing with" and "the faculty of moral discernment."[16] C. S. Lewis has an illuminating essay on the development of these two senses.[17] The unusual expression here has given rise to the textual variant "a good conscience," (P72 al). The sense in this

---

12. Martin, *2 Corinthians*, 302.
13. Stibbs and Walls, 114. Aristotle *NE* 5.10. *TDNT* 2.588–90. Cf. Phil 4:5.
14. Michaels, 142, Achtemeier, 196.
15. for Χάρις in 1 Peter see Goppelt, 200.
16. Davids, 107.
17. Lewis, *Studies in Words*, 181–213.

passage is that the consciousness of God and the values of his kingdom lead to the radical non-retaliatory and creative behavior commended in what follows.

you endure pain while suffering unjustly. The word for *unjustly* (ἀδίκως) may have been chosen in contrast to the use of *justly* (δικαίως) in verse 23. The suffering is unjustly deserved, but the God in whom they trust judges justly. God's just judgment is in contrast to all unjust systems, be they imperial, (2:13–17) the slave-based economy, (2:18–25) or patriarchal (3:1–7). The use of this passage in previous generations to condone slavery, or of the following section (3:1–7) to justify patriarchy or male dominance is wholly unwarranted and entirely misses the subversive quality of the parenesis in this section, indeed in the whole letter.[18] It is the example and achievement of the submissive Christ that is truly subversive of the world's oppressive systems and behavior.

2:20

If you endure when you are beaten for doing wrong, what credit is that? But if you endure when you do right and suffer for it, you have God's approval.

If you endure when you are beaten for doing wrong, what credit is that? The mention of credit, a word used here only in the NT[19] and meaning *fame, glory,* points to the "honor/shame culture" in which the letter was written.[20] The word for beaten (κολοφιζόμενοι) *strike with the fist,* is used of Jesus during his trial (Mark 14:65) and anticipates Peter's emphasis on the passion in the following verses.[21]

But if you endure when you do right and suffer for it, you have God's approval. Here Peter introduces the theme that will be the major concern in the remainder of the letter.[22] Every word is important. The verb for *suffer* (πάσχειν) is used 11 times in the latter[23] as are four of the sixteen NT occurrences of the cognate noun *suffering* (πάθημα). How Christians respond to udeserved suffering is a major theme of the letter.

18. Williams, *Good Works,* passim.
19. BDAG, 547.
20. Campbell, *Honor, Shame and Rhetoric in 1 Peter,* Elliott, *Disgraced yet Graced.* Elliott provides a valuable list of honor/shame terminology in the letter, 80–86.
21. Hillyer, 88.
22. Witherington, 153
23. Possibly 12 times, but see notes on the text, 165. There are 40 NT occurrences.

The word for *endure* (ὑπομονεῖτε) has the sense of "to maintain a belief or course of action in the face of opposition, stand one's ground, hold on, endure."[24] This patient endurance is expressed in terms of practicing *good works* (ἀγαθοποιία). Travis Williams has recently demonstrated that good works are not merely apologetic but subversive.[25] To cite Brittany Hale's fine phrase, Christian slaves (like the wives of 3:1–6) are to practice "subversive submission in society."[26] However, submission, though strategic, is much more in 1 Peter. It is Christological. Christians are called to follow in the steps of Christ, who *emptied himself and humbled himself and became obedient unto death, even death on a cross* (Phil 2:5–11, 1 Pet 5:6–7).

The phrase *you have God's approval*, (τουτο Χάρις Πάπα Θεω) is the same wording as at the beginning of verse 19 (forming an *inclusio*). Whereas the first occurrence meant something like *this is commendable*, this second use, in light of what follows, probably includes the more technical Christian sense of *grace*. Goppelt has shown how the word has a variety of different connotations within the letter.[27]

2:21

For to this you have been called, because Christ also suffered for you, leaving you an example, so that you should follow in his steps.

For to this you have been called. Note the same wording in 3:9. Following Christ in his suffering is a calling; to follow Christ in his non-retaliatory behavior is to obtain a blessing from God (3:8–9). Calling refers primarily to God's choice rather than ours,[28] for God is the one who calls believers (1:15, 2:9, 5:10).[29] Many scholars have proposed that 1 Peter is here citing an early Christian hymn or creed.[30] While the passage incorporates material from a variety of traditions, Elliott is correct to question the letter's dependence on a creed or hymn.[31] Although the passage reflects the household codes (*haustafeln*) as a series of subordinate clauses, suggesting

24. BDAG, 1039.
25. Williams, *Good works in 1 Peter*.
26. Hale, 79.
27. Goppelt, 200.
28. Goppelt, 201, Achtemeier, 198 n. 128.
29. Elliott, 523.
30. Elliott, 543–50 offers full discussion and bibliography.
31. Elliott, 525. Feldmeier, 167–8.

a hymnic form, the outstanding influence is Isaiah's "fourth servant Song" (Isa 52:13–53:12). The passage is a direct Christological meditation on that song. This Isaianic song is never quoted, and perhaps not even alluded to in Jewish pre-Christian literature, but it becomes one of the key *testimonia* for the Christian gospel, and its use may be traced back to the teaching of Jesus (Mark 10:45, Luke 22:37). 1 Peter makes the most extensive use of this passage in the NT, and it is surprising that Peter's midrashic treatment of Isaiah 53 has been given insufficient attention in studies of NT theology and of the use of the OT in the NT. The four quotations and several allusions from Isaiah 53 are conveniently listed in several recent commentaries.[32] They are as follows:

1 Peter	Isaiah 53
2:21	4,5,6,8,10,11,12
2:22	9
2:23a	7
2:23b	3–5,7,8,11,12
2:23c	6, 12
2:24a	4, 11, 12 (cf 53:5)
2:24b,c	5,11
2:24d	5
2:25a	6a[33]

Because Christ also suffered for you, leaving you an example, so that you should follow in his steps. Some manuscripts read *Christ died,* but *suffered* is certainly the original reading, as it suits a context in which suffering is central.[34] The word for *example* (ὑπογραμμὸν) was regularly used in the ancient world of a child's tracing book, "a pattern of letters of the alphabet over which children learning to write would trace."[35] Followers of Christ need to follow closely (ἐπακολουθήσητε) in his steps.

---

32. Elliott, 547, Jobes, 194.
33. Adopted from Elliott, 547.
34. See the excursus on textual variations in 1 Peter, 165.
35. Achtemeier, 199, Jobes, *195,* Green, 84.

2:22

> "He committed no sin, and no deceit was found in his mouth."

Significantly, the verses from Isaiah 53 quoted in 1 Peter 2 do not follow Isaiah's order, but that of the passion narrative. For Peter, the passion of Jesus is the hermeneutical key to Isaiah 53. During Jesus' earthy ministry Peter totally missed this (Mark 8:32). When he writes the letter it is clear and central to his theology.

2:23

> When he was abused, he did not return abuse; when he suffered, he did not threaten; but he entrusted himself to the one who judges justly.

Peter follows the step parallelism of Hebrew poetry in telling the story of Jesus' passion in the words of Isaiah 53. The progression makes the transition to verse 24 from Christ as example to Christ as sin-bearer more natural. The rhetorical effect is of the story being carried to its climax, on a tree. The focus of verse 23 is the passion narrative, although Isaiah 53:7 may be in view as well. Peter is calling his readers to emulate Jesus' non-retaliation and trust in God. (3:9). Cranfield finely remarks: "no bitter threats or prayers of vengeance escaped His dying lips, but instead a prayer to His Father to forgive His enemies."[36] Jesus entrusting himself to God who judges justly anticipates the call to entrust ourselves to a faithful creator (4:19).

2:24

> He himself bore our sins in his body on the cross, so that, free from sins, we might live for righteousness; by his wounds you have been healed.

No commentary does justice to this magnificent statement of Christ's vicarious suffering. A full-length study is long overdue. The need for such a monograph is all the more urgent since the publication of the creative study by N.T. Wright.[37] Commentators note the sense that Christ bore our

---

36. Cranfield, 67.

37. Wright, *The Day the Revolution Began*. This splendid study, however, does not mention 1 Peter 2:18–25.

sins *right up to the cross*.[38] Some have seen in the expression that Christ *bore our sins* a background in the scapegoat of Leviticus 16,[39] while others a reference to the sin offering.[40] Still others focus attention on the allusion to Deut 21:23, *Anyone hung on a tree is under God's curse*, a strand of early tradition found in Acts 5:30, 10:39, 13:29, Gal 3:13.[41] The expression *on the tree* is *metaleptic*, that is, it becons the reader to examine the context and background of Deuteronomy 21, and presupposes his/her competence to do so.[42] The *combination* of Deut 21:23 in these instances, as here in 1 Peter, with other OT texts deserves further study, and suggests sophisticated midrashic technique.[43] Some focus on the cultic significance and Christ's role as the sacrificial animal.[44] Add to these the theme of the "righteous sufferer," so prevalent in second temple Judaism,[45] and indicated by the linguistic and thematic link between Psalm 34 and Isaiah 53 in 1 Peter.[46] These suggested backgrounds, each inadequate on its own, all contribute in some way to the richness of Peter's teaching on the vicarious and substitutionary nature of Christ's death. For 1 Peter the death of Jesus finds its focus in the Suffering Servant of Isaiah 53.[47] Peter's purpose is both kerygmatic (to proclaim Christ's death for sin) and paraenetic (to apply it to the pattern of Christian living, especially under trial). A faithful interpretation of this passage will emphasize equally Christ our example and Christ our sinbearer.[48]

So that free from sins we might live for righteousness. While Peter's thought is "close to Paul" in Rom 6:11,[49] the chief influence is probably Isaiah 53:10: *The righteous one, my servant, shall make many righteous, and he shall bear their iniquities*. Note again the verbal link with Psalm 34 (cited in 3:10–12) through the catchword *righteous* (δίκαιος).

By his wounds you have been healed. This clear allusion to Isaiah 53:5 changes the first person to the second person plural, giving direct application

---

38. REB: *He carried our sins in his own person*. Cf. Phil 2:8.
39. Wand, 83.
40. Bigg, 147. Cf 3:18.
41. TDNT 5, 39.
42. Hays, *Exhoes of Scripture in the Gospels*, 84.
43. See excursus on the Old Testament in 1 Peter, 176.
44. Spicq, 112.
45. See the fine treatment of Carey, *Jesus Cry from the Cross*, 94–125.
46. Note the link word deceit (δόλον) in in Psalm 34 and Isaiah 53 (cf. 1 Pet 2:1).
47. See the especially insightful discussion in Elliott, 543–50.
48. Jobes, 195 uses the phrase "Christological paraenesis."
49. Michaels, 148. Lightfoot, *2 Corinthians and 1 Peter*, 95 notes "The most Pauline passage is 1 Peter 2:24."

to the recipients of the letter. And the application of Isaiah 53, which began with the example of Jesus and moved to his vicarious suffering now shifts again to focus on the healing ministry of Jesus (cf. Matt 8:17).

2:25

> For you were going astray like sheep, but now you have returned to the shepherd and guardian of your souls.

Once again we have an allusion to Isaiah 53:6, *All we like sheep have gone astray.* The idea of sheep and shepherd is a major theme in scripture. For Christ as shepherd see 1 Pet 5:4, Luke 15:1–7. John 10:11, with OT antecedents in Psalm 23, Isaiah 40:11, Ezekiel 34, and Zech 13:7.[50]

But now you have returned to the shepherd and guardian of your souls.

The precise translation of *you have returned* has been much debated. Should it be translated as an active or a passive/middle?[51] Achtemeier noting the divine initiative opts for the passive.[52] Perhaps the best solution is to see behind the phrase the Hebrew intensive of Psalm 23:3, *He brings me back, He causes me to return.*[53] Of the love of God in Christ that caused this return Bede comments, "Jesus wanted to redeem us so much that he put our sins on his shoulder and bore them for us on the tree, in order to give us eternal life as well as blessing in this world."[54]

---

50. See Bailey, *The Good Shepherd, passim.*
51. Dubis, 82–83.
52. Achtemeier, 204 note 205.
53. Bailey, *Finding the Lost*, 68. *The Good Shepherd*, 44–45.
54. Bede, ACC, XI, 96.

1 Peter 3:1–7
by Brittany K. Hale

3:1–2

> Wives, in the same way, accept the authority of your husbands, so that, even if some of them do not obey the word, they may be won over without a word by their wives' conduct, when they see the purity and reverence of your lives.

These seven verses are challenging for modern interpreters. I would entitle the section, like the previous one, "subversive submission in society."

Likewise (ὁμοίως) points back to 2:18–25 in which slaves are instructed to "submit" to their earthly masters, whether they are gentle or harsh. *Submit* (ὑποτάσσω), is used six times in 1 Peter (2:13, 18; 3:1, 5, 22; 5:5). The first appearance is in the exhortation for all Christians to *be subject to every human authority* in 2:13. These human authorities, then, whether they be the emperor, masters, or non-believing husbands, are not assumed to be just authorities. In fact, there is a tacit understanding that any human institutions are likely to be unjust precisely because they are of humans and not of God. Slaves are given the example of Jesus, who suffered unjustly, but who *entrusted himself to the one who judges justly,* and Jesus' trust was not in vain (2:23). God vindicated Jesus when he raised him from the dead (Acts 2:36). Furthermore, 1 Pet 2:12 encourages Christians to conduct themselves honorably, "so that, though they malign you as evildoers, they may see your honorable deeds and glorify God *when he comes to judge*" (emphasis mine). There is no guarantee the Gentiles will be convinced and converted before Christ returns, though that is the hope. Rather, the Gentiles will at least have witnessed the conduct of Christians, and so will recognize God's glory when he is fully revealed at the end.[1] Therefore, the author is not assuming divine backing for Rome or its patriarchal structure. The act of submission to (potentially) unjust governors, masters, and husbands serves a specific purpose, i.e. to evangelize them. As the *Logos* humbled himself, became human flesh, and submitted himself to the unjust human institutions of the world in order to save the world, so too, are wives instructed to practice this voluntary *kenosis* of their freedom for the sake of winning their husbands.

If any do not obey the word (εἴ τινες ἀπειθοῦσιν τῷ λόγῳ). Disobey (ἀπειθέω) is used in Acts to refer to Jews who did not believe in Jesus. In Romans, Paul quotes Isaiah 65:2: "Of Israel he says, 'All day long I have held out my hands to a *disobedient* and contrary people'" (Rom. 10:21; emphasis mine). He also uses ἀπειθέω in reference to Jews who reject Christ (15:31), and for any who "do not *obey* the truth . . . the Jew first and also the Greek" (2:8-9; emphasis mine). The husbands in mind in 1 Peter 3:1, whether Jew or Gentile, are most likely those who do not believe in Christ, not Christian men who fall into sin.[2] Later in the letter, those of the "household of God" are contrasted with those "who *do not obey* (ἀπειθέω) the gospel of God" (4:17), strengthening the case that these husbands are nonbelievers. Therefore this instruction in 3:1-6 does not apply to marriages in which both parties are Christians.

Submission is both a strategy for survival (1 Peter 2:13-17) and for evangelism (that unbelieving husbands *may be won without a word*), in a society structured on the pagan concept of *paterfamilias*. The Christian family is a dismantling of, and therefore a threat to, the *paterfamilias*. This counter-cultural Christian "family" is another controlling theme of 1 Peter, with familial language sprinkled throughout the epistle: "new birth" (1:3, 23; 2:2), a new "inheritance" (1:4; 3:7, 9), God is "invoked as Father" (1:17), Christians are "obedient children" (1:14), they are now "a holy nation, God's own people" (2:9), and the "household of God" (4:17). Feminist scholar Elisabeth Schüssler Fiorenza sees this threat to patriarchy as the primary attraction for women (and slaves). Schüssler Fiorenza notes, "The Christian message was so attractive and convincing for women and slaves, precisely

---

1. Achtemeier and Jobes agree on this point. Selwyn, Goppelt, and Green believe this refers to the conversion of the Gentiles.

2. There are still Christian leaders who call upon this passage as a proof text for ordering wives of "Christian" men who abuse them, who cheat, or who are disobedient to God in any way, to stay and submit to their husbands as their "spiritual leader." These women are told to be gentle with their husbands, and to pray for them. The onus for the man's spiritual restoration is put on the wife's prayers. If she is not submissive, it is viewed as a hindrance to his ability to assume his calling as her spiritual leader. The damage this teaching has done to both the wives and husbands in this situation is incalculable.

because it promised them liberation from the patriarchal order and gave them a new freedom in the community of equals."[3] Women who identified as free and equal members of this Christian household or family "constituted a potential political offense against the patriarchal order."[4] Their faith already constituted an act of rebellion to the *paterfamilias*. The author of 1 Peter is not directing them to submit themselves "again to a yoke of slavery," for these are daughters of the free woman, Sarah, as we shall see below.[5]

The author gives the reason for submission in no uncertain terms (διὰ τῆς τῶν γυναικῶν ἀναστροφῆς ἄνευ λόγου κερδηθήσονται, [*that*] *they may be won without a word*). This is a rhetorical device (so that even if any do not obey the word, they may be won without a word), not an injunction for women to keep silent. Ironically, the goal of evangelism via submissive conduct is truly an act of subversion of the entire pagan, patriarchal system. For it is fear of God, not of emperor, master, or husband which drives the Christian's "pure conduct." The common value placed upon honorable or pure conduct by Christians and Roman, pagan cultures alike, is the key to this witness. Elliott notes, "Given their subordinate status, wives were hardly in a position to coerce their husbands."[6] The husbands will see that other than worshipping Christ, the wife does not act in any other way to bring tension or embarrassment to the household. Thus, "this 'winning' is not a process of compulsion but of attraction."[7] Christian conduct in general should surpass that of even the most honorable pagans, for they follow the example of Christ, who *when he was abused, he did not return abuse; when he suffered, he did not threaten; but he entrusted himself to the one who judges justly* (2:23). Thus, the "pure conduct" of wives will inevitably point their husbands to the one in whom they trust, Christ.

---

3. Schüssler Fiorenza, *In Memory of Her*, 265.

4. Schüssler Fiorenza, *In Memory of Her*, 265.

5. Galatians 4–5:15 is applicable to more than circumcision and justification by faith. This freedom was of a literal quality, *as servants of God, live as free people* (1 Peter 2:16). Though 1 Peter is not emphasizing Sarah's freedom, but her trust in God and her courage as she submits to Abraham's selfish schemes.

6. Elliott, 558.

7. Ibid.

3:3–4

Do not adorn yourselves outwardly by braiding your hair, and by wearing gold ornaments or fine clothing; rather, let your adornment be the inner self with the lasting beauty of a gentle and quiet spirit, which is very precious in God's sight.

Women's dress and adornment has been, historically, one of their few outlets for free expression. It has also been of great concern to men.[8] Jobes notes that this historical fixation on women's adornment, in the OT as well as Greco-Roman culture, partially stems from the perception of outward adornments "as instruments of seduction ... [and] use of cosmetics was viewed as an attempt to deceive," as well as expression of vanity.[9] Jobes sees this as instruction against outward adornment in general for the sake of appearing chaste when wives leave their homes and husbands to participate in worship. The purpose here (as elsewhere in the household codes of the NT), is not to tell women what is proper dress, but what is proper motivation in dress. The text does not read "do not braid your hair or wear gold jewelry," but "do not *let your adorning be external*, [e.g.] the braiding of hair and the putting on of gold jewelry, or wearing fine clothing" (3:3, emphasis mine). External ornamentation is not to be the source of adornment. The word for adornment is κόσμος, which is the same word for the universe, the celestial bodies, the world in general, all of humanity, and it is often used in the Septuagint to translate the "host" (צָבָא) of heaven (either stars or angels). This is not a term for merely dressing oneself, but for decking oneself. Κόσμος represents the creative flair of God. How women adorn themselves (external ornaments vs. internal qualities) reveals their true nature as created beings who share in the image of God.

The author of 1 Peter rejects the notion (still held by many) that a woman's external beauty constitutes worth. Rather it is the adornment of the hidden or secret *person* (ἄνθρωπος), which pleases God. It is disappointing that Elliott so readily sees in 1 Peter 3:3–4 a call for women to remain within patriarchal gender norms: "the external-internal contrast also replicates the conventional identification of the female with the internal sphere of the home in contrast to the male's responsibility for the external affairs

---

8. Though outside of the purview of this paper, the history of men's desire to control how women clothe themselves is by no means a thing of the past. As Virginia Woolf observed, "the history of men's opposition to women's emancipation is more interesting perhaps than the story of that emancipation itself." Woolf, *A Room of One's Own*, 55.

9. Jobes, 204.

of public life."[10] However, the qualities of the *hidden person* do not support Elliott's interpretation. By using ἄνθρωπος rather than γυνή, the implication is that these hidden qualities are not exclusively feminine, but are the true adornment of women and men. The internal adornment is described as: 1) "hidden" or "secret" (κρυπτός), which is the same word Jesus uses in Matthew for giving alms and praying in secret, so that only the Father sees (Matt. 6:4, 6); 2) of the *heart*: i.e. the seat of thought and the will, out of which behavior comes; 3) *imperishable* (ἄφθαρτος), which is the same quality of the inheritance promised in 1:4 and the seed of new birth in 1:23; and 4) *precious in the sight of God*. The secret, imperishable qualities of the heart which God values in all Christians are a *gentle and quiet spirit* (τοῦ πραέως καὶ ἡσυχίου πνεύματος). The *spirit* here is not the Holy Spirit but "a person's frame of mind, disposition, temperament," etc.[11] Πραέως, gentle, is the same term Jesus uses in Matt. 5:5 *Blessed are the gentle/meek, for they will* inherit *the earth*. The emphasis on inheritance is hardly a mistake; in verse 7 the men will be reminded that women are co-heirs. Jesus also uses πραέως to describe himself in Matt. 11:29: *I am gentle and humble in heart*. Ἡσυχίου, quiet or tranquil, is no more distinctly a feminine quality than *gentle*. Achetemeier finds that "a 'quiet' spirit is the ideal both for the Christian community (1 Tim 2:2) as well as for individual Christians (1 Thess 4:11; 2 Thess 3:12)."[12]

3:5-6

> It was in this way long ago that the holy women who hoped in God used to adorn themselves by accepting the authority of their husbands. Thus Sarah obeyed Abraham and called him lord. You have become her daughters as long as you do what is good and never let fears alarm you.

The reference to holy women of the past, exemplified by Sarah, has puzzled many scholars. Sarah only calls Abraham her "lord," once (Gen. 18:12), and she is not speaking directly to him. Moreover, she is not particularly obedient. By contrast she commands Abraham twice: take Hagar (Gen. 16:2), send Hagar away (Gen. 21:10). God also tells Abraham to obey her, *whatever Sarah says to you, do as she tells you* (Gen. 21:12). Yet Jobes argues that

---

10. Elliott, 568.
11. Elliott, 566.
12. Achtemeier, 214.

despite how this seems to have "embarrassed both Philo and Josephus . . . the submission of Sarah to Abraham was a long-standing element of Jewish tradition."[13] The best candidate for the source of Sarah's submission to Abraham are the sister-wife narratives of chapters 12 and 20.

In *Gender, Power, and Persuasion*, Mignon Jacobs focuses on the complete absence of Sarah's power for self-determination.[14] Though Abraham insists she has power over his life (Gen. 12:13), this power is an illusion. It is intriguing that the imaginative retelling of Abraham and Sarah in Egypt in the Dead Sea Scrolls depicts Sarah with a great deal of personal autonomy. In the Qumran mindset, Sarah was an active participant, and risked herself to save her husband, who is drawn in a highly sympathetic light.[15] In Genesis 12, she does not speak at all, and in chapter 20, though Abimelech tells God that Sarah had said (of Abraham) *he is my brother* (20:5), she never speaks directly. "Sarah's situation parallels that of the Christian wives Peter addresses, living as foreigners and resident aliens in a hostile society."[16] There is little doubt that she would have been in no position to resist Pharaoh, Abimelech, or Abraham. It is God who steps in to rescue Sarah, twice, from Abraham's faithlessness. One might say Abraham was acting in disobedience to the word, and yet, Abraham is never punished for his lack of faith in God's protection and his willingness to risk her. Though it is a stretch to say the author of 1 Peter has in mind Sarah's obedience to a husband who is ἀπειθέω, she is submissive in at least these two situations in which she suffers for the sake of her husband.

Can this submission to cruelty be regarded as proper internal adornment of the secret person? Is 1 Peter guilty of sanctioning domestic abuse as some readings by liberation theologians have alleged it to be? David Horell cautions readers against either of two possible extremes: 1) the text upholds patriarchy, and we should too; 2) the text upholds patriarchy, and we should remove it from the canon. He finds Achetemeier's egalitarian reading to be a tad too optimistic, but denies that 1 Peter upholding patriarchy, nor sanctioning domestic abuse. The trouble is that "1 Peter *can* be read in ways which legitimate the suffering of slaves and women . . . a key question is how—if it is possible—to guard against such uses of the Bible."[17] The key for these verses is to look at the qualifying statements: "the holy women *who hoped in God*," and "*if you do not fear* anything that is terrifying." Though

---

13. Jobes, 205. Sly, "1 Peter 3:6b in light of Philo and Josephus," 126–29.
14. Jacobs, *Gender, Power, and Persuasion*, 73–102.
15. 1QapGen XIX–XX, DSSE, 484–87.
16. Jobes, 205.
17. Horrell, *1 Peter*, 110.

the Neronian persecutions had not yet begun, women would soon need this encouragement, for they were martyred as well as men. Clement informs us that "Christian women had to play the part of Dirce (a figure in Greek mythology) and be torn apart by two bulls."[18] The holy women of the past, and Sarah, hoped in God, as Christ "entrusted himself" to God. God rescued Sarah from the foreign kings in both narratives. Christian women are then called her children, if they do not fear. 1 Peter 2:17 has already invoked the command to fear God, tacitly implying Christians are to fear no one else. At the end of this extended argument (1 Peter 2:13–3:17), the author will encourage Christians: *but even if you do suffer for doing what is right, you are blessed. Do not fear what they fear* (3:14). In other words, it was the gentle and tranquil spirit of Sarah and the other holy women who hoped in God (even when their husbands did not), and who did not fear though they were also vulnerable foreigners. This is what makes these wives "children of Sarah" (3:6).

3:7

Husbands, in the same way, show consideration for your wives in your life together, paying honor to the woman as the weaker sex, since they too are also heirs of the gracious gift of life—so that nothing may hinder your prayers.

As the wives of unbelieving husbands are pointed back to the charge in 2:13–17 to submit to human institutions, and to honor everyone including the emperor, husbands are likewise charged to honor women. Unlike the husbands of 3:1 who *disobey the word*, these Christian men are expected to live with their wives (and presumably any other females in their households, who would be under their protection in Roman society), according to their knowledge of the Gospel. This knowledge or understanding (γνῶσις) is translated by Elliott and the NRSV as *considerately*. The "knowledge" is qualified by the two ὡς clauses: *as the woman is the weaker vessel . . . as they are co-heirs with you of the grace of life*. The tension is the reverse of the situation for the slaves and the women. Whereas women are internally free now, but not yet recognized as equals in the sight of the world (the now and not yet of the kingdom), and so are given survival strategies, men are told to be aware that women are now their co-heirs in the kingdom of God. However, because women are still vulnerable in the Greco-Roman world (and because their bodies are physically smaller and weaker), men are charged to honor

---

18. Reicke, *The New Testament Era*, 249.

women, and essentially to look out for them. A *vessel* (σκεῦος) is simply a created being. It is more often used for men in the NT, but the choice may have been intentional, to highlight the similarity between women and men as created beings, despite the woman being physically more frail than the man.[19] This is not the initiation of chivalry, but the same call for all in the Christian family with more freedom, resources, and worldly power to care for those who are oppressed and vulnerable.

As co-heirs to the imperishable inheritance of 1:4, women are afforded equal dignity and worth, both socially and legally within the Church.[20] Rodney Stark's research directly contradicts Elliott's claim that "there is little if any evidence to indicate that within the Christian community any attempt was made to establish 'equal legal or social or political rights' of males and females."[21] Both men and women were expected to live chastely, infanticide and abortion were prohibited, wealthy widows kept their husband's estate, and poor widows were cared for by the church so neither group needed to remarry. Women also had greater choice in who they married, and they married older than pagan women were often forced to (which contributed to their survival, as young girls often died in childbirth). Clearly, "the Christian woman enjoyed far greater marital security and equality than did her pagan neighbor."[22] It was extremely rare for women to inherit anything. Job giving his daughters a share of their brothers' inheritance was a striking statement about the realignment of his values. The use of co-heirs in 1 Peter carries more weight as a statement about all Christian women.

Finally, men are warned that their "prayers might be hindered" if they fail to honor women as co-heirs. Green cautions against writing this threat off as superstition, "for failure to communicate with God is tied to a comprehensive misunderstanding of God and God's ways."[23] Indeed, Green reminds us that "divine justice is tilted in the direction of society's marginal," and men are to "take their cues from the head of the household of God."[24] However, Green does not find any connection between maleness and inherent superiority of status (headship). It is no accident that men are required here to honor women, just as they are to honor the emperor in 2:17. These men are called to an awareness of the vulnerability of women within society; the disparity between the sexes is a social construct which cannot (nor has

---

19. Achetemeier, 217.
20. See textual note on 3:7, 165.
21. Elliott, 580–81.
22. Stark, *The Rise of Christianity*, 105.
23. Green, 100–01.
24. Ibid, 101.

been) entirely subverted overnight. If men participate in this oppression of women, rather than using the power society confers upon them to aid women, God will not listen to their prayers. The warning recalls the terrifying passage in Matt 25:31–46, when Jesus warns that any who do not care for the *least of these* (hungry, thirsty, a stranger, naked, sick, or in prison), *will go away into eternal punishmen."* (verses 45, 46). Therefore, it is not too much to argue that for Peter the husbands' spiritual wellbeing hinges on their treatment of their wives. Verse 7 acts as a valuable safeguard against a patriarchal misreading of verses 1–6.[25] The best way forward in interpreting this passage is to begin with the new creation vision of verse 7, and not to lose sight of it.

---

25. Such as we see, unfortunately, in 1 Timothy 2.

1 Peter 3:8–12
By Janet C. Hanson

3:8

Finally, all of you, have unity of spirit, sympathy, love for one another, a tender heart and a humble mind.

With the idiomatic phrase *Finally* (τὸ δὲ τέλος,) we conclude the parenesis begun in 2:11, with general instructions for all (πάντες) members of God's household.[1] The main verb absent,[2] five unusual adjectives are listed in a chiastic fashion,[3] defining the unique contours of the cross-shaped character of the Christian community. Virtue lists, often used for the purpose of moral instruction, were popular in the ancient Greco-Roman world, and can be found elsewhere in the New Testament.[4] Peter deliberately lists qualities widely admired (but for the last) in the surrounding culture, but also associated with the ministry and teachings of Jesus Christ, perhaps in order to lead us past a mere ethical ideal to a unique Christian reality, where "character is stamped with the die of the nature of the thrice-Holy God."[5] While most English translations smooth out the awkward-sounding adjectives, when read in their original form the "being" that leads to coun-

---

1. Stibbs and Walls, 128 suggest the use of the phrase τὸ δὲ τέλος points to the climax or "crowning point" of the previous discussion.

2. According to Achtemeier, 222, the participial, ὄντες, "being" is implied, referring back to the imperatives of 2:17.

3. So, Elliott, 603, Forbes, 108.

4. See Fitzgerald, "Virtue/Vice Lists" in *ABD* 6: 858 for a complete listing. Similar NT passages to ours frequently noted by commentators: Rom 12; 1 Cor 13; Eph 4:3, 31–32; Col 3:12–15.

5. Henry, *Christian Personal Ethics*, 474.

ter-cultural "doing" can more readily be discerned.⁶ At the chiastic center Peter places the *genuine mutual love* of 1:22, from which all other thought and action must flow.⁷

Have unity of spirit (ὁμόφρονες). The compound adjective "like-minded" is used only here in the Bible,⁸ while the equivalent Pauline phrase, αὐτὸ φρονεῖν, *to be of the same mind*, is more common.⁹ The cognates appear in OT Wisdom literature in reference to human discernment as well as to the "creative understanding of God."¹⁰ The call is not to uniformity, but to "a unity of aim and purpose, a oneness in attitude,"¹¹ so often discarded in favor of schisms and divisions. As Davids astutely notes, "This is not the unity that comes from a standard imposed from without, such as a doctrinal statement, but that which comes from loving dialogue and especially a common focus on the one Lord."¹² By sharing the mind of Christ we share his unity.

Sympathy (συμπαθεῖς). Literally, "who has fellow-feeling with another," as in the Latin translation: *compatientes*, "compassion." The adjective is unique here in the NT, but reflects a highly valued affection in Greco-Roman and Jewish literature in reference "to the sharing not just of grief or pain, but of a whole range of emotions and experiences."¹³ Thus, Paul will admonish Christians to *rejoice with those who rejoice, weep with those who weep* (Rom 12:15, see also 1 Cor 12:26). 4 Maccabees employs συμπαθεῖς to celebrate the love of siblings (4 Macc. 13:23), and of mothers, *who because of their birth pangs have a deeper sympathy toward their offspring*. But it is Christ's willingness to participate in our human frailty, to genuinely *sympathize with our weaknesses* (Heb 4:15), that informs the familial mandate to "each be constantly and charitably open to the other in such a way that the other's failings are covered."

Love for one another (φιλάδελφοι). Literally, "loving as brothers," here we find the crowning characteristic and *raison d'etre* for the familial harmony so crucial to the church's survival. While the adjective is found only here in the NT, the related imperatives of 1 Peter 1:22; 2:17, *love one another*

---

6. "Persons can only *do* what they *are*." Green, 102.

7. "For God himself is love, is compassionate and tender-hearted, and to be like-minded, humble-minded is to view ourselves in proper relationship with that God." Henry, *Christian Personal Ethics*, 474.

8. The word does occur in classical literature, see Elliott, 603.

9. Cf. Rom 15:5; 2 Cor 13:11; Phil 2:2; 4:2.

10. φρονέω, NIDNTTE 618, Cf. Prov 3:19; Isaiah 40:28; Jer 10:12.

11. Hillyer, 100.

12. Davids, 124.

13. Michaels, 176.

deeply from the heart, and *love the family of believers,* as well as the reminder to *maintain constant love for one another* in 4:8, join the rest of the NT in attesting to this fundamental Christian virtue.[14] The love for God the Father, demonstrated in love for one another and supremely exemplified in Jesus Christ, represents the mark of a true Christian.[15] The adjective places believers, as children of the same Father, in relationships of both tangible support[16] and mutual affection formerly reserved for blood relations,[17] compatriots, and fellow members of religious communities.[18]

A tender heart (εὔσπλαγχνοι). Literally translated "good entrails," referring to the ancient association of the bowels and other inward organs with deep, often impulsive passion.[19] In later use the word group described "tender feelings and caring concern for others, especially for kin, natural or fictive."[20] While not common to the LXX, but used in pseudepigraphal writings, the noun, σπλάγχνα, is applied to God's eschatological acts of compassion and mercy.[21] The adjectival form is found only here in the NT, yet this gut-wrenching, profoundly moving affection, which flows from *the tender mercy of our God* (Luke 1:78), is closely associated with the ministry and parables of Jesus, the one uniquely endowed with this divine compassion.[22] As one of the virtues distinctly characteristic of those "in Christ" (Phil. 2:1),

---

14. Cf., Rom 12:10, 1 Thess 4:9, Heb 13:1, 2 Pet 1:7.

15. Cf. John 13:34-35; 1 John 2:9-11; 5:1-2. Although Goppelt, 233 and Achtemeier 222-3 remind us the focus here is specifically love within the Christian family, not mere abstract love for all humanity, Jesus' exhortation in Matt 5:43-48 points ahead to God's inclusive intentions, as we will discover in 1 Pet 3:9.

16. "In Greek, brotherly love involves obligation rather than feelings. This obligation includes personal loyalty but focuses upon the material support of food and shelter and upon the provision of protection and aid in public life." Donelson, 98.

17. The compound word, ἀδελφός, literally means "one born of the same womb." Wilkings, "Brother, Brotherhood," *ABD* 1: 782-3.

18. See *TDNT* 1:144-146 for the significance of the word group in Jewish and Classical, as well as Christian writings.

19. *TDNT* 7: 548-557.

20. Elliott, 605.

21. T. Zeb. 8.2 "In the last days God will send his compassion on the earth, and whenever he finds compassionate mercy, in that person he will dwell." Charlseworth, *OTP,* 1, 807.

22. Cf. the use of the verb form, "to be moved with pity" (σπλαγχνίζομαι), referring to Jesus: Matt 9:36; Mark 1:41; 6:34; 8:2; 9:22; Luke 7:13, as well as in the Parable of the Wicked Servant, where it is used in conjunction (as in Luke 1:58) with ἐλεέω, "to have pity, mercy" (Matthew 18: 27, 33) the response of the Samaritan (Luke 10: 33), and the father of the Prodigal Son (Luke 15:20).

"this good-heartedness is a quality that knows no frontiers, and so prepares the way for those qualities which especially face towards the outside world."[23]

And a humble mind (ταπεινόφρονες), "humble-minded."[24] In the highly competitive, honor/shame–based Greco-Roman society, the word group implied "lowly, mean, insignificant, weak, poor, of trivial power or significance."[25] As Elliott affirms, it represented "a detestable position to assume, unworthy of true men."[26] The adjective is found in the Bible only here and in Prov 29:23 of the LXX, although the noun, ταπεινοφροσύνη, occurs 7 times in the NT.[27] In the OT and other Jewish tradition, to be humble-minded is to recognize one's proper relationship with God.[28] This virtue, so crucial to church unity, is modeled on the teachings and conduct of Jesus who *came not to be served but to serve* (Mark 10:45, Phil 2:5-8). Because he is "gentle and humble in heart," Jesus can promise rest for souls battered and bruised by the arrogant, selfish conceit characteristic of fallen humanity, and so destructive to community. "In a deft restructuring of 'the way the world works,' Peter takes a label that might well have been used by unbelievers in a smear campaign against followers of Christ and uses it positively as a characteristic disposition of Christians."[29]

3:9

> Do not repay evil for evil or abuse for abuse; but on the contrary, repay with a blessing. It is for this that you were called—that you might inherit a blessing.

Following this brief listing of virtues essential to Christian harmony, in verse 9 we are introduced to "the centerpiece of the ethical teaching of the entire epistle."[30] A like-minded community, characterized by compassionate love and tenderhearted humility, will be prepared to respond to evil

---

23. Selwyn, 189.

24. Support for ταπεινόφρονες is superior to alternative manuscript witness to φιλόφρονες, "hospitable" or the conflation of the two. See Green, 101.

25. *TDNT* 8:1–26.

26. Elliott, *A Home for the Homeless*, 128.

27. Acts 20:19; Eph 4:2; Phil 2:3; Col 3:12 and 1 Pet 5:5b in a positive sense, Col 2:18, 23 in a polemical context.

28. Cf. Psalm 18:27; Proverbs 3:34, Isaiah 58:5. See *TDNT* 3:369–71 for a thorough treatment of ταπεινόφρονες and its cognates.

29. Green, 103.

30. Michaels, 178.

provocation and reviling in a counter-intuitive, non-retaliatory manner.[31] Called to solidarity with their Lord, who *did not return abuse; when he suffered, he did not threaten* (1 Peter 2:23), and in response to his teaching,[32] these Jewish-Christians would have already been familiar with OT wisdom literature's call to a non-retaliatory response.[33] While κακός, *evil* can denote any injurious or morally reprehensible behavior,[34] λοιδορία (speech that is highly insulting, abuse, reproach, reviling)[35] may reflect circumstances especially pertinent to the cultural milieu of 1 Peter.[36] As Elliott proposes, "The nature and weapons of the attack on the Christians is a classic example of public shaming designed to demean and discredit the believers in the court of public opinion with the ultimate aim of forcing their conformity to prevailing norms and values."[37] Without patronage or social position on their side, few options, legal or otherwise, would have been open to Peter's readers. Yet resigned passivity is not what the author has in mind. Christians are supernaturally empowered "to break the cycle of evil that spirals ever downward."[38]

but, on the contrary, repay with a blessing. Two verbs, ἀποδίδωμι (to render, reward, recompense)[39] and εὐλογέω (to bless), comprise a negative and a positive command. The secular understanding of the Greek, εὐλογέω, goes no further than "to speak well of, praise, extol."[40] But here under Old Testament influence and the reiteration of εὐλογίαν later in the verse, the more demanding teaching of Jesus comes into view.[41] In following their Lord, Christians must reject both passive resignation and *lex talionis*, and instead demonstrate love of, prayer for, and kindness toward those who

---

31. It would be a mistake to sharply differentiate between verses 8 and 9. Jesus commands not mere self-restraint but love for enemies (Luke 6:27). See also the response of the compassionate Samaritan directed towards one of his traditional enemies in Luke 10:33. In addition, intra-church hostility and tensions were clearly present in the early church (Cf. 1 Cor 11:17–20; Eph 4:25–32; Col 3:8–11), and are present today.

32. Matthew 5:43–44; Luke 6:27–28.

33. See Prov 20:22; 24:29; 25:21–22. Oft-mentioned similarities to Romans 12:17 and 1 Thess 5:15 also suggest a common parenetic tradition.

34. BDAG, 501.

35. BDAG, 602, its NT use is limited to here, and 1 Tim 5:14.

36. Cf. 1 Peter 2:12, 23; 3:16; 4:4.

37. Elliott, *Disgraced Yet Graced*, 170.

38. Jobes, 218.

39. BDAG, 110.

40. BDAG, 407–8.

41. Matthew 5:38–48; Luke 6:27–36.

mistreat them. "Enemy love advocates a refusal to differentiate between friends and enemies."[42]

It is for this that you were called.[43] Using the same exhortation given to slaves in 2:21–3, Peter reminds all Christians of the vocational nature of our counter-cultural response.[44] The prepositional phrase *because to this* (ὅτι εἰς τοῦτο) points ambiguously, either backward, referring to 9a, "you were called to this, to repay with blessing," or forward to what follows.

that you might inherit a blessing. This grammatical uncertainty raises questions about the nature of the blessing (εὐλογία) and its apparent contingency on human obedience. The backward focus of the same phrase (ὅτι εἰς τοῦτο) in 1 Peter 2:21 makes a strong case for the same in 3:9, and is favored by the majority of commentators.[45] Some scholars, objecting to any hint of "salvation by works," contend the grammatical construction bears greater similarity to 1 Peter 4:6; pointing forward, the "to this" refers to eschatological blessing, *kept in heaven for you* (1 Pet 1:4).[46] Thus, Selwyn concludes, "The Christian's attitude of goodwill towards those who inflict personal insult or injury is grounded in a thankful realization of God's mercies and promises to himself."[47] As Green contends, "A hard choice need not be made."[48] Comprising both unearned inheritance and a robust ethical demand, "the Christian hope is also the Christian rule."[49] The peculiar Christian identity is formed in following in the footsteps of Jesus (2:21), so the refusal to heed the call to be a bearer of God's blessing, despite hostile treatment, raises questions as to the genuineness of our calling and love for Christ.[50] But at the same time, "we shall enter increasingly into the full enjoyment of the blessing of God's forgiveness and goodwill only if we learn ourselves to extend similar forgiveness and good will to others."[51]

---

42. Green, 105–6.

43. ὅτι εἰς τοῦτο ἐκλήθητε. Some later witnesses precede the conjunction with the participle εἰδότες (*knowing*), "transforming ὅτι into a marker of a clausal compliment" (*knowing that*) M. Dubis, 99.

44. Καλέω, in the sense of "to choose for receipt of a special benefit or experience" (*BDAG*, 503) is a frequent topic in 1 Peter (1:15; 2:9, 21; 3:6, 9; 5:10).

45. Elliott, 609 (Cf. Achtemeir, 224, Donelson, 99, Grudem, 127, Jobes, 219, Michaels, 178).

46. Cf. Davids, 127, Goppelt, 234, Selwin,190 for this latter view. For a more detailed discussion of the argument, see Elliott, 609–610.

47. Selwyn, 190.

48. Green, 106.

49. Bigg, 156.

50. See 1 Peter 1:7, 14–17; 2:1–3.

51. Stibbs and Walls, 131.

3:10-12

For "those who desire life and desire to see good days, let them keep their tongues from evil and their lips from speaking deceit; let them turn away from evil and do good; let them seek peace and pursue it. For the eyes of the Lord are on the righteous, and his ears are open to their prayer. But the face of the Lord is against those who do evil."

With the conjunction *for* (γὰρ), the author moves directly into an extensive Old Testament quotation, lifted, with minor stylistic changes, from Psalm 34:12b-16 (LXX 33:13b-17).[52] While the psalm's influence on early Christian parenesis and liturgy has been widely noted,[53] in a recent article, Sean M. Christensen presents a compelling case for a close relationship with 1 Peter in particular, a theory first explored by Wilhem Bornemann a century ago.[54] According to Christensen, the psalm quotation in 1 Peter 3:10-12 is strategically placed in the center of the letter, providing clarification and support for the previous ethical discussion, and preparing the reader for the exhortation to follow.[55] The instructional material in verses 8-9 and the psalm quotation in 10-12 contain striking similarities, as well as forming together a chiastic pattern.[56] Psalm 34 had traditionally been applied to David and Israel's affliction,[57] and now to the righteous suffering of Jesus.[58] Beleaguered Christians are thus encouraged to stand firm in obedience, "while awaiting the ultimate blessing of vindication."[59]

"*Those who desire life and desire to see good days (3:10a).*[60] Originally referring to temporal prosperity, the New Testament context suggests to some

---

52. Allusions to this Psalm are found in 1 Peter 2:3 and echoed throughout the book. See Jobes, 220-3 and Excursus, "The Use of the Old Testament in 1 Peter," 171-72.

53. Selwyn, 190. See also *1 Clement.* 22:2-8.

54. Wilhelm Bornemann, based on linguistic and thematic parallels, proposed the book was a baptismal sermon dependent on Psalm 34 according to Sean M. Christensen, "Solidarity in Suffering," 335.

55. Ibid. 337.

56. Christensen, "Solidarity in Suffering, 341, credits Richard Bauckham for this literary observation.

57. Cf. 4 Macc 18:15, and the superscription of the psalm, referring to David's experience.

58. 1 Peter 3:13-18 links the psalm quote in verses 10-12 to the example of Christ. See also, John 19:36.

59. Christensen, *Solidarity in Suffering,* 351.

60. Psalm 33:13 LXX reads, "What person is he who wants life, coveting to see good days?" (NETS) The author or authors of 1 Peter have made minor changes in the syntax

commentators a more distant, eschatological longing.⁶¹ This view, however, ignores the seamless and unqualified movement between verses 9 and 10. Goppelt's description of *the gracious gift of life* (ζωή) as "the abiding and whole existence of the creature with its Creator"⁶² provides helpful clarity.

In verses 10b-ll, five imperatives, covering both speech and conduct, direct the way to this quality of life:

"*let them keep their tongues from evil and their lips from speaking* (παυσάτω) *deceit; let them turn away* (ἐκκλινάτω) *from evil and let them do* (ποιησάτω) *good; let* them **seek** (ζητησάτω) *peace and pursue* (διωξάτω) *it.*"⁶³

The quotation ends with the assurance, "*the eyes of the Lord are on the righteous, and his ears are open to their prayer. But the face of the Lord is against those who do evil,*"⁶⁴ leaving unaddressed the second half of the psalm verse.⁶⁵ The warnings of 1 Peter are directed not toward God's enemies, but toward discouraged Christians, tempted to forsake the Jesus way when suffering unjustly.⁶⁶ The choice is between God's blessing or opposition. Jobes concludes, "Each choice is a microcosm of life or death."⁶⁷

---

perhaps for editorial purposes. Some scholars surmise Peter was working from a different textual tradition than that of the LXX. Cf. Michaels, 180.

61. "To 'see good days' is to see what is now unseen, the glory in store for Christians at the revelation." Michaels, 180. See also Elliott, 612 and Dubis, 100.

62. Goppelt, 236. See also Jobes, 224, "Good days for the Christian are those that enjoy the fellowship of God. . . ."

63. For the frequent NT admonition to the pursuit (διώκω) of peace, see Rom 14:19; 2 Tim 2:22, Heb 12:14, reflecting Jesus in Matt 5:9 (Hillyer, 103).

64. "The Old Testament always sees behind every moral demand made upon man the will of God, who in the eyes of the sinners is their enemy, but in the eyes of the righteous is their friend and helper in adversity." Weiser, *The Psalms*, 299.

65. "to cut off the remembrance of them from the earth" Psalm 34:16b (LXX 33:17b).

66. The author refers to κακός (evil) five times in 3:9-12 within a discussion of Christian ethics. See also 1 Peter 2:1, 16.

67. Jobes, 224. See Deuteronomy 30:19-20 for similar themes.

1 Peter 3:13–17
by Amanda Van Vliet Snyder

For many readers 1 Peter will have a very contemporary feel. In 1 Peter 3:13–17, Peter is addressing the issue of a Christian's response to non-believers, especially those who reject, persecute, and may even cause them physical harm. This section demonstrates that Peter is primarily concerned with the believer's response to persecution and intimidation. His focus in this section is how a follower of Christ should react to specific attacks from the non-Christian world.[1] According to the Apostle Peter, the Christian response to the world should be full of kindness and respect. Their response should point non-Christians toward the love of Christ. I. Howard Marshall sums up this section by stating, "Though we Christians will have to respond to some hostile forces in an unbelieving world, we must live lives of a character that can be recognized for its quality even by non-Christians."[2]

3:13

Now who will harm you if you are eager to do what is good?

In the preceding section, Peter informs his audience that God is responsive to the "suffering of the righteous."[3] This, however, leads to a contradiction in the lives of the recipients that Peter must confront in verse 13. Although the Lord promises to hear the prayers of the righteous and set His face against those who do evil, yet persecution still remains.[4] Peter's uses the word *now* (καὶ) to transition from God's promises in verse 12 to his

---

1. David Walls and Max Anders, *I & II Peter, I, II & III John, Jude*, vol. 11, 53.
2. Marshall, 78.
3. Jobes, 222.
4. Green, 109.

statement to his audience that their current suffering is limited and cannot inflict real harm to the followers of Christ, those who are eager to do what is good (τοῦ ἀγαθοῦ ζηλωταί). The theme, and the influence of Psalm 34 from the previous verse (3:12) carries over into verse 13; the people who are described in verse 12 as "those who do evil" (ποιοῦντας κακά) are the very same people who will harm (τίς ὁ κακώσων) those who are doing good.[5]

Since verse 12 refers to God's face being against those who do evil, it is possible that Peter's audience may begin to question why God's people suffer. Peter refers to the persecution they were experiencing, addressing the possiblity that the audience was experiencing a "pronounced existential experience of theodicy on their parts."[6] It is possible that the preceding verse leaves his audience questioning that there are only two explanations for the hardship they face. Either, they are actually wicked, and therefore, they are experiencing God's wrath, or that the Lord "will not or cannot protect His own."[7]

However, Peter is arguing in this verse that there is a third explanation for the plight of the readers. Peter is making the case that no one can ultimately harm those who are zealous for what is good. Through his rhetorical question Peter simply makes the point that no one can bring lasting and eternal harm upon believers.[8] Moreover, he is further reiterating the point he made in verse 12, God will reward those who are faithful.[9] Peter is encouraging those who are facing persecution, allowing them to see that if God is on the "side of the righteous and against those who do evil, what harm can possibly come to those who do good?"[10] It is important to note that Peter is here echoing Isaiah 50:9.[11]

---

5. Ibid. 111
6. Ibid.
7. Ibid.
8. Jobes, 226.
9. Schreiner,170.
10. Michaels, 185.
11. Focus on the echo of Isa 50:9 may be the key to solving any tension between verse 13 and verse 14.

3:14

But even if you do suffer for doing what is right, you are blessed. Do not fear what they fear, and do not be intimidated,

Verse 14 begins with the conjunction *but* (ἀλλ'). It is likely that this conjunction is used as a clarification for the previous verse.[12] Believers have been harmed, and some even killed, by opponents. Therefore, Peter likely uses the conjunction to link the two verses, suggesting that when someone is harmed for doing good, there will be eternal consolations.

Peter is indicating in verse 14 that the suffering of believers does not contradict the claim of verse 13, but that those who *suffer for doing what is right* (πάσχοιτε διὰ δικαιοσύνην), enduring opposition because of their zealousness, are *blessed* (μακάριοι).[13] He wants to reassure his readers that even present suffering is not a sign of "punishment but of God's blessing both now and especially in the future, in the day when he rewards his people with eternal life."[14] Peter is stating that those who do what is right are blessed even when they are suffering; their ultimate fate is better than "that of evildoers even when the will of God permits those evildoers to oppress them."[15]

Peter used the Greek *blessed* (μακάριοι) to proclaim the state of those who are persecuted for doing righteousness. This word can be translated as "being fortunate or happy because of circumstances, fortunate, happy."[16] However, it must be understood that Peter was not telling his readers that suffering should bring happiness. He did not say that "sufferings are themselves pleasant, for then, obviously, they would not be sufferings."[17] It was likely that Peter was referring to the words of Jesus, who proclaimed that those who suffer are blessed because of the eschatological reward they will receive, an adaptation of the "eighth beatitude in Matthew 5:10-11, *Blessed are those who are persecuted for righteousness sake* (μακάριοι οἱ δεδιωγμένοι ἕνεκεν δικαιοσύνης).[18] Therefore, it was more likely that Peter's should use the word μακάριοι in the same way that Jesus used it in the beatitudes, meaning "privileged recipients of divine favor."[19] Peter was agreeing with the words of

12. Schreiner, 171.
13. Ibid., 171.
14. Ibid.
15. Michaels, 186.
16. BDAG, 610.
17. Schreiner, 171.
18. Michaels, 185.
19. BDAG, 610.

Jesus, declaring that those who "suffer for the sake of righteousness, actually dwell in a state of blessedness."[20]

Peter may also be making the point that those who choose do what is right in the eyes of the Lord may actually bring unwanted attention upon themselves. Joel Green argues that those who attempt to imitate Christ, those who are "eagerly zealous for the good, find themselves out of step with the conventions of wider society."[21] Because they do not conform to the norms and expectations of society, Peter's audience may be inviting malice from those who do not believe.

The second half of this verse is the imperative, *do not fear what they fear* (τὸν δὲ φόβον αὐτῶν μὴ φοβηθῆτε). Peter is alluding to the text in Isaiah 8:12-13, where the Lord exhorts Isaiah not to have fear of their enemies because the Lord is with them. This text in Isaiah appears to be important to Peter; it is also quoted earlier in the epistle in 1 Peter 2:8.[22] Even though there are differences between this verse and the text found in Isaiah, the heart of the quotation remains intact. Peter is contrasting the fear caused by humans in verse 14 with fearing and revering God in verse 15. Peter is stating that ultimately no one can harm believers. Since their suffering is a "sign of God's blessing, then it follows that they should not fear what others can do to them."[23]

3:15

> but in your hearts sanctify Christ as Lord. Always be ready to make your defense to anyone who demands from you an accounting for the hope that is in you;

Verse 15 continues Peter's allusion to Isaiah 8 by calling his readers to *sanctify Christ as Lord* (κύριον δὲ τὸν Χριστὸν ἁγιάσατε). In the LXX, the use of Lord (κύριος) in Isaiah 8 clearly refers to YHWH, but here Peter used the word to refer to Christ (Χριστὸν). The change Peter makes from *him* (αὐτόν in the LXX) to Christ "reflects the conviction that Jesus the Messiah deserves the same honor as YHWH."[24] In the same way that God's holiness was made known among the Gentiles through the Israelites, Peter was

---

20. Green, 112.
21. Ibid.
22. Jobes, 229.
23. Schreiner, 172.
24. Ibid, 173.

calling believers to make Christ's holiness be known "even in the face of interrogation and threats."[25]

Also added to the original writing in Isaiah 8:13 is the phrase *in your hearts* (ἐν ταῖς καρδίαις ὑμῶν). This gives personal application to the command. For Peter, the heart (καρδία) was the "innermost center of the human being and hence the source of Christian love."[26] Therefore, Peter is telling his audience that they need not only to acknowledge Christ's sanctity with their words, but within the depths of their inner lives.

The beginning of the next sentence, *always be ready* (ἕτοιμοι ἀεὶ) seems out of place. In the previous sentence, Peter refers to the inner life, a great contrast to his next statement in verse 15. Some biblical scholars state that it is difficult discern how the "next sentence relates to the previous one."[27] However, Peter seems to be suggesting that when believers are doing what is good and righteous, it will cause the secular world to see something different. It will cause non-believers to ask questions and want to know why. When believers live an inner life where Jesus Christ is sanctified, it will be reflected in their outer lives. Peter is simply stating that the *hope* (ἐλπίδος) that "animates believers will become so evident that unbelievers will ask for an explanation."[28]

The readers are being asked to be ready always to provide a *defense* (ἀπολογίαν) to anyone who asks about their faith and hope in Christ Jesus. As Christians respond to the world in a way that is strikingly different from those around them, they become a curiosity. Peter is emphasizing that his audience should always be ready to provide an answer to anyone who sees the way they live and asks about the Christian faith.[29]

Peter's use of ἀπολογίαν may lead some to believe that Peter was referring to a formal court case in which believers were responding to legal accusations. However, Peter clears this up by using the phrase, *to anyone who demands from you an accounting* (παντὶ τῷ αἰτοῦντι ὑμᾶς λόγον). Peter is speaking here of anyone who may question a believer's faith, not just government authorities. Peter is not just referring to a courtroom, but instead is using legal language to describe the "informal exchanges that can occur between Christian and non-Christian at any time and under varied circumstances."[30] It is possible that Peter used the language of the court-

---

25. Michaels, 187.
26. Achtemeier, 233.
27. Schreiner, 174.
28. Ibid,175.
29. Ibid,174.
30. Michaels,188.

room because he understood that the suffering believers were facing caused them to be scrutinized and tried on a daily basis.

It is also important to understand that Peter is not calling believers to be argumentative and to initiate a debate with the secular world; he is not referring to "syllogistic reasoning or presentation of indisputable evidence to support the truth of the Christian faith."[31] Rather, he is asking believers to be ready to give a "positive, reasoned presentation of the gospel."[32] Peter was not asking his audience to offer a defense to scoffers, but to offer a reasonable account to those who asked,[33] those who sincerely want to understand the differences in how believers live. Peter is assuming that believers do in fact have "solid intellectual grounds for believing the gospel,"[34] and was exhorting his readers to be ready to defend those grounds in public. He was expecting all believers to understand the essential elements of their faith and to be equipped to explain that to others.

Unfortunately, many believers use Peter's words as a justification to argue with the nonbelieving world and to engage in debates in the public arena. Those believers often forget or overlook Peter's final command in this verse, *yet do it with gentleness and reverence* (ἀλλὰ μετὰ πραΰτητος καὶ φόβου). What Peter is saying is that when believers are faced with hostility and persecution, it is tempting to respond harshly. He is reminding his readers that their response should be filled with "gentleness toward other people and reverence before God."[35] He is teaching that those who fear God and are humble will treat those who oppose them with love, demonstrating the gospel of Christ they are proclaiming.

3:16

> yet do it with gentleness and reverence. Keep your conscience clear, so that, when you are maligned, those who abuse you for your good conduct in Christ may be put to shame.

This verse begins with the proclamation that believers must *keep [their] conscience clear* (συνείδησιν ἔχοντες ἀγαθήν). συνείδησιν refers to the "inward faculty of distinguishing right and wrong."[36] Here Peter is reminding his

---

31. Green, 117.
32. Marshall, 116.
33. Lange, *Holy Scriptures: 1 Peter*, 59.
34. Schreiner, 175.
35. Ibid., 176.
36. BDAG, 967. See also on 1 Peter 2:19. For a different sense of the word.

audience to remain blameless and pure and not to resort to anger when they are asked to defend their hope. This is the attitude from which believers must make their defence.[37]

Peter explains to his audience the reason they are to maintain a good conscience before God using the particle *so that* (ἵνα).[38] He states that when believers remain in good standing before God and display righteous behavior, those who have *maligned* (καταλαλεῖσθε) them will *be put to shame* (καταισχυνθῶσιν). When this letter was written, the readers were likely being mistreated and maliciously slandered by their secular nieghbors. However, Peter is calling his audience to not use these attacks as an excuse to respond in kind, but instead to constantly live by a "higher ethical standard than quid pro quo."[39]

There is some disagreement as to what Peter meant when he used the term καταισχυνθῶσιν. Some state that unbelievers will be put to shame within their lives after recognizing their unjust treatment of Christians, while others believe Peter is referring to shame felt on the Day of Judgment.[40] Either way, Peter is arguing that it is "exactly at those moments when a believer may feel the least like responding with a gracious testimony of hope in Christ that it is most important to do so."[41]

3:17

For it is better to suffer for doing good, if suffering should be God's will, than to suffer for doing evil.

Peter begins verse 17 with the phrase *for it is better* (κρεῖττον γὰρ), echoing words found in Jesus' teachings.[42] One example can be found in Matthew 5:29, *It is better for you to lose one of your members than for your whole body to be thrown into hell.*[43] In the same way that Jesus set up two eschatological alternatives, Peter might be using this phrase to offer similar alternatives: Are you suffering now for *doing good* (ἀγαθοποιοῦντας)? Or will you suffer later for *doing evil* (κακοποιοῦντας)? Since it is likely believers will not escape

---

37. Michaels, 190.
38. Schreiner, 176.
39. Jobes, 231.
40. Schreiner, 177.
41. Jobes, 232.
42. Ibid.
43. NRSV, Matt 5:29.

suffering, then it is important that the "opposition Christians receive must be for good behavior, not their shortcomings."[44]

---

44. Schreiner, 179.

1 Peter 3:18–22

By Stephen R. Rodriguez

First Peter 3:18–22 is among the most difficult passages to interpret in the New Testament. The issues are many and complex. One is left to try and unravel a myriad of puzzles.

3:18

For Christ also suffered for sins once for all,[1] the righteous for the unrighteous, in order to bring you to God. He was put to death in the flesh, but made alive in the spirit.,

How should we read this text? Should it read that Christ *died* or that he *suffered*? To be sure, most modern scholars agree that "suffered" is the original/initial[2] reading. First, as seen in our excursus, we have fully analyzed the external/internal evidence and have deemed that ἀπέθανεν should be the preferred reading and thus the original/initial reading.[3] Second, it must be stated that Isaiah 53 is in concert with 1 Peter. It is ever present in the background. And recently, scholarship has shown that περὶ ἁμαρτίας can actually be translated as sin-offering.[4] Here we have an allusion to Isaiah 53:10 and Leviticus 16:9. Jesus is the offering for sins and no less than his death is

---

1. Or could be better translated, "For Christ even died as an offering for sins once for all time." With the emphasis on Christ dying and being an offering for sins.

2. We used original/initial understanding the debate as to whether or not we can even get to the original text.

3. See text-critical excursus below 166 for a greater detailed explanation as to why ἀπέθανεν is the preferred reading here and why it is adopted in this commentary as the original/initial reading in 3:18.

4. Wright, *The Climax of the Covenant*, 220–25. Recently, Wright, *The Day the Revolution Began*, 332.

required. The final teleological-eschatological punishment of the wicked is annihilation, namely the second death. Jesus, then, as our substitute, must take upon himself this exact same second death. Thus, it is inadequate to state that Christ took our place of eternal conscious torment because Christ is not being tormented as we speak. Moreover, we must note that the sin offering and sacrifice was not to be tormented, but rather totally consumed in death (cf. Lv. 16:27). Lastly, verse 18 and 22 may be a creedal–hymnal fragment, which, in part, may account for the deviation from the lexical theme of suffering.[5] Therefore we note a chiastic structure in 2:21, 3:18, and 4:1, namely, *suffered–died–suffered* (πάσχω–ἀποθνῄσκω–πάσχω) which is supported by both external and internal textual evidences. The emphasis is thus drawn in this section to the creedal confession of Christ's death in his *crucifixion*, life in his *resurrection*, and power/authority in his *session*. All of which speak of the victory achieved over the powers of evil by the risen Christ.

How does *died* (ἀποθνῄσκω) enhance Peter's argument in the midst of suffering? First, while Christ's suffering led to death at the hands of men, he was made alive by the Spirit. In 1 Peter the suffering servant of Isaiah is in concert with the writer of the letter. The servant would not only suffer, but also be led to death (cf. Isa. 53:8,12, ἤχθη εἰς θάνατον and παρεδόθη εἰς θάνατον). Those who were suffering presently knew that even if death came, victory and vindication would follow. Christ died, was raised, and was vindicated. And so too would it be for the persecuted/martyred believer. Second, it connotes a dying to self and to sin (cf. 2:24) as seen in the Pauline tradition (cf. Rom. 6:2, 7, 8; 2 Cor. 5:14, 15; Phil. 1:21; Col. 2:20; 3:3, etc.).[6] The call to holy living in the midst of an unbelieving world is evident in this letter (cf. 1:16; 2:16; 3:16; 4:2–3; 4:15–16). Peter urges the churches to suffer for good and not for wrongdoing. He exhorts them not to turn back to the passions of the world. Why? As the early church believed, they had been crucified and had died with Christ (cf. Gal 2:20). Thus, we can say that the inclusion of ἀπέθανεν was twofold in its rhetoric to persuade the persecuted churches. It was used to provide encouragement that the same vindication experienced by Christ would be experienced by them *and* that Christ has died for them and they have died with Christ, thus dying to themselves and to sin.

The righteous for the unrighteous, in order to bring you to God. Here we come back to another portion of the creedal–hymnal fragment. It is probably

---

5. For more regarding this cf. Kazuhito Shimada, *Studies on First Peter*.

6. To be sure this is primarily a Pauline usage of ἀποθνῄσκω, but this does not negate its orthopraxial inclusion and usage in the early church.

better translated, "A righteous one on behalf of the unrighteous in order that believers might be brought to God." The anarthrous δίκαιος makes *the righteous one*[7] less of a probability than *a righteous one*. Arguments can rightly be made to interpret it as *righteous on behalf of the unrighteous*, however, with a potential allusion to the Suffering Servant in Isaiah (δικαιῶσαι δίκαιον)[8], a righteous one, seen as substantival, is to be preferred. Peter has already made an emphatic allusion to a Suffering Servant in 2:22–25. It appears that the Isaianic text and the chiastic πάσχω-ἀποθνήσκω-πάσχω[9] should be seen as in concert. The *hapax legomenon* προσαγάγῃ τῷ θεῷ here is indeed an indication of the elevated rhetoric, which would further support this being a creedal–hymnal fragment. Moreover, the author appears to be drawing together two narratives: Lev 16:9 where Aaron is told bring the goat *as a sin offering* (καὶ προσάξει Ααρων...περὶ ἁμαρτίας), and the Passover/Exodus story. Jesus is, in fact, the high priest *and* the sin offering, fulfilling these roles found within the Day of Atonement. In other words, it is the sin offering who was brought to death, who now brings a people through a new exodus to God (cf. Exod 19:4 προσηγαγόμην ὑμᾶς πρὸς ἐμαυτόν). It is by dealing with the problem of sin that this new exodus from the exile from the garden is achieved. The exile from the Garden is, of course, the "exile prime," against which all other exiles are to be measured. The author merges the Day of Atonement and the Exodus/Passover narratives, in a fashion similar to John 1:29.[10] Through this new Exodus sin is dealt with, forgiveness is granted, and we are brought to God.

He was put to death in the flesh, but made alive in the spirit. Though the verb ἀποθνήσκω is not seen throughout the letter, neither is its kin θανατόω. Both serve as examples of *hapax legomena* within this letter. The introduction of the ἀποθνήσκω/θανατόω construct should not be seen as superfluous. Rather, it is an emphatic case wherein, Christ's suffering ultimately led to death (ἀπέθανεν), which was done *by* the hands of men (θανατωθεὶς μὲν σαρκὶ), but who was made alive *by* the Spirit (ζωοποιηθεὶς δὲ πνεύματι). Again, we see the overtones of the Suffering Servant who bore our sins, suffered, and was led/given over to death (Isa. 53:8, 12).

The participle "having been put to death on the one hand" (θανατωθεὶς μὲν) points to Messiah's crucifixion. The following participle "but having been made alive" (ζωοποιηθεὶς δὲ) refers to Messiah's resurrection. But how then shall we interpret these datives σαρκὶ and πνεύματι? There are many

---

7. Achtemeier, 239, 247–48.
8. Isa 53:11.
9. For more on this chiastic structure see excursus 1, 166
10. Wright, *The Day the Revolution Began*, 138, 209.

competing views. Is this a dative of sphere or dative of reference, i.e. "having been put to death in the flesh. . .having been made alive in the s/Spirit"?[11] Is it a combination of a dative of sphere and a dative of means, i.e. "having been put to death as a human, but made alive by the Spirit"?[12] Could it be a combination of a dative of sphere and a dative of agency, i.e. "being put to death in respect to the body, but made alive by the Spirit?"[13] Or might this be considered a dative of instrument/agency, i.e. "having been put to death by humans, but made alive by the Spirit?"[14] It is probably best to take it as it referring to this latter category. Achtemeier is correct in drawing out the distinction between the Christ's own flesh and the agency by which the death came, namely, at the hands of the men, i.e. flesh. The dual-passive participles indicate that Christ was the receiving agent of the force of the participle.[15]

3:19

In which also he went and made a proclamation to the spirits in prison.

This might be the most difficult single verse to interpret in the New Testament. *What* is the antecedent of ἐν ᾧ καὶ found in verse 19 and how should it be interpreted? *Who* are the spirits mentioned here, *what* was it that Christ proclaimed to them, *when* did he proclaim it to them, and *where* was it that he proclaimed it? Does this passage allude to a *decencus ad inferos* (i.e. the so-called harrowing of hell) or not? These are all questions that yearn to be answered.

First, much speculation has been given to what is meant by ἐν ᾧ καὶ. What is its antecedent? There are those who say that the original/initial text read ενωχ (Enoch). The relation of 1 Peter to 1 Enoch will be treated below and while the connection between these two literary works is indeed

---

11. Selywn, 196.; Dalton, 134.; Jobes, 235.
12. Green, 118.; Wallace, 343.
13. Dubis, 118.
14. Achtemeier, 250.
15. This reading gives the clearest indication of what is meant, i.e. *Christ was put to death at the hands of men, but he was made alive by the Spirit.* Further evidence might be found in P72 where Spirit is written as a *nomen sacrum* (see also CS193 in both places). Thus, from our earliest extant witness to the text we see that by the Spirit was implied. This is echoed in 4:6 when it is said that those who are dead were judged according to men of the flesh, but made to live to God by the Spirit.

apparent, the textual conjecture is unwarranted.[16] P72, the oldest extant manuscript of the letter, displays the *nomen sacrum* for both Noah and Enoch in Jude, yet when one would expect to find it in 1 Peter it is absent. Many interpretations of the antecedent of ἐν ᾧ καὶ have been proposed. Selwyn argued that its antecedent is the whole of verse 18, which would give it a sense of "in which process," referring to Christ's passion, death, and resurrection.[17] Jobes, sees ἐν ᾧ καὶ as a temporal conjunction, i.e. "at which time."[18] Dalton saw the antecedent as πνεύματι with ἐν interpreted as a locative, whereby "Christ preached to the spirits in the spiritual realm."[19] Whereas Achtemeier, while seeing πνεύματι as the antecedent, understands ἐν in an instrumental sense so that "Christ to the spirits by the Spirit."[20] After observing the dative of agency already employed, it would be safe say that this latter interpretation is the most likely and would be better translated, *By whom he also proclaimed after going to the spirits in prison.*

Second, we must ask: who are these spirits? Generally speaking, the interpretation of the identity of these spirits can be placed into two camps, viz., those who believe they are *human beings* and those who believe they are *fallen angels*. Those who object to the former raise the fact that πνεύματα is never used for human beings without a qualifier (cf. Heb. 12:23). Instead, in Scripture πνεύματα is mainly used to reference spiritual beings. Modern scholarship has looked outside the New Testament to help understand the eschatological framework that is found in this passage. Most commentators now see the connection between 1 Peter and 1 Enoch. It was Enoch who was to proclaim the message of the fallen angels' defeat (cf. 1 Enoch 12:4–13:2; 15–16). Moreover, we see that fallen angels are detained forever in the prison house (cf. 1 Enoch 21:10). These connections should not be overlooked when attempting to identify these spirits.

Third, what was preached/proclaimed and when did he do it? Whatever this message is it seemingly goes hand in hand with the individuals who were the recipients of it. Was it a message of *salvation* or one of *condemnation*? If these "spirits" refer to human beings, then ἐκήρυξεν could be seen as a preaching of the good news of salvation. However, if these "spirits" refer to fallen angels, then what we have here is not a preaching of salvation; rather, ἐκήρυξεν is interpreted as a proclamation of condemnation. Considering the

---

16. See Achtemeier, 253, for a full discussion of this conjecture.
17. Selwyn, 197, 315.
18. Jobes, 242–43.
19. Dalton, 141–43.
20. Achtemeier, 252.

context of the passage, the point that the author is trying to achieve, and its appealing connection to 1 Enoch, this latter option is preferred.

Fourth, where is the location of this prison? Again, how one interprets "spirits" and how one interprets what is "preached/proclaimed" will determine what and where this prison is. Interestingly, φυλακῇ is never used in the New Testament in connection with a final abode for human beings. Moreover, we must note the striking parallelism found in 2 Peter 2:4 (cf. Jude 6) and 1 Enoch 20:2. Both mention Tartarus[21] as the abode of the fallen angels. The connection of this with Noah in 2 Peter 2:5 should also be weighed in the conversation. Surely this Tartarus is the prison mentioned in 1 Peter 3:19.

Thus, we have the following main considerations and options before us when interpreting this verse:

(1) The term "spirits" refers to human beings during the time of Noah. And Christ descended into Hades (i.e. harrowing of hell) preaching a message of salvation to those in this prison in between the time of his death and resurrection. (2) The term "spirits" refers to human beings who died during the time of Noah. And Christ, by the Holy Spirit, preached a message of salvation through Noah to those imprisoned by their own sin and wickedness before the flood. (3) The term "spirits" refers to fallen spirits who are in the prison for their rebellion against God. Thus, this victorious proclamation did not occur during the *triduum mortis*. Rather, it was seen throughout the collectivity of the Messiah's resurrection (v.18—ζωοποιηθεὶς δὲ πνεύματι), ascension (v.19—πορευθεὶς), and session (v.22—πορευθεὶς), and thus he proclaimed a message of condemnation (much like Enoch) *against* and victory *over* these fallen spirits. Considering and weighing the evidences of the overall context and intent, this latter option best fits what the author is seemingly trying to convey throughout the letter.[22]

---

21. This is wrongly translated as hell by most English versions (cf. NRSV, ESV, NIV, NASB, etc.). Tartarus acts as a temporary place of holding until the awaited judgement takes place much like Hades.

22. This view, put forth by Dalton has persuaded most contemporary scholars, but not all. See the thoughtful comments of Metzger, *Apotolic Letters of Faith, Hope and Love.* 53.

3:20

who in former times did not obey, when God waited patiently in the days of Noah, during the building of the ark, in which a few, that is, eight persons were saved through water.

If the spirits mentioned above are indeed fallen angels in Genesis 6, then the mention of Noah is quite fitting. The account of the deluge and Noah, along with Sodom and Gomorrah, serve as the two archetypes of destruction experienced by the wicked and salvation/rescue received by the righteous.[23] In the so-called Enochian corpus, Noah and the flood are well attested in its material and thus its importance to our section should be noted.[24] The punishment given in 1 Enoch 67 indicates an imprisonment of the angels who brought defilement upon humankind through knowledge of secret things.[25] The flood was seen here as waters of judgment (Cf. 1 Enoch 67:13). Rather than a baptismal catechism, what we have here is a continuation of the judgment narrative found in 1 Enoch. The transition from the spirits in prison (v. 19) to Noah (v. 20) is a natural segue of thought showing the punishment of what is evil and the vindication/rescue of what is good. It was the angels who would "burn punitively under the ground"[26] while of Noah it was said "I shall strengthen your seed before me forever and ever as well as the seeds of those who dwell with you."[27] Clearly, the author is continuing his reflection on the Enochian narrative to help show his audience the outcome of those who were *persecuting* and the vindication of those being *persecuted*.

During the building of the ark, in which a few, that is, eight persons, were saved through water. There is dispute about whether one should take δι' ὕδατος as instrumental (i.e. by means of water), or locative (i.e. through water), or a combination of the two. The question remains, what was it that the eight were saved from: the water, the wicked, or both? The author is surely trying to draw a parallel between his audience and Noah, to encourage them that they too, being few, will be brought safely through and delivered like the eight mentioned. The rhetorical function of what we see here must be kept within the oppressive context in which his audience resided. In both cases wickedness of the day was being encountered and in the former it was dealt with by means of the flood, while the ark allowed for safe passage. The

---

23. cf. Flood | Mt. 24:37–38; Lk. 17:26–27; 2 Peter 2:5; Sodom and Gomorrah | Mt. 11:23–24; 2 Peter 2:6; Jude 7.

24. Cf. 1 Enoch 10.2–3; 54.7–10; 65.1–12; 66–67; 83–84; 89.

25. 1 Enoch 67.4; 69.1.

26. 1 Enoch 67.7.

27. 1 Enoch 67.3.

judgment that faced the wicked was certain death by means of the water and the eight were rescued from this very judgment being carried through the water while in the ark. So, the eight's salvific deliverance was two-fold, viz., deliverance from the coming judgment and deliverance from the wickedness in the world. And it was by means of the water and through the water that their deliverance was found. The author's focus in this case is on the fate of the both righteous and the wicked.

3:21

And baptism, which this prefigured, now saves you—not as a removal of dirt from the body, but as an appeal to God for a good conscience, through the resurrection of Jesus Christ,

Again, the translations of the Greek here are numerous. What is the antecedent to ὅ?[28] How should ἐπερώτημα be translated and should συνειδήσεως ἀγαθῆς be rendered as an objective or subjective genitive? Forbes draws out the grammatical options at this point.[29] Amongst the options before us related to the antecedent of ὅ, ὕδατος has been seen as the best fit. However, Selwyn's view of ὑμᾶς being the antecedent is quite attractive and should not be overlooked. The connection it makes between Noah and the audience of this letter is evident. But even if we take ὕδατος to be the antecedent, this still leaves open the possibility that the audience is being referenced as a type of people experiencing something like that of Noah. These options are not in opposition to each other.

So, the question often asked is whether or not the author indicates that individuals are saved by means of baptism? The parallelism found in the two δια clauses: δι' ὕδατος and δι' ἀναστάσεως Ἰησοῦ Χριστοῦ would seem to state otherwise. Ultimately, Noah was saved by means of water through the ark and believers are saved by means of the resurrection through Jesus Messiah. It is clear that the baptism here referenced has certain qualifiers attached to it. It is not a removal of dirt from the flesh, rather it is found in both "the pledge to God from a good conscience" (subjective genitive) and "a pledge to God to maintain a good conscience" (objective genitive). A plenary genitive is most likely in view here as neither contradict each other, but rather complement each other.[30] Thus, it is best rendered in the ambiguous "pledge to God of a good conscience." The clause συνειδήσεως ἀγαθῆς ἐπερώτημα εἰς

---

28. Interestingly, P72 and Codex 01* both omit ὅ.
29. Forbes, 128–30.
30. Cf. Wallace's view on the Plenary Genitive, 119–21.

θεόν δι' ἀναστάσεως Ἰησοῦ Χριστοῦ is in apposition to βάπτισμα and serves epexegetically to further clarify the author's intent. Thus, we see baptism here as an immersion into a life pledged to God through the power of the resurrection of Jesus.

3:22

who has gone into heaven and is at the right hand of God, with angels, authorities, and powers made subject to him.

Here we have a close to the creedal-hymnal fragment that began in verse 18. We also must note the clear parallelism that is found in *who has gone* (πορευθείς) here and the πορευθείς found in verse 19 above. Christ brought proclamation of victory over the spirits in prison through his death and resurrection. So too, through his ascension and session, a message of victory is proclaimed against the angels, authorities, and powers who are subject to the Messiah. In this we have a crucial use of subjection (ὑποτάσσω), which has been seen throughout the letter (cf. 2:13, 18; 3:1, 5, 5:5).[31] Peter calls those who are the presently-suffering-exile-sojourner people to be in subjection to the governing authorities. Household servants are called to be in subjection to their masters, whether good or crooked, and wives are to be in subjection to their unbelieving husbands. Now, Peter gives theological focus to this theme by stating that all authorities and powers are in subjection to the exalted and victorious Messiah (ὑποταγέντων αὐτῷ ἀγγέλων καὶ ἐξουσιῶν καὶ δυνάμεων). Though believers might be in submission at the present moment, it is in *that* present moment that all would-be authorities and powers are in subjection to the risen Messiah. Thus Peter's thought rests on the fact that the Messiah was vindicated with his victory over death, evil, and suffering. The powers and authorities thought that they had triumphed over the Messiah in his death, but it was actually the Messiah who triumphed over them through his resurrection, ascension, and session. So too, the royal-priesthood people are and will be the vindicated *Christus-victor* people who will rule and reign as cultivators of God's new creation in the age to come.

---

31. This is credited to Peter R. Rodgers who brought to my attention its final significance in this place. Here it is in an echo of Psalm 110:1, the most frequently used Old Testament text in the New Testament.

1 Peter 4:1–6
by Corbett Cutts

4:1

> Since therefore Christ suffered in the flesh, arm yourselves also with the same intention (for whoever has suffered in the flesh has finished with sin),

With a single adverb (οὖν) Peter returns to the preceding section of his letter, anchoring what follows in the wake of Christ's sufferings described in 3:18. It is precisely because Christ suffered for humanity, as a righteous and sinless man, that Christians should expect nothing less in their own lives. As Feldmeier indicates, a number of variants exist for *suffered in the flesh* (παθόντος [υπερ ημων] σαρκί) to incorporate the atoning death of Christ.[1] Despite the textual variations, the concept of substitution is found in 1 Peter (c.f., 1 Pet 2:21–25) and the b clause of the verse lends support to this conclusion. We will return momentarily to the unique subtext that undergirds Peter's dual usage of *flesh* (σαρκί) when ascribed first to Christ and second to the believer, but here its use is plain: Christ suffered physically and has set forth the example concerning suffering that the believer should follow.[2]

Peter urges his listeners to follow Christ's example with alacrity. Invoking visions of a militant–like response, the use of ὁπλίσασθε (literally: to make ready, especially by engaging, to arm) is noteworthy in that the word is only used once in the NT and its use elsewhere frequently indicates

---

1. Feldmeier, 211. See excursus on the text of 1 Peter 166.
2. John Phillips, *Exploring the Epistles of Peter*, 165.

military preparation.³ Peter's exhortation is augmented by his selection of a seemingly odd weapon of choice: mental fortitude. He calls on Christians to arm themselves with the same mind or *intent* (ἔννοιαν) toward suffering as Christ had. The juxtaposition of Christ's attitude towards physical suffering and Peter's call to wage war in solidarity with the Messiah seems strange if left unexplained, but fitting when set in the context of the end verse 1, and along side Paul's discourse in his letter to the Romans (cf, Rom 7:14–25).

The ὅτι clause has long been a point of contention in understanding Peter's meaning here, since grammatically this clause can be attributed either to Christ or to the believer. In his commentary on 1 Peter, John Calvin traces the exegetical debate back to Erasmus, arguing Erasmus incorrectly uses ὅτι to ascribe *the suffering* (ὁ παθὼν) to Christ when the sentence is indefinite and extends generally to all believers, again echoing Paul in Romans 6:7.⁴ Following Calvin, Greg Forbes and other exegetes understand this clause as identifying the believer with a clear implication that suffering has a positive ethical effect.⁵ We are facing suffering in Christ.

Even with the focus on the believer, Peter's implied meaning of *suffering* (ὁ παθὼν) is still ambiguous. Davids notes that while the sin-suffering equation was prominent in the OT, its varied usage in the NT requires greater discernment on the reader's part.⁶ Given Peter's Christological focus on Jesus' suffering and death as the means of redemption and the basis for Christian living (c.f., 1 Pet 1:3, 18–19; 2:21–25; 3:18; 4:1) and his emphasis in verses 2–4 on abandoning a pagan lifestyle at all costs, the most obvious conclusion is that *suffering in the flesh* (ὁ παθὼν σαρκὶ) is an unambiguous sign that one is no longer living a sinful mindset.⁷ One has truly turned to God.⁸

Feldmeier rightly attributes the awkward construction at the end of verse 1 to Peter's reformulation of the apostle Paul's participative Christology (cf Romans 6) replacing baptism for suffering. He is using participation in Christ's suffering as an expression of community, a prevalent analogy in 1 Peter (c.f., 1 Pet 2:19ff; 3:13ff; 4:13ff; 5:1).⁹ This participative Christology coupled with our rendering of *suffering in the flesh* (ὁ παθὼν σαρκὶ) above echoes the remembrance and commemoration motif anchored in

---

3. BDAG, 716.
4. Calvin, 298.
5. Forbes, 136.
6. Davids, 36, footnote 53.
7. Jobes, 265.
8. Forbes, 136.
9. Feldmeier, 212.

God's command to keep the Sabbath in Exod 20:8. Peter's usage here, and his continued emphasis in verses 2–4 that suffering is a mark of separation from the world, draws parallels with the OT emphasis of the Sabbath as a covenantal sign that Israel has been set apart by God to be his chosen people (c.f., Exod 31:12–17; Deut 5:15). While certainly the mode is different (rest / suffering), both actions set apart the believer from the world and bring the believer in line with God's will.

4:2

so as to live for the rest of your earthly life no longer by human desires but by the will of God.

Peter provides some much needed clarity as the opening preposition of verse 2 expresses the purpose of what precedes it, *done with sin* (πέπαυται ἁμαρτίας), with the sense that one ceases with sin so as to devote the remainder of this life to doing the will of God.[10] This clarification further bolsters Peter's exhortation that to suffer with Christ is a permanent sign of life in Christ for the *remainder of one's life lived on earth*[11] (τὸν ἐπίλοιπον ἐν σαρκὶ βιῶσαι χρόνον) and is made explicit in the juxtaposition between *the will of God and the lusts of humanity* (ἀνθρώπων ἐπιθυμίαις ἀλλὰ θελήματι Θεοῦ). Calvin notes that this contrast underscores both the believer's total depravity and the need to become obedient to God by renouncing the greed of humanity and forming one's life according to the will of God. This is an inexhaustible act which requires total commitment of the believer for the remainder of their life.[12]

The permanency of Peter's participative Christology strengthens and continues the motif of remembrance and commemoration prevalent in Sabbath keeping. P.A. Barker notes the eschatological dimension of the Sabbath laws in the OT as anticipating the ideal life in God's place and under his rule. While Sabbath keeping was a practice that carried sociopolitical ramifications in this life, it also looked forward with great anticipation to

---

10. Dubis, 132.

11. Another translation of the Greek text is also often used: *the remaining time to live in the flesh*. However both this translation and the one used here raise unintended eschatological questions that are worth noting but marginally out of scope for this commentary. If it is the remainder of one's life lived on earth, the implication is that the life to come is not earthly; whereas, if it is the remaining time of life lived in the flesh, the implication is that the future life is not bodily. Dubis argues that the phrase, "this mortal body" can be used as it allows for a future, imperishable, resurrected body (Dubis, 132).

12. Calvin, 300.

the full and final redemption of the people of God in the life to come.[13] So too does Peter's call to *no longer live by human desires but by the will of God* (μηκέτι ἀνθρώπων ἐπιθυμίαις ἀλλὰ θελήματι Θεοῦ). By participating with Christ in their sufferings, the believer is both reminded of their depravity and God's act of deliverance in Christ. Moreover, the contrast between God's will and the lusts of humanity again signals the believer as set apart—as someone who lives in the flesh but not to the flesh.[14]

4:3

You have already spent enough time in doing what the Gentiles like to do, living in licentiousness, passions, drunkenness, revels, carousing, and lawless idolatry.

The adjective that begins verse 3, *is sufficient* (ἀρκετὸς) receives the emphasis. It is used ironically, indicating that they have participated in the ungodly behavior listed below and have done so for far too long. The use of ἀρκετὸς is rare in the NT, found only three times outside of 1 Pet 4:3, and is often understood as a note of encouragement (c.f., Matt 6:34; 10:25).[15] Yet here, Peter uses ἀρκετὸς in a manner parallel to Ezek 44:6 where Israel is being chastised by God for their ungodly behavior which included allowing foreigners to guard the temple, introducing idolatry and desecrating God's sanctuary.[16] The parallel between Peter's usage of ἀρκετὸς and Ezekiel emboldens the remembrance motif in that such abhorrent behavior is antithetical to the Lord and has gone on for far too long and has significant consequences.

Peter's emphasis that suffering with Christ is a permanent sign for believers in this life continues in verse 3 with Peter's contrast of the will of God and *the will of the Gentiles* (τὸ βούλημα τῶν ἐθνῶν). Dubis contends that the construction of the three perfect verbs: *the past* (παρεληλυθὼς), *having carried out* (κατειργάσθαι), and *having walked* (πεπορευμένους), emphasizes that this past of theirs, marked by ungodly actions, is a closed chapter.[17] Similar to verse 2, this pagan lifestyle is diametrically opposed to the believer's new life in Christ that can only be experienced if the believer practices total abstention from their former lifestyle.

13. Barker, "Sabbath, Sabbatical Year," DOT, Pentateuch, 705.
14. Hart, 70–1.
15. BDAG, ἀρκετὸς, 131.
16. Ibid., 70–1., BDAG, 472.
17. Dubis, 133.

By shifting from using the term *human desires* (ἀνθρώπων ἐπιθυμίαις) in verse 2 to *the will of the Gentiles* in verse 3 (τὸ βούλημα τῶν ἐθνῶν), Peter gives the previous life of the believer a cultural–societal dimension which he uses to emphasize the "otherness" of the believer in the world.[18] While such an emphasis sits in the foreground of the text, undergirding it is an echo of the OT. The contrast of the former life of the believer, described as the ungodly acts of the Gentiles, and the believer's new life in Christ, uses the remembrance motif. Peter leverages the strong emotional ties of his audience in remembering YHWH as the only God, who abhors idols and has set his people apart for a purpose (c.f., Exod 20:3–5).

The contrasting severity of the inequity imbued in Peter's usage to the term, "the will of the Gentiles" is further explicated through a list of vices that underlies the futility (1:18) and darkness (2:9) of the previous life and is generally categorized as unrestrained excess and idolatry.[19] The catalogue of vices: *licentiousness, passions, drunkenness, revels, carousing, and lawless idolatry* (ἀσελγείαις, ἐπιθυμίαις, οἰνοφλυγίαις, κώμοις, πότοις καὶ ἀθεμίτοις εἰδωλολατρίαις) that conclude verse 3 has influenced the discussion of the ethnic identity of 1 Peter's audience. Many scholars have used this list to conclude that the readers were predominately Gentiles because Jews would never participate in such ungodly acts. Jobes rightly contends that such a conclusion reflects an idealized and romanticized view of Jewish piety.[20] Jobes points to the golden–calf incident in Exodus 32 as one example that highlights Israel's propensity for idolatry, even in the very beginnings of their covenantal relationship with God. This was idolatry that included eating, drinking, and revelry similar to the behaviors listed in verse 3.[21]

4:4

They are surprised that you no longer join them in the same excesses of dissipation, and so they blaspheme.

Peter writes that the Gentiles are *surprised* (ξενίζονται) that the believer *no longer swims in the flood of depravity with them* (μὴ συντρεχόντων. . . .εἰς τὴν αὐτὴν τῆς ἀσωτίας ἀνάχυσιν) and they are now *hostile* (βλασφημοῦντες) to them for their abstention.[22] The inclusion of hostility illuminates Peter's call

18. Feldmeier, 213–14.
19. Ibid., 213.
20. Jobes, 268.
21. Ibid.
22. Feldmeier, 214–15.

to *arm oneself* (ὁπλίσασθε) with the expectation of suffering in verse 1 and gives further support to the remembrance motif present in the pericope. Goppelt writes that verse 4 is the turning point in the chapter at which Peter begins to answer the question of how the believers are to conduct themselves as foreigners, alienated because they are no longer ruled by the lusts of humanity.[23] The believers are again the Exodus community, only this exilic experience is not geographic but sociological.[24] As such, Peter's usage of the remembrance motif acts to comfort the reader and remind his audience that like their ancestors, God remembers his people and will deliver them from their bondage. For the believer, this new deliverance began with Christ, continues as the believer participates with Christ in their suffering, and will come to its glorious conclusion upon Christ's return in the life to come.

Dubis argues that despite the apparent connection between Noah and the flood and Peter's usage of *the flood* (τὴν. . .ἀνάχυσιν) here, this construction is a NT and LXX *hapax legomenon* and should be understood as a play on words.It is not meant to explicitly draw on the flood narrative as *the flood* (κατακλυμός) is typically used (c.f., LXX Gen 7:17; 2 Pet 2:5).[25] Following Michaels, Feldmeier furthers this argument positing that the entire metaphor is a cosmic exaggeration of pagans running and plunging themselves into a flood of debauchery who are then surprised that the Christian believers are no longer following suit.[26]

However, grammatical construction is but one variable in discovering OT echoes and allusions in the letter. Therefore one should not rule out the presence of the flood motif on this basis alone, especially when verse 4 is related to what precedes it in verse 3, what follows in verse 5, and the rest of 1 Peter. Jobes notes that the minority status of the believer who is *blasphemed* (βλασφημοῦντες) by the Gentiles in verse 4 parallels Noah and his family being minorities surrounded by hostile unbelievers.[27] Additional parallels are also found in Peter's call to remain faithful despite the wickedness of the world around them in verses 3–4. This echoes Noah's righteousness despite the inequity of the world, and Peter's warning of impending judgment in verse 5 is certainly reminiscent of the Noah's awareness of God's imminent judgment upon the world.[28] This is yet another instance where it is quite

---

23. Goppelt, 153.
24. Ibid.
25. Dubis, 135.
26. Feldmeier, 214.
27. Jobes, 258. See textual note on 4:14, 166–67..
28. Ibid.

plausible that the predominant Jewish audience of the letter would make the connection between Peter's words and OT imagery. This vivid rehearsal of the flood narrative fits the primary purpose of the letter, adding a depth of cultural richness that supported Peter's exhortation to deny their old life marred by the lusts of humanity and live for the will of God.

4:5

But they will have to give an accounting to him who stands ready to judge the living and the dead.

While rendered as a separate sentence in both the Greek and English texts, Peter's warning of the coming judgment of humanity serves as both a warning and a comfort for the reader and should be considered as a continuation of thought from verse 4. The idiom, *to give an account* (ἀποδώσουσιν λόγον) literally translates *to repay a word/matter* and is used elsewhere in the NT in a legal sense to give a defense for one's action (or inaction) in court (c.f., Matt 12:36; Lk 16:2) and here is applied to the final judgment.[29] Forbes notes the interesting eschatological reversal of 1 Pet 3:15 where it is now the unbelievers who will have to give an account for themselves.[30] Calvin asserts that this alteration is meant to be a point of encouragement to the believers who now find themselves in sociological exile as Peter sets before them the judgment of God[31] as a reminder that those who stand opposed to the will of God will one day be punished for their actions.[32]

Peter's note of encouragement is further bolstered by the immediacy of God's pending judgment. Forbes argues that Peter's contention that unbelievers must be *ready* (ἑτοίμως) to give their account to God is a Greek idiom that carries the expectation of an imminent end (c.f., 1 Pet 4:7, 17; 1:6).[33] Several textual variations exist seemingly to smooth out the text because of this idiom, but *to him who is ready to judge* (τῷ ἑτοίμως ἔχοντι κρῖναι) is favored due to the support of ℵ A C2 P Byz, and because of the idiom's

---

29. Dubis 136, quoting Achtemeier.

30. Forbes, 141.

31. There is some debate as to whether the account given by the unbelievers is to be given to God or Christ. Hart argues *to him* (τῷ) refers to Christ rather than God citing Rom 14:10, while both Forbes and Jobes contend *to him* (τῷ) refers to God the Father (c.f., 1 Pet 2:23) (Hart, 71; Jobes, 270). Given Peter's assignment of both Christ and God the Father earlier in the Epistle, ascribing *the one* (τῷ) to God the Father is most fitting.

32. Calvin, 301.

33. Forbes, 141.

inherent difficulty.³⁴ By emphasizing the coming judgment of God, the remembrance motif continues as Peter offers the believer comfort in knowing that God will not pass over without punishing those who have persecuted Christians.³⁵

4:6

For this is the reason the gospel was proclaimed even to the dead, so that, though they had been judged in the flesh as everyone is judged, they might live in the spirit as God does.

Dubis argues that Peter intends to connect verse 6 with either verses 4 or verses 1–5 through his usage of *for* (γάρ) despite the literal connection with verse 5 vis-à-vis the repetition of *judge* (κρίθῶσι) and *dead* (νεκρός).³⁶ Whether the connection is to a specific verse is of secondary importance as the full pericope of verses 1–5 comes clearly into view: God hears the cries of his people, will deliver them from their suffering, and punish the wicked for their inequities. Feldmeier further supports this rendering by also connecting verse 6 with 3:19 (although this is often disputed). God as judge punishes the unjust, but through Christ salvation is offered even to those who once lusted over the will of the Gentiles.³⁷ Here we see the capstone of Peter's usage of the remembrance and commemoration motif. For Israel, to be set apart was a call not to isolation but to purpose (c.f., Gen 12:2). Because they were called to be holy (1:16), Israel was challenged to be faithful to the will of God even in the face of exile, persecution, and death. So too is the new community of believers in Christ.

Certainly one of the oddest statements Peter makes is his proclamation that the gospel was preached *even to the dead* (καὶ νεκροῖς εὐηγγελίσθη). While a plain reading of *the dead* (νεκροῖς) may lead one to conclude that Peter is positing that the gospel was preached to the dead in Hades, Forbes convincingly argues that νεκροῖς refers to those who, while alive, heard and responded to the gospel but have since passed away. This aligns with Peter's repeated concern to encourage his readers that divine vindication awaits those who suffer for doing good.³⁸

---

34. Ibid.
35. Feldmeier, 215.
36. Dubis, 137.
37. Feldmeier, 216.
38. Forbes, 142. See, however, Horrell, *Becoming Christian*, 73–99, who argues in favor of the view that Christ preached to those "already dead," not to those who have

While Peter's intentions in using καὶ νεκροῖς εὐηγγελίσθη may seem a bit peculiar, one should not let it detract them from the poignant conclusion of verse 6, that though *they had been judged in the flesh as everyone is judged, they might live in the Spirit as God does* (ἵνα κριθῶσιν μὲν κατὰ ἀνθρώπους σαρκί, ζῶσιν δὲ κατὰ θεὸν πνεύματι). Forbes writes that Peter is establishing a comparative analysis between human standards and God's standards. God's litmus test for judging the believer is based on very different criteria than what is used by their pagan neighbors.[39] Peter's juxtaposition here connects verse 6 with verses 2–3 as he implores his readers to permanently reject the lusts of humanity in favor of the will of God. It also runs parallel to both verse 4 and the overall theological essence of the epistle in that despite the suffering experienced at the hands of the pagans, they are chosen and honored by God and will one day be vindicated.[40] Peter's usage of the otherness of the believer again alludes to both the OT motifs of exile and remembrance. The new exilic experience of the believer is coupled with Peter's plea that God has set them apart for a purpose and that they should remain faithful to their new life in Christ. God will not only deliver them from their sufferings, but also punish the unrighteous.

"since died."

39. Ibid., 142–43.
40. Ibid., 142.

1 Peter 4:7–11
by Amanda Beuerman

4:7

The end of all things is near; therefore be serious and discipline yourselves for the sake of your prayers.

In verse 7 *end* (τέλος), has an eschatological sense. *Near* is relative, considering this letter was written about 2,000 years ago. However, every day does bring us closer to the end. It is not about the day but rather the era that the original audience lived in. The Messiah had come and ushered in a new era, one that would continue until the return of Christ. According to Karen Jobes, "Peter is saying that because of the resurrection of Jesus Christ, his readers are living in the last stage of God's great redemptive plan, and the goal of that plan is being realized."[1] Today's reader also lives in that era: the *end of all things* is still near. The idea is to be ready, to think in light of eternity. Keeping this in mind should prevent complacency.[2] Regardless of when Jesus returns, the known world, no matter how long its duration, is temporary when placed on the timeline of eternity. Peter wanted his readers to think not only about the day they were living in, but also to keep in mind things that are eternal, not just temporal. In doing so, one should be serious, also translated as *be of sound mind*, that is, sound judgment. And one should be disciplined, also translated to be sober and self-controlled. As Selwyn nicely remarks, the impending judgment is "no vague and distant matter;

---

1. Jobes, 275.
2. Stibbs and Walls, 153.

it is at the door."[3] One should live life making wise and reasonable choices. Our choices and actions reflect our Christian profession.

Joy is a part of the Christian life, and God invented fun.[4] The quest in life should not be first and foremost pursuing merriment, pleasure, and material things. Rather, by remembering what is temporal, one can remember what is important and live with purpose. We see from the text that how we live our lives affects our prayers. "Sobriety is indispensable to full prayerfulness."[5] According to Elliott, "Sound judgment and alertness do not bring about prayer as much as they determine and aid its effectiveness."[6] Jobes writes that the result of this eschatological understanding should be prayer, as εἰς indicates purpose, and the knowledge that the end is near should motivate prayer.[7] The understanding that Jesus is returning should energize a person's prayer life.

4:8

Above all, maintain constant love for one another, for love covers a multitude of sins.

Love one another continuously, persevere in loving one another, because love covers, conceals, and takes away from sight, a multitude of sins. Loving others and persevering in that love, enables us to overlook sins, to avert our focus from sins done against us. There is a choice to ignore or forgive the offense because of the love for that other person. To do something constantly, is to persevere in it. Perseverance has a connotation of the task being difficult. Generally there is no need to persevere through the things that may be easy and refreshing. Rather it is required to persevere through things that may be more challenging, although still not bad such as a workout at the gym or a difficult assignment for school or work. These things are beneficial and may require perseverance in the task, to carry on even when it is challenging and difficult. In the case of exercise, perseverance in the exercise routine for that day is needed, but to do so daily, in order to have the full benefit. Perseverance for that time of exercise, then again, and again, will develop the habit and add health benefits more than just physically. Loving

---

3. Selwyn, 216.
4. 1 Timothy 6:17.
5. Stibbs and Walls, 153.
6. Elliott, 749.
7. Jobes, 277.

others continuously also has benefits physically, emotionally, mentally, and spiritually. It strengthens love for others and keeps away bitterness.

According to Selwyn, "Whenever the causal ὅτι occurs in 1 Peter, it introduces the theological ground of an ethical injunction."[8] Following ὅτι, is the phrase *love covers a multitude of sins*. The Old Testament has some references to the covering of sin as well. In Ps 32:1, and 85:2, covering of sins is related to forgiveness.[9] *Happy are those whose transgression is forgiven, whose sin is covered* (Psalm 32:1). Prov 10:12 *Hatred stirs up strife, but love covers all offenses*. In the New Testament there is also reference in Rom 4:7 (citing Ps 32:1) as well as Jas 5:20 about covering of sins. Loving others continuously to cover a multitude of sins has to include forgiveness, it would include extending forgiveness to them. It does not mean to have no boundaries or let people treat others badly, but it does mean offering more grace to the mix. Being quicker to forgive, slower to get angry, and slower to take offense. It does not mean to pretend someone is not rude, it means choosing to let some things go, lovingly address others, and forgive quickly (Jas 1:19). As Paul Achtemeier writes, "a love that can be quickly cooled, or that is not able to withstand the rigors of an outside persecution intent on destroying the community, is of little use."[10]

4:9

Be hospitable to one another without complaining.

A common understanding of hospitality is having someone over for dinner, maybe occasionally entertaining overnight guests, or weekend guests if we live someplace interesting where people tend to visit, or if we live further away from family who in order to visit need to stay a few days. Some families understand hospitality to mean extended stay for members and lots of good food. Hospitality in antiquity was not just sharing a little of what you had to offer. It was generosity without complaining, without grumbling. This instruction not to complain may imply that hospitality was challenging at times.[11] It may also be an echo of the grumbling of God's people after leaving Egypt. In order to avoid complaining or grumbling, hearts have to be in the right order. It is not just instruction to keep silent. It is instructions to have a right heart that makes it possible to not complain about the oppor-

---

8. Selwyn, 217.
9. CNTUOT, 1039.
10. Achtemeier, 295.
11. Stibbs, 155.

tunity to serve another person. There should be no complaining internally in the heart either.

The original audience would have known that there were not a lot of reliable and safe places to stay when traveling. Inns were often not safe and full of questionable and immoral dealings.[12] Hospitality offered would have extended for the duration the traveler was in the region.[13] Hospitality was a vital part of communication.[14] Hospitality and the passing of letters and information was the means whereby the Christians could know how their brothers and sisters in other areas were doing, and share needs and assistance.[15] Such hospitality was vital for early Christian missionaries to do their work.[16] Travelers would need to bring provisions, but many were walking and would face limitations on how much they could carry in a pack, and even preserved food eventually becomes perishable. The roads and inns were not necessarily safe. Hospitality was not only necessary in saving money on a hotel, but was also a tangible need for safety, food, and water.

The Greek word found in verse nine, φιλόξενος, translates as *hospitality*. The Greek word ξένος, means stranger or foreigner, and is most often associated with hospitality.[17] Hospitality is not just for the friend, but the stranger as well. In 1 Tim 3:2, and Titus 1:8, Paul claimed hospitality among the qualifications of a bishop.

There were also no church buildings at that time, and the churches would have met in smaller groups in people's homes. It was not necessarily an easy task to be a host, especially during times of persecution. The host may have faced undesirable consequences.[18] Part of hospitality was to reach out to the traveler. But it had a greater importance within the community of those who would hear the letter. The text reads *one another*, ἀλλήλους from the word ἀλλήλων, meaning *each other*. This implies mutuality and hospitality needed among the congregation.[19] Hospitality was expected in the Christian community at large (Heb 13:2). Hospitality was a theological matter as well as a practical one, an opportunity to show grace, love, and care for others.[20] The original audience would have been living in ways dif-

---

12. See Thompson, "The Holy Internet," 55.
13. Sakenfeld, NIDB, 2, 901.
14. See Thompson, "The Holy Internet," 55.
15. Ibid., 58.
16. Sakenfeld et al. NIDB, 2, 901.
17. Koenig, *ABD*, 3, 299.
18. Jobes, 280.
19. Achtemeier, 296.
20. See Thompson, "The Holy Internet," 56.

ferent from the culture around them; as such they needed fellowship with one another. Some Christians may have been separated from family and faced persecution because of their faith. This is all the more reason why their fellow believers should open their homes to each other.[21] There were social boundaries of status within the culture that Christians should not have adhered to, and inviting others to join at the table was "tantamount to extending familial ties to them."[22]

4:10

Like good stewards of the manifold grace of God, serve one another with whatever gift each of you has received.

Peter now shifts his attention to the exercise of spiritual gifts. A steward is a manager, an administrator. A steward is not the owner, but rather someone who is entrusted with responsibility on behalf of another. The gifts given by God are for his glory, to be used first and foremost not for personal gain, but rather to do the Lord's work. This does not mean gifts given by God cannot benefit his people personally, but that this should not be the highest priority and goal. Such gifts should not be used to manipulate or hurt others, but rather to bless others. The controlling factor should be love. David Watson noted, "This is always the supreme mark of the Spirit of God."[23]

All persons, not just some, have spiritual gifts. The spiritual gifts are listed in Rom 12:6–8, 1 Cor 12:7–11, and Eph 4:11, as well as here. Spiritual gifts have taken on a new importance in the contemporary church.

4:11

Whoever speaks must do so as one speaking the very words of God; whoever serves must do so with the strength that God supplies, so that God may be glorified in all things through Jesus Christ. To him belong the glory and the power forever and ever. Amen.

This is in reference to the spiritual gifts mentioned in verse ten. *Whoever speaks* is referring to someone using any spiritual gift that involves speaking.

---

21. Jobes. 281.
22. Green,145.
23. Watson, *I Believe in the Church*, 113.

The Greek word used is λόγια from the word λόγιον, often translated as *sayings,* or *oracles*. In this context some translations also have *utterances*. It is more than just prophesy, but it is the sayings of God, his teaching, shared for the benefit of the Christian assembly. In the Old Testament, λόγιον had the sense of being an oracle from God with a person as the messenger. In verse 11 there is still that sense of a messenger, but those who bear the Spirit and the λόγιον are still inspired by the Spirit.[24] Selwyn noted that "the preacher is not the purveyor of his own notions, but the transmitter of the utterances of God. The minister must not be setting forth his own competence or importance, but regard himself as acting from resources which God supplies."[25]

Those who have the spiritual gift of serving should do so in the strength of the Lord, thereby glorifying God. When not relying on the strength of the Lord it is easy to become overwhelmed, and serving feels burdensome instead of life-giving. When using our spiritual gifts in the Lord's strength we can grow tired, but it should not feel burdensome. No matter what gift a person is given it should be used in the way the Lord desires, in line with the character and heart of God.

God provides whatever his stewards need. As God supplies the strength, he also supplies what is needed for those who speak.[26]

Him in 11b refers to God, as is more common in the New Testament doxologies.[27] The use of "amen" does not indicate the conclusion or the letter (cf Rom 9:5). It is rather the indication that a train of thought has ended and a new section is about to begin.[28]

---

24. *TDNT,* 4,139.
25. Selwyn, 219.
26. Elliott, 760.
27. Ibid., 762.
28. Ibid., 766. See also Introduction 6 for a possible explanation of a new situation after 4:12.

1 Peter 4:12–19
by Aubrey Freely

4:12

> Beloved, do not be surprised at the fiery ordeal that is taking place among you to test you, as though something strange were happening to you.

Beloved: This section is offset from the rest of the letter by the address, which connotes an intimate shift in tone from the generalized sufferings of Christ to the specific sufferings of the Anatolian Christians. Peter has carefully demonstrated his ecclesial theology of the unity between Christ's paschal experiences and the trials of the local church[1], and now he begins to emphasize the logical eschatological conclusion of this unity of suffering.

Do not be surprised: This sentiment follows 1:7 in asserting the necessity of local suffering under God's new eschatological schema. As will be discussed later, the necessity of suffering affirmed here does not imply God's pleasant desire for it but God's engineering it into the eschatological goal for the world. The admonition that Christians ought not to be surprised is in pointed contrast with the "surprise" of the Gentiles in 4:4 that the Christians no longer behave *like the Gentiles do.* These surprises and sufferings are intricately connected, for the Christians are suffering as a direct result of surprising the Gentiles with their new codes of conduct.[2]

At the fiery ordeal that is taking place among you to test *you.* This trial by fire, following a similar phrase in 1:7, is the first direct reference to the

---

1. See especially 2:4–5, 2:18, 4:1–2.
2. Green, *1 Peter*, 154. See Introduction, 6 for a possible reason for the shift in tone at 4:12.

local situation. It was likely not a literal incendiary experience, and given the treatment in later verses of the honor/shame dichotomy, it is even unlikely that it was violent in nature[3]. Rather than detailing the precise nature of the suffering, Peter simply explains the reason for it. Comparing it to the fiery test mentioned in 1:7 is an attractive, but ultimately fruitless option. While the two sections have certain linguistic similarities and employ similar frameworks of thought,[4] there is divergence worth noting. 1:7 appears to indicate an evaluation of worth, similar to an appraisal of a precious metal. The ordeal here, however, is meant to *test* the church, in the sense that it is an opportunity to remain faithful or relapse back into the conduct they so recently left behind.

4:13

But rejoice insofar as you are sharing Christ's sufferings, so that you may also be glad and shout for joy when his glory is revealed.

But rejoice insofar as you are sharing Christ's sufferings. Coupled with the kind of *test* 4:12 calls to mind, it becomes clear that this segment of the letter is diverging slightly from 1:7. Here the suffering of the church is linked with the suffering of Christ, thereby making theological sense of the "test" imagery. God is not leaving the Anatolian Christians to see if they founder. Rather he is allowing them a period of struggle that will more closely identify them with Christ. A controlling theme of the letter is God's assured presence in the midst of suffering, and here Peter makes the climax of his case. The ostracism faced by the local church, that suffers in innocence as Christ did, can be a source of deepening joy and bliss as much as it can be an impediment to life[5]. The fact of human suffering would not be a surprise to this community, as it was under the control of the Roman Empire. The shock, just like the shock of Christ's cross, is that the suffering they endure can result in good. It need not be pointless. To Peter, innocent suffering presents an opportunity to act faithfully that deepens the church's actual experience of God in Christ. The letter therefore urges the readers away from the idea that the suffering is a "surprising" monstrosity and towards an understanding of the devotional and eschatological possibilities that proximity to God through innocent suffering creates.

---

3. See Liebengood's excellent treatment of this topic, pp 130–53.
4. Liebengood has drawn these parallels out, especially pp 145–6.
5. Green, 155.

So that you may also be glad and shout for joy when his glory is revealed. This intimacy is not for the present macabre moment alone, but exists in what is clearly an eschatological schema. We support Leibengood in his assessment of the point of the fiery suffering. It is not to merely refine or assess the faith of the church, but to link them in identification with Christ in order to bring them into the joy of the eschaton in a fashion after a new exodus.[6] Keeping in step with the letter's tendency to link suffering and glory, verse 13 indicates the necessity of the suffering mentioned in verse 12, together with the Christians' share in the glory of Christ's revelation. The will of God, further indicated in 4:19, is that the church follow the example (2:21) of Christ's suffering not as an end in itself, but as a wilderness experience that inevitably leads into the joy of promised glory.

4:14

If you are reviled for the name of Christ, you are blessed, because the spirit of glory, which is the Spirit of God, is resting on you.

If you are reviled for the name of Christ. Achtemeier has drawn out the unique phrasing of suffering ἐν ὀνόματι Χριστοῦ, which combines a negative experience with a positive designation for an action the followers of Christ perform.[7] This text does not support the modern interest in characterizing authentic religion by one's willingness to suffer "for" or "on behalf of" Christ, or enduring unpleasantness simply because Christ suffered "for" humanity. This is neither a measure of one's devotion nor a "tit for tat" theology of suffering. Instead, it refers to suffering that, as Achtemeier points out, occurs both because of one's designation as a Christian as opposed to "some other kind of person,"[8] and as a unification with the sufferings already endured by Christ. This odd phrase continues Peter's argument that the church's sufferings are redemptive insofar as they are like the sufferings of Christ, because they are experiences that deepen the local church's intimacy with Christ. Though the church has not initially chosen these kinds of experiences, they are nevertheless a way of tracing the grooves of the *example* (ὑπογραμμὸν) left behind in the wake of the Passion (2:21).

You are blessed. It naturally follows in Peter's theological schema that if one's experiences of suffering provide deeper unity with Christ, then that unity will continue into the next phase of the narrative of Christ's life, which

---

6. Leibengood, *Eschatology*, 141.
7. Achtemeier, 307–08.
8. Ibid. See also Horrel, *Becoming Christian*, 164–210.

is characterized by joy. Although μακάριοι is combined with a ὅτι phrase, this is not a formal beatitude in the style of the Gospels. Familiarity with these texts is mostly assumed, but the similarity is probably more cultural than literary.[9]

The Spirit of glory, which is the spirit of God is resting on you. This allusion to Isaiah 11:2, is a messianic reference, here applied to the Messianic people.[10]

4:15

But let none of you suffer as a murderer, a thief, a criminal, or even as a mischief maker.

Peter continues to explain the nature of Christian suffering by offering a contrast of four vices. These function in the argument as rhetorical sins, not ones likely committed by the community[11]. Asia Minor is not Corinth. The first three are straightforward in meaning: one who unjustly kills, one who claim's another's possesions by stealth (as opposed to the λῃστής—violent bandits—who were crucified along with Christ), and one who does evil. The fourth rhetorical sin is a rare word that has been difficult to translate. The common suggestions are *meddler* or *mischief maker* in the sense of a person who inserts himself into business that is not his own. Another possibility is *spy* or *informant*. These latter suggestions are more serious crimes, and given that Peter uses ὡς to emphasize the smallness of the fourth sin relative to the first three, *meddler* is the best choice.

The list of sins, in the context of the imperative to identify one's sufferings with those of Christ, lends to this passage a great sense of irony. Christ himself suffered a punishment reserved for those who committed the crimes Peter listed. The Anatolian church is to follow precisely in the footsteps of Christ to his cross being associated with the accusation of shameful practices while truly remaining innocent of them (2:21-23).

---

9. So Achtemeier, 308 and Mbuvi, Temple, Exile and Identity, 115-22.

10. See Mbuvi, *Temple, Exile and Identity*, 115-22, For the text of 4:14 see the excursus, "The Text of 1 Peter" 166-67.

11. Boring, 158.

4:16

> Yet if any of you suffers as a Christian, do not consider it a disgrace, but glorify God because you bear this name.

Here is the final clarification of the nature of Christian sufferings and their logical conclusion. With the illumination the rhetorical sins of the previous verse has given, the reader now understands that the call to suffering is actually a call to forsake the traditional understanding of that culture's honor and shame. As Boring points out, to be called a "Christian" was to be socially shamed by the culture outside of the church[12]. Thus the letter describes a surprising reality in which the inner truth is the opposite of the outward circumstances: The label of "Christian" was shame to those outside, but glory or pride to those within the church.

This dichotomy of inverted honor/shame reflects the kind of suffering Christ endured on the cross. Outwardly, death by crucifixion was a shameful mark on a person's final moments, and likely their legacy after death. However, those who came to worship Christ recognized the crucifixion as his most honorable achievement. With this in mind, the Anatolian Christians are not to imagine the public ostracism one of them might receive *as a Christian* means that they have been scorned by God. Peter, as Boring explains, "wants his readers to grasp that, while there is a kind of suffering considered shameful by the society that is indeed disgraceful (suffering as a thief, murderer, or criminal), there is also a kind of suffering that brings no dishonor."[13] It is precisely this kind of innocent suffering that aligns Christians with Christ and brings them into fellowship with him. This fellowship, brought about by "bearing" the Christian name,[14] is what provokes the Christians to *glorify God*.

---

12. Ibid.
13. Ibid.
14. On the reading *name*, see excursus, "The Text of 1 Peter," 167.

4:17

For the time has come for judgment to begin with the household of God; if it begins with us, what will be the end of those who do not obey the gospel of God?

For the time has come. The term *time* (καιρὸς) refers not to chronological time, but to a critical point in time (the God-given moment) giving further emphasis to the eschatological tone of the letter, and particularly of 4:7.

For judgment to begin: Frequently this is considered an allusion to the OT[15]. Several texts are cited,[16] the most plausible being Ezek 9:6. While Jobes considers the allusion to be a rebuttal of the notion of God's abandonment in Ezekiel, it is instructive to consider the narrative arc in that book to understand 4:17. The frightening judgment occurs in Ezek 9:6 and is followed by the departure of the glory of the Lord from the temple and the city in Chapter 10, but ultimately resolves in the return of the Lord's glory in Ezekiel 43. Peter's citation of the phrase is set in the context of this larger story, and the ultimate message is one of hope. Judgment is not the last word (see comments on verse 18). Thus the rhetorical questions that follow may not warrant so bleak an interpretation as is often given. The keynote of the whole letter is salvation and hope. In light of this observation, perhaps the question at the end of the verse and of verse 18 ought not to be interpreted as negatively as it often is.[17] Carson notes that "the conceptual background of the OT passages which is bound up with condemnation is absent.[18]

The household of God (τοῦ οἴκου τοῦ θεοῦ) was taken by J.H. Elliott to refer to the "household" rather than to the temple.[19] He has not been widely followed in this, and "house of God," a common OT designation for the temple, would be a better translation.[20] Although 1 Peter has great interest in the church as the household of God, the cultic and temple references in the context (especially 4:14) convincingly point to this being a reference to the temple imagery so prevalent throughout the letter.[21]

---

15. So Achtemeier, Green, and Jobes.
16. Ezek 9:6, Jer 25:29, Zech 13:7–9, Amos 3:2, Mal 3:1–5 are often proposed.
17. Eg. Grudem,, 183.
18. Carson, CNTUOT, 1042.
19. Elliott, A Home for the Homeless, 165–233.
20. See especially the critique of Achetemeier, 158–159. Mbuvi, *Temple, Exile and Identity in 1 Peter*, 90.
21. See Mbuvi, *Temple, Exile and Identity in 1 Peter*, passim, and see the excursus by Vince Conroy pp. 190–200..

4:18

And, "If it is hard for the righteous to be saved, what will become of the ungodly and the sinners?"

If it is hard for the righteous to be saved. Verse 18 offers a successive and parallel rhetorical question to the one posed in the previous verse. To support his argument from the previous verse, Peter draws from Prov 11:31: *If the righteous are repaid on earth, how much more the wicked and the sinner?* The LXX replaces *on earth* with *it is hard* (μόλις) to indicate the difficulty (for God or for humans, it is not clear) by which humans experience salvation, and Peter follows the LXX. Carson argues that this use of μόλις indicates that, while God is not burdened by the offer of salvation, God's people will find that the way of salvation is a narrow road.[22] However, this pericope operates with the scope of the cross readily in mind in order to assist the Anatolian Christians in identifying with their experience of suffering. Indeed, coupled with the temple imagery that flows throughout the letter, it is clear that the difficulty of sacrifice, and the cost of the atonement, are closer to the forefront of Peter's mind than has perhaps been previously acknowledged. Christ's difficulty must at least be as poignant as the narrow road through persecution which the local church must travel, because the pericope up to this point has taken great pains to equate them with one another.[23]

What will become of the ungodly and the sinners? This final portion of the twin rhetorical questions indicates that, while the fate of the persecutors will be different than the fate of the household of God, it will nevertheless be intertwined. Joseph notes that "it is clear that the author sees a connection between the suffering of the audience and their future on the one hand, and between their suffering and the fate of their detractors, on the other hand"[24]. This connection forms a chiastic seesaw: one group suffers now and experiences glory later, while another is dominant in the status quo but will suffer later. Because of the connection between them, there is perhaps no indication that this future suffering will entail worse experiences than the shame the Anatolian Christians are advised to reject. It is not a clear picture of eternal conscious torment, but simply an assertion that "crime does not pay,"[25] for the proverb quoted here occurs in a segment of similar maxims regarding payment and wealth. If we are to follow our argument in

---

22. Carson, CNTUOT, 1042.

23. On the idea of "messianic woes" see Dubis, *Messianic Woes*, and the convincing critique of Leibengood, *Eschatology*, who argues for a background in Zechariah 9–14.

24. Joseph, *A Narralogical Reading*, 90.

25. Carson, 1042. (Waltke, *Proverbs 1–15*, 513).

4:17, we conclude that interpretations of this rhetorical question must be flexible in the degree to which they assign condemnation to the persecutors, particularly since the controlling theme of 1 Peter is one of love for enemies and the redemption that follows suffering.

4:19

Therefore, let those suffering in accordance with God's will entrust themselves to a faithful Creator, while continuing to do good.

Therefore, let those suffering in accordance with God's will. Having fully explained the reasons why Christian suffering is not a surprising or wholly negative event, Peter brings his thought to a conclusion (ὥστε καὶ). Those who *suffer in accordance with God's will are*, of course, the ones who suffer innocently as a result of bearing the name and ostracism associated with Christ. This God-appointed suffering is not suffering for doing wrong, like committing murder or stealing, as the pericope has shown. Here, innocent suffering is now described in a new way: that which is *God's will*. Achtemeier shows that this kind of suffering "will inevitably result from following God's ways rather than those of secular society,"[26] which brings the minds of the reader back to the reasons for their suffering in the first place. They have followed God's will, surprising their pagan neighbors, and are beginning to pay the inevitable price. If their initial behavior had the approval of God, then suffering at human hands on account of that behavior also must fit into God's schema of the new reality in Christ. This is how suffering can be the will of God; not issuing from a neglectful or vicious deity, but from obedience to that deity in a hostile culture.

Entrust themselves to a faithful Creator. Those who suffer are to *entrust themselves*, one of two imperatives that offer conclusion to the theological arguments of the pericope. Achtemeier shows that the imperative implies one party giving something to another party as a guarantee that object will remain safe.[27] In this case, the valued object is the Christians' very personhood. They are not instructed to entrust their livelihoods, their reputations, their security, or any other portion of their lives, but simply *themselves*, indicating a totality of trust. The one in whom Christians place their trust is the *faithful creator* (πιστῷ κτίστῃ) who of course by the very nature as the Creator is the only one qualified to accept such a trust. The creator of the self is the guarantor of the self's continued care. This is the only New Testament

---

26. Achtemeier, 1 Peter, 2:23; Cf Luke 23:46, Psa 30:6 LXX.
27. Achtemeier, 318.

use of *creator* (κτίστῃ), and it significantly occurs in a passage with several temple images.²⁸

While continuing to do good: The second imperative of the conclusion reminds the readers of their purpose and goal in the midst of suffering. Just as Christ entrusted himself to God and continues on with his miracles and teachings, so the Anatolian Christians are to conduct themselves in such a way. This is a remarkable imperative when paired with the πιστῷ κτίστῃ of the previous clause, for it implies a connection between the creative acts of God and the faithfully "good" acts of God's people. Certainly a theme throughout the letter, the injunction to repay blessings for curses may also have been apparent in the allusion to Ezekiel 9:6 in 4:17, if one takes the entire narrative arc of the Temple in Ezekiel into account. In that prophetic book, the glory does in fact leave the house of God, leaving the suffering of God's people in its wake. But by the end of the story, living waters gush forth from the altar that was once the center of a killing field and flow out into the world, re-creating the stagnant waters with freshness. The faithful, unsurprised suffering of the Anatolian Christians, and the regenerative good they continue to do in the midst of their trials, is their opportunity to identify with the Savior and Creator and participate in the divine life.

---

28. See excursus on Temple imagery in 1 Peter, 190–200.

1 Peter 5:1–7
by Brian Lucas

A number of commentators recognize that this section reflects Peter's personal experience.[1] Cranfield wrote, "There is a special intimacy about this section. The personality of Peter seems to come forward, though with a notable modesty and restraint...we seem to feel the humility and gentleness of one who was self-reliant and impetuous, but has been chastened and refined."[2] The profound shaking that Peter experienced from his brashness and confidence, his misunderstandings, his denials of his lord and the ensuing despair witnessing what Jesus endured with arrest and trial, how he (Jesus) reacted, and then, the post-resurrection encounters and Peter's restoration, all this stands behind this passage. Cranfield reflects, "We may guess that behind these words there lies the memory of the conversation recorded in John 21:15–19."[3] Selwyn notes similarly: "So much from Peter's witness of what he saw, the indelible impression which the lonely figure of his master standing in meek silence before his accusers" stands behind this passage.[4] Cranfield captures this emotional impact with the following description: "the personal poignancy of that second descriptive phrase in I Peter 5:1, μάρτυς τῶν τοῦ Χριστοῦ παθημάτων, will easily be recognized by referring to the following passages (in this order). Mark 14:29; Luke 22:31f; Mark 14:32–42, 47; John 18:10f; Mark 14:50, 54, 66–72; Luke 22:61. How deeply must what he witnessed have been engraved on his memory. The indelible impression of that uncomplaining Sufferer had broken down his self-reliance and arrogance and transformed his character."[5] With the angel's words to the woman at the tomb we know that Peter had

1. Selwyn, Cranfield, , Jobes, Feldmeier.
2. Cranfield, 108.
3. Cranfield, 108.
4. Selwyn, 95.
5. Cranfield, 109.

a special place in his master's affection: Mark 16:7 *But go and speak to his disciples and to Peter.*

5:1

Now as an elder myself and a witness of the sufferings of Christ, as well as one who shares in the glory to be revealed, I exhort the elders among you

Therefore (οὖν) is used throughout the letter. It functions here as an inferential particle, leading to a conclusion that follows from a preceding argument or indicating the next in a sequence. Given the situation Peter has described he here sets out the action that must follow.[6] With a brief restatement for those listening who are elders he rehearses the trials they face and that the *judgment is to begin with the house of God.* He exhorts them to commit themselves to their Lord, the faithful Creator, aware of the suffering that may also reflect the nature of their calling.[7] Peter now addresses those who have the charge to care for the church, with respect to the nature of their pastoral call and relationships within the church.[8]

Elders (Πρεσβύτερους) As we see in the LXX this is a term with a long history in Jewish writings, descriptive of leaders in ancient Israel and the second temple period. In the early Christian church it clearly has an official connotation. On the one hand, it must not be understood in too definite or limited a sense. It probably includes all those who have some sort of pastoral function and responsibility.[9] Calvin offers a similar perspective: "by this word he means pastors and all those who are appointed for government in the church."[10]

I Exhort (Παρακαλῶ) See also 2:11. Here Peter makes his appeal "not in a tone of command...(but he) places himself on the same level as the elders he addresses, even using a term *fellow elder* (συμπρεσβύτερος) for the purpose."[11] Feldmeier then adds that Peter, "rather than stressing his authority, he stresses his empathy with the elders in their task...Peter's approach to

---

6. Bailey, *The Good Shepherd*, 253.
7. Cranfield, 107.
8. Selwyn, 227.
9. Cranfield, 107.
10. Calvin, 315; Jobes, 302.
11. Feldmeier, 232.

his hearers can as well be read as an example of humility, which is the goal of the whole exhortation" (see 5:5–6).[12]

In referring to himself as a *fellow elder* Peter avoids the appearance of coming across in an authoritative or heavy handed manner, expressing more a sense of mutuality in the call that they share. This manner of approach conveys to them a sense of the vital importance of their call. Elevated to a par with Peter's call, they would sense all the more the seriousness their own call and the apostle's charge. This is re-enforced the three contrasts, or polarities, he addresses to them in verses 2 and 3, as to how specifically they need to respond to their challenge.

Jobes reflects as well on the personal nature of this section. She notes that both phrases begin with the definite article; *the fellow-elder, the sharer* (ὁ συμπρεσβύτερος and ὁ κοινωνός) which are in apposition to each other, re-enforcing the call they share, that is, "ministry with its attendant suffering and the glory to follow." She then adds that "the definite article combined with the preposition συμ may be understood as a possessive: 'your fellow elder, drawing Peter and the elders he is addressing even more deeply into their shared calling and experience."[13]

A witness of the sufferings of Christ (μάρτυς τῶν τοῦ Χριστοῦ παθημάτων). With the term *witness* (μάρτυς) we enter the dense shrubbery of ambiguity, both with regard to the sense intended for the term μάρτυς as well as for the following genitive phrase τῶν τοῦ Χριστοῦ παθημάτων. Is it to be construed as subjective or objective genitive? In Acts 9:4 we appear to meet another layer of complication. There in Saul's initial encounter with the risen Jesus we read: *Saul, Saul, why are you persecuting me?* (ESV) In seeking to clarify the meaning of μάρτυς here Danker establishes some parameters for us.

B μάρτυς may be used in the NT "of witnesses of events which they know about (1 Thess 2:10; 1 Tim. 6:12; 2 Tim.2:2; Heb.12:1), without having experienced them personally."[14]

C "of witnesses who bear a divine message (Rev.11:3; Acts 1:8; 13:31)...In this sense, above all, of Jesus' disciples as the witnesses of his life, death and resurrection -"you are my witnesses (μάρτυρες) Acts 1:8— with the objective genitive of the things witnessed. And under this category Danker includes this 1 Peter 5:1 phrase.

For a number of commentators, including Calvin, Goppelt, Jobes and Feldmeier, the syntactical point shedding light on this term 'witness' is the parallel phrase which follows: a) *Witness of the sufferings of Christ* (μάρτυς

---

12. Ibid.232.
13. Jobes, 300.
14. BDAG, 619.

τῶν τοῦ Χριστοῦ παθημάτων) then b) *Who shares in the glory to be revealed* (ὁ καὶ τῆς μελλούσης ἀποκαλύπτεσθαι δόξης κοινωνός). Calvin comments that he "prefers to regard it as referring to his own (Peter's) life...because (then) these two clauses will be more in harmony."[15] For Calvin then both clauses reflect the duality that repeatedly emerges not only here in 1 Peter. Centering in Jesus' own teaching it finds expression throughout the New Testament. Calvin cites a specific examples from Paul, in 2 Timothy 2:12, *if we suffer together, we shall also reign together.* "Peter, then, probably had this (passage) in view, so as to be heard as the faithful minister of Christ, proof of which he gave in the persecutions he had suffered and in the hope of the life to come."[16]

In her comments introductory to this section, Jobes writes, "the pastoral motif of the shepherd provides the background against which (Peter's) final instructions to the church are to be read."[17] More specifically Peter construes μάρτυς as emphasizing witness by participation, paralleling the affirmation of his being a *sharer/participant* (κοινωνός) in the glory to be revealed. Further Jobes asserts that the theme of participation extends throughout—fellow elder, fellow witness and fellow heir of glory, with the prepositional prefix συμ- imparted to all three.[18] Goppelt follows essentially the same course (see Calvin also). "Here the idea of personal observation could be included, but the emphasis is not on a position of eyewitness but on the testimony that leads to participation in the suffering and, therefore, in the glory."[19] And Bishop Leighton agrees also with the this interpretation maintaining that "(Peter) did indeed give witness to Christ, by (himself) suffering for him the hatred and persecution of the world in the publishing of the Gospel, and so was a witness and martyr....But more particularly intended, is, his certain knowledge of the sufferings of Christ in his own person as an eyewitness of them.. and a publisher of them."[20] But Peter here makes no reference to his death.

---

15. Calvin, 315.
16. Ibid 315.
17. Jobes, 299.
18. Jobes, 301.
19. Goppelt, 342.

20. Leighton, 465. Leighton cites Luke 24:45–48, where Jesus says, You are witnesses to these things (verse 48).

5:2

to tend the flock of God that is in your charge, exercising the oversight, not under compulsion but willingly, as God would have you do it—not for sordid gain but eagerly.

In verse 2 Peter challenges the elders to "shepherd the flock of God." As Jobes comments, "it is not surprising that Peter is drawn to the shepherding motif found in Isaiah and Ezekiel, when one remembers his reconciliation with Christ, in John 21:15–19, where Jesus asks Peter to feed and care for his sheep. Jesus, the great (and good) shepherd, commissions Peter in his role as under shepherd; Peter in turn commissions fellow elders as under shepherds, shepherding and overseeing the Christian believers in their locale."[21] Indeed in the LXX this image bears a rich heritage in Proverbs, the Psalms and the prophetic literature, including Ezekiel, Jeremiah, and Zechariah. The root ποιμν interestingly carries these associations in all its forms: shepherd or leader (ὁ Ποιμήν), the one who tends the flock; (ἡ ποίμνη or τό ποίμνιον) the flock (metaphor for people of Israel); the verb form meaning to tend or to herd; to guide or govern; to protect, care for, or nurture (ποιμαίνω).[22] The Old Testament passage that most compactly utilizes all three expressions of this one root is Isaiah 40:11. *as a shepherd shepherds his flock* (ὡς ποιμὴν ποιμανεῖ τὸ ποίμνιον).[23]

The flock of God (Ποίμνιον τοῦ Θεοῦ). That is, not our own flock, but "that committed to our own custody by Him who...will require an account of us concerning it,...his purchased flock at so dear a rate...Paul expresses it (Acts 20:28) the flock of God that he bought with his own blood."[24] Peter here addresses our image of the shepherd, the tasks he is to undertake and the manner in which he undertakes them. As Selwyn states, "this word ποίμνατε includes the whole of a shepherd's care for his flock and not feeding only...the charge to the elders here derives a special poignancy from the charge which Peter himself had received."[25] Jesus' parabolic teachings in the Gospels, so deeply grounded in the Old Testament (see Ezekiel 34, Zechariah 11, Jeremiah 23, Psalm 23, chief among others), introduces all the players: the flock itself, God's people, ever prone to wander and ever so needy of care; the shepherds of Israel appointed to tend, feed and protect

---

21. Jobes, 304.
22. Lust, Eynikel, Hauspie, 502–3.
23. Rahlfs-Hanhart LXX, 619.
24. Leighton, 469.
25. Selwyn, 229.

them, themselves ever prone to be faithless and self-serving. And then, the true shepherd, who promises to intervene, call the wayward shepherds to account and establish a faithful shepherd over his people. "While, on the one hand, the metaphor depicts the waywardness and helplessness of the people, it is used, on the other hand, to depict God's care for his people."[26] We must realize how formative this tradition was for Peter, who through failure, restoration and commission experienced Jesus as the Good Shepherd. Within those accounts closing the Gospels, apart from Peter's own report and actions, we pick up other hints. Mark 16:7 The angel addresses the two Marys: *Go tell his disciples* and Peter *that he is going before you into Gallilee. There you will see him.* When we turn to Peter himself, in that agonizing conversation with Jesus, we find him being restored, receiving his calling as shepherd, *tend my sheep*, while himself also being addressed as one of the flock, (John 21::22), in Peter's wondering about John, *what is that to you; you are following me).*

As we turn to consider the three polarities, the contrasting qualities held up before the elders, Peter once more focuses our attention with ever greater detail upon the Old Testament shepherds, deepening our understanding and vision of what these Christian elders must seek to replicate in their lives and ministry.

Exercising the oversight (ἐπισκοποῦντες). As to its inclusion in the text Goppelt writes "as to the evidence for or against its inclusion there is myriad of views." The textual evidence appears to him "equal in weight for both readings."[27] Yet in Goppelt's analysis he also points us toward 2:25, where since it is evident that "the connection of 'shepherd and overseer' was familiar to the writer of 1 Peter it seems then even more likely that the ἐπισκοποῦντες is original."[28] To this I would add, and I would think perhaps most telling of all, the additional evidence in the conjoining of these words and images in the prophetic tradition from which Jesus had taught, as well as Peter.[29]

Not under compulsion, etc. (Μὴ ἀναγκαστῶς ἀλλὰ ἑκουσίως κατὰ θεόν). The New Testament parallel aiding us in explicating the sense of this stated polarity is Philemon 14[30] The derivative ἀναγκαστῶς here in 1 Peter 5 according to Louw and Nida assert would be rendered ". . .obligatory on the

---

26. Cranfield, 109.
27. Goppelt, 344. See excursus on the text of 1 Peter, 167.
28. Goppelt, 344, who notes the concurrence of Selwyn and Kelly.
29. See, for example, Ezekiel 34:11.
30. Louw and Nida show, 671, sec. 71.30 and 71.31. ἵνα μὴ ὡς κατὰ ἀνάγκην τὸ ἀγαθόν σου ᾖ ἀλλὰ κατὰ ἑκούσιον.

basis of being imposed...out of obligation." Not on such a basis exhorts Peter, *but rather willingly* (ἀλλὰ ἑκουσίως Given the broader context of the letter, as he continues to prepare and equip them to face and endure suffering in hope, this sense seems clear. Both Peter and the elders know that in this role as shepherds of their flock, they would be all the more exposed to the dangers of threats and persecution. As Cranfield writes, "The reluctance which may make constraint necessary, may be due to the fear of danger (in times of persecution to be a leader is to run greater risk) and it is unworthy to hold back from responsibility for fear of danger."[31] This first negative is followed by the contrasting positive exhortation. The ἑκουσίως κατὰ θεόν addresses the "right spirit and motive...willingly, as being in God's service."[32] This expression *according to God*, or *in God's service* might become clearer for us in the subsequent contrasting couplet, indeed being *as God would*. In following this line, *for sordid gain* (αἰσχροκερδῶς) may not be referring primarily to shameless gain in financial terms, but more in the sense of seeking personal gain, advantages or prerogatives that might accrue from being "on the inside," of which money would be only one *desideratum*. And, *as God would* would then not only hold a conjectural sense, but seek to connect our thinking to what he has in fact done, the manner in which he has acted on our behalf. Taking this approach serves also to lead us to the last of the couplets. And the contrasting positive *willingly* (προθύμος) re-enforces this as well, with the sense of "being eager to be of service, freely, (and also) readily to suffer (πάσχειν)" in Hermas 9,28, 2:4.[33]

5:3

Do not lord it over those in your charge, but be examples to the flock.

This third polarity makes more explicit the line of thought into which Peter has been leading us with *willingly* (ἑκουσίως) and *eagerly* (προθύμως). The foundation upon which all three polarities rest now becomes clear. Peter uses Jesus' own manner of expression, *not lording it over* (Μὴ κατακυριεύοντες) but *being examples to the flock* (ESV) (τύποι γινόμενοι τοῦ ποιμνίου.) Τύποι clearly is a word most apt.[34] As Feldmeier concludes, "the use of the catch-

31. Cranfield, 128.
32. Selwyn, 230.
33. BDAG, 870, Jobes "eager for service," 304.
34. Jobes, 305; Leighton, 472; Selwyn, 231; Cranfield 113. BADG 1020 "embodiment of characteristics or function of a model....an object formed to resemble some

word κατακυριεύειν for the misuse of power, the formulation reminds one of a word of Jesus in the synoptics (see, for example, Matt.20:25; Mark 10:42).[35]

5:4

And when the chief shepherd appears you will win the crown of glory that never fades away.

This word of promise to the elders we must place in the context of the entire letter. The nature of the ministry to which they are called, shepherding this particular flock of God, will most likely continue to engender resistance and consequent suffering, a fact of which they are all aware. Peter, and of course Paul as well in relation with other communities of faith, have lived this pattern, experiencing for themselves what their chief shepherd encountered. But as Jesus himself was vindicated, raised from the dead and exalted in glory at the right hand of God, so when he appears, these shepherds, called of him, will receive that unfading crown, sharing and participating in the glory of Jesus himself (taking τῆς δόξης as an epexegetical genitive). The motif of *glory* (δόξα) is an expression for the award that will be granted to those at the Parousia who have followed Christ in suffering and therefore will be glorified as Christ himself is (1:11,21; 4:13). "This motif plays a decisive role in the whole letter (1:7; 4:13f; 5:1, 10)."[36]

5:5

In the same way, you who are younger must accept the authority of the elders. And all of you must clothe yourselves with humility in your dealings with one another, for "God opposes the proud but gives grace to the humble."

Here Goppelt sees a return to a theme already approached from several angles, "After these directives for the work of the elders in the congregation, one expects to hear a word about the relationship of the congregation to the elders."[37] With *in the same way* (Ὁμοίως) then, Goppelt sees a general indication of correspondence—i.e. "just as the elders have their duties, so

---

entity…an archetype serving as a model, type (or) pattern…example."
35. Feldmeier, 235, n.19.
36. Feldmeier, 236.
37. Goppelt, 350.

too do those who are younger." He concludes, regarding the identify of these "younger people," that the reference is not only to younger people in terms of age, but these "νεώτεροι are surely named here as representing all church members in relation to the elders" and which he affirms seems consistent with Paul's teaching that obligated all members to subject themselves to the leaders (1 Cor. 16:16; 1 Thess. 5:12).[38] Leighton translates the term as 'novices', that is also construing it as not merely a reference to age distinctions.[39]

The call here for *all* (πάντες) to mutual humility in the above passage finds its rationale or justification in the reference to God himself, who resists the arrogant, but gives grace/shows favor to the humble. It is a special point with the New Testament that the command of humility is based in Christ's self-degrading on our behalf, the Christ who described himself as gentle and *humble in heart* (πραῢς καὶ ταπεινός; Matt. 11:29; Phil 2:6–8). As a believer within this new life, this new reality "shows itself precisely in that one does not look on his or her own things, but what serves the other. . . From there it is no longer far to the ideal of humility. . .as the response of the believer to God's turning toward them in his Son, which then on their part becomes the model for dealings among people."[40] Kingston, in his TDNT article on slave (δοῦλος), makes reference to the foot washing in John 13; and Phil 2:7, and directing us to Gal.5:13 "A permanent basis of the obligation of mutual service is laid on all Christians: *through love act as servants or slaves of one another* (διὰ τῆς ἀγάπης δουλεύετε ἀλλήλοις). This is not in spite of, but on the basis of the fact that they are called to freedom (cf 1 Pet 2:16)."[41] Cranfield re-enforces this connection. "We have already heard of humility in 3:8. The word translated 'gird' is a curious one; it means 'to tie on securely' and it is probable that the substantive formed from it referred specially to the apron worn by slaves. It seems likely that Peter has in mind the memorable occasion when Jesus girded himself with a towel to wash his disciples' feet, John 13:1–15."[42] Leighton renders this section of verse 5 "'all of you be subject to one another." This further clarifies the duty, making it universally mutual: 'one subject to another'. The very company of Christ and all his exemplary lowliness. . .all (this) did not bar this frothy, foolish question, 'who shall be the greatest?' (Luke 22:24). Now this rule is just the opposite. Each is to strive to be the lowest, 'subject to one another.'"[43] The

38. Goppelt, 351.
39. Leighton, 425
40. Feldmeier, 240.
41. TDNT II, 277–8.
42. Cranfield, 117.
43. Leighton, 474.

wide range of relationships Peter addresses throughout this letter certainly reflects not only those vis-à-vis the surrounding hostile society and culture, but also those of every sort within the body. As Paul, so also Peter here alludes to the tensions that can surface in the struggles to integrate our new and real freedom in Christ over against the repeated calls for submission and service. These tensions are with us to this day. This call is not only directed to the brothers and sisters in their own relationships, but with reference to their example, and also to Christ himself. Paul seems best to capture this tension in 1 Cor 9:19: *"For though I am free from all, I have made myself a servant to all, that I might win more of them* (ESV).

In his essay, 'First and Second Things' C. S. Lewis provides a helpful conceptual framework to perhaps recast this struggle and attempt to reflect upon it from a different vantage point. We often experience confusion over what within a given issue is most essential, the call which we cannot afford to ignore. In then attempting to realize what appears on offer, in not considering or in refusing the only road which provides entrance, our way remains blocked. We long to realize what is in actuality the 'second thing', without addressing the 'first'.[44] Here is such a tension. We desire the release and freedom that is ours in Christ, but the door through which we must go to enter into that freedom is that of surrender and submission, one of the lanes of obedience. That this is the 'first thing' in our passage is re-enforced here in verses 5b-6 with three appearances of the root ταπεινο*, reflecting the quality, a person exhibiting it, and the verb of its expression, which verb is not only imperative, but in the passive voice as well. As Bishop Leighton pointed out to us earlier on, this call to all urging mutual humility and submission cuts across both sides of the dilemma. On the one side there is the desire to elevate ourselves over against others. Within this brief section Peter not only speaks to this specifically (in 5:3 *not lording it over, but being examples for the flock*), but to do so employs expressions of great personal weight from the Lord himself, while also reaching back into the prophetic traditions from which Jesus had drawn. We naturally resist subordinating, submitting ourselves to another, whatever the relationship. And Peter directly addresses this in 5:5, though this is only the last of several pointed calls to submission.

F. D. Maurice offers a helpful summary of this theme, which he also affirms is a theme frequently appearing in and foundational to the letter. "I need not point out to anyone how carefully St. Peter constitutes all relationships...upon the basis of the common relation to Christ; how all the obligations of elders and their flocks, the duty of not being lords over God's

---

44. Lewis, "First and Second Things," in *God in the Dock*, 278–81.

heritage…all mutual services and obligations…are placed on the same ground; how the whole framework of human society is shown to rest on Him who gave up Himself, to rest upon self sacrifice."[45]

Dietrich Bonhoeffer also makes clear, this is not a "leadership principle." Rather it is Christ himself who now stands in between, our mediator in all our relationships. It is his life that must come to expression in and through us.[46] Bonhoeffer addresses this also in *Nachfolge* (*Discipleship*), where he affirms this service not as a principle, but rather, it is Christ himself within us.[47] Put on humility, clothe yourself in humility, with clear reference to the core of the new way of life that is to characterize our lives and relationships. Thus for Bonhoeffer this living Christ not only indwells each of us individually, but it is he himself who now stands between us as brother and sister. "He is in the midst. . . .He is not only the mediator between God and man, but between man and man. Between son and father, between man and wife, between the individual and the community stands Christ, the mediator, whether they are able to recognize him or not."[48]

5:6

Humble yourselves therefore under the mighty hand of God, so that he may exalt you in due time.

This re-emerging emphasis on humility serves both to center it as a 'first thing' that we must pursue, the life (his) through which we find the road to the 'second things'. We see once more how we are to act, what kind of people we are to be in our relationships with others; but second, it also affirms with equal weight to whom, before whom or under whom we are to humble ourselves. "Be humbled under his mighty hand"; trust in him, in his vindication, and he will lift you up at the proper, fitting, appropriate time– a message recast once more in verse 10.

"When it is demanded that believers should 'humble' themselves under this hand, it is also about 'submitting' oneself to that decreed by God. First Peter associates this with God's power and control, explicitly praised in both doxologies (4:11 and 5:11), not subjugation but rescue."[49] See also 4:19, that those who suffer should entrust their souls to the faithful creator."

---

45. Maurice, *The Unity of the New Testament*, 306–7.
46. Bonhöffer, *Life Together*.
47. Bonhöffer, *Nachfolge*, 48.
48. Ibid, 48–9.
49. Feldmeier, 243.

As Leighton assures us, Peter makes it clear that "submission is our only course."⁵⁰ There is no other road ahead of us in Christ but this one. And then, once more, we must see that for what we seek to gain, exaltation in and with him, sharing in his glory, this is the only way, the 'first thing' through which alone we gain the 'second,' and desired, thing. "This humble submission is the only way to gain your point. What would you have under any affliction, but to be delivered and raised up? Thus alone can you attain that."⁵¹

And, as Cranfield reminds us, even that final phrase in verse 6, *in due time* (ἐν καιρῷ) expresses not only some vague "at some time later," but rather "these words 'in due time' point to the coming again of Christ."⁵² He is the one who trusted himself to his father and gained his vindication, and the encounter with whom for Peter brought his restoration and calling to this same life.

5:7

Cast all your anxieties on him because he cares for you.

Peter is echoing Psalm 55:22. Here we find the contrasting image over against Jesus' words in John 10:13 *because he is a hired hand the cares of the sheep are not a concern to him.* (ὅτι μισθωτός ἐστιν καὶ οὐ μέλει αὐτῷ περὶ τῶν προβάτων). Peter now, with full confidence and assurance, urges those to whom he writes to themselves have this assurance and confidence in the true and good shepherd. (See also Psalm 55:22; Matthew 6:25–34; Philippians 4:6).

---

50. Leighton, 480.
51. Ibid. 480.
52. Cranfield, 118.

1 Peter 5:8–11
by Keith Calara

5:8

Discipline yourselves, keep alert. Like a roaring lion your adversary the devil prowls around, looking for someone to devour.

Be self-controlled, be alert: Self-controlled (νήψατε) literally means "be sober," but *self-controlled* better reflects the sentiment of avoiding physical, emotional, and spiritual excesses.[1] Earlier in 5:6, Peter makes a direct reference to the Exodus narrative, *the mighty hand of God*, drawing the narratival motif into the peroration. The command to be somber-minded echoes Peter's exhortations in 1:13, where he explains that "the girding of their minds" is accomplished through self-control.[2] The command "be alert" carries an eschatological undertone. In the NT γρηγορέω is often used eschatologically as in the parable of The Faithful and Unfaithful Servant in Matthew 24 and the parable of The Ten Bridesmaids in Matthew 25. The Apostle Paul uses it eschatologically in 1 Cor 16:13 and 1 Thes 5:10, and the book of Revelation does the same in Rev 3:3 and 16:15. The phrase *so that he may exalt you* in verse 6 further supports an eschatological reading of peroration.

Your accuser the devil: The word *accuser* (ἀντίδικος) is normally employed in legal settings as in one who brings legal accusations or a plaintiff, though not necessarily a prosecutor.[3] In the NT the devil (διάβολος) could

---

1. BDAG, 672.
2. Jobes, 111.
3. LSJ, 155.

literally refer to a "slanderer" or "adversary," but in verse 8, and most other passages, it likely refers to a personified transcendent evil being who stands in direct opposition to the divine will of God.[4] This is the first time in the letter that Peter speaks of a personal evil. Introducing the devil as the Christian's adversary changes how the Church ought to view evil and humans who inflict suffering on others. As Feldmeier notes,

> One should observe that everything previously addressed with respect to evil... was concretely named as desire, sin, doing evil, cunning, hypocrisy, and the like, and thus did not need a reference to the personification of evil. Nor was the devil used to demonize the opponents; on the contrary, they are to be respected along with all people.[5]

Green agrees that Peter likely seeks to deemphasize the complicity of the aggressive Gentiles, painting them as victims duped into committing evil by a skilled opponent.[6] Jobes suggests that Peter has the corrupt social systems in mind, thinking that the devil himself does not necessarily destroy humans.[7] Manipulation of social systems does not seem outside the realm of possibility, as the scripture does not deny it. But Peter does not seem to believe that the devil has authority over social systems outside of the Church.

is prowling about like a roaring lion, seeking someone to devour. No other author in the NT employs the image of a lion to describe the devil. Jobes notes that the book of Revelation does employ images of dangerous wild beasts to depict corrupt governments. However, this phrase seems to stand opposed to the notion that Peter is referring to systemic evil and corruption.[8] At the same time, this passage does not necessarily say that the evil does not operate through systems. Peter's depiction of the devil as a frightening lion seeking to destroy individuals does not necessarily pit the church against the world. In the earlier chapters of the letter, Peter does not encourage his audience to disengage from the culture and cloister themselves; instead he instructs them to accept their position in the culture, whether it be as a slave, wife to a non-believer, or other role, because while in those roles they are to act as missionaries. At 2:12 he even believes that there will be non-believers who will convert upon witnessing the holy life lived by his audience, implying that he believes the values held by non-be-

---

4. BDAG, 226.
5. Feldmeier, 245.
6. Green, 180–181.
7. Jobes, 314.
8. Jobes, 314.

lievers and the values held by Christians have corresponding points.[9] The lion image acknowledges that evil is ever present, but it does not govern the whole of the culture with which the Church engages.

5:9

Resist him, steadfast in your faith, for you know that your brothers and sisters in all the world are undergoing the same kinds of suffering.

Resist him, firm in the faith: The subject of verse 8 *adversary* (ἀντίδικος) functions as the antecedent of *resist him* (ᾧ) signaling that verse 9 does not shift topics, but rather expands upon the subject of the devil by addressing what the believers are experiencing. Peter declares that resisting the devil requires a firm faith. He pairs his command to resist the devil with a word of encouragement, invoking a call of solidarity.

the same burdens of sufferings are being accomplished: In the NT ἐπιτελέω renders in English as to establish or to perform, but these meanings do not fit what Peter attempts to describe at 1 Pet 5:9.[10] Instead "to accomplish," found in the LXX seems more appropriate. One does not usually think of suffering as something "to accomplish," but the New Testament writers, including Peter, developed a theology of suffering that reflects this reality. The persecution and suffering of the Christians throughout Anatolia prompts Peter to write this letter, and he acknowledges this suffering as a temporal reality. Because of the audience's new loyalties and way of life, they will inevitably experience suffering. Suffering, like sin or evil, is not part of the cosmic order. Suffering exists as a consequence of the humanity's falling out with God, and in this context, suffering comes about as a result of living a holy life in the midst of a broken world. This perspective resonates with Gospel tradition including John 15:18–24 where Jesus explains to his disciples that the world will hate them because he was hated (Matt 10:22). Peter banishes any false hopes that an easy escape exists, and instead focuses his audience on the eschatological hope presented in the next verse.

your family of believers throughout the world: Peter's use of *world* (κόσμῳ) likely refers more to the world than to the whole of the cosmos.[11] Here the theological motif of family and the narratival motifs of Creation, Exodus, and the Temple come together in Peter's use of the word for *broth-*

9. Volf, "Soft Differences" 20–21.
10. *TDNT* VIII, 61–62.
11. Achtemeier, 343.

ers and sisters (ἀδελφότητι) in reference to the audience's fellow Christians throughout the world.[12]

The term *family of believers* (ἀδελφότης) appears only here and at 2:17 in the New Testament. Elliott highlights Peter's intentions to emphasize the familial aspect of the Christian community. Though this study disagrees with Elliott's position that the term *house* (οἶκος) has nothing to do with the Temple, it does agree that First Peter seeks to emphasize household and familial images, and that proclivity likely grows from the Creation narrative and the theology undergirding the Temple.[13] During the scene where YHWH creates the woman in Gen. 2:22 the YHWHist uses the word *made* (בָּנָה) in reference to "fashioning" the woman out of the man's rib. The YHWHist employs various types of word play in the Genesis 2–3 creation account like the pairing of *man* (אָדָם) with *ground or earth* (אֲדָמָה) or the relationship between *naked* (עָרוֹם) describing the man and the woman at 2:25 and *crafty* (עָרוּם) describing the snake at 3:1. The YHWHist seems to employ a bit of word play in his use of *built* (בָּנָה) as it usually pertains to the construction of buildings, but it can also refer the building of a family as it does in Deut 25:9 where Moses pronounces the Levirate law pertaining to marriage.[14] By God "fashioning" the woman in Gen 2:22 he constructs both a household and a family.

To further illustrate the point, YHWH brings the woman before the man at Gen. 2:23, and the man speaks the words, *This is now bone of my bones, and flesh of my flesh; she shall be called Woman, because she was taken out of Man*. In the OT these words are used to speak of familial relationships, much like how English speakers refer to "blood relations."[15] Many interpreters often relegate the significance of this text to the context of marriage, but the words carry much broader implications. Walter Bruggeman argues that these words follow a covenant formula, but the covenant in Genesis 2 is between YHWH and humanity, not between the Man and the Woman.[16] In other words, humanity can find unity and intimacy through family bonds and through unity in purpose, specifically service to God. The Exodus narrative draws from this narratival and theological motif as Moses declares that the Israelites have become God's people, and the NT writers draw from

---

12. See excursus on Temple Imagery, 190–200. The word is also used in 2:17, and not elsewhere in the NT.

13. Elliott, *A Home for the Homeless*, 202.

14. HALOT, 810–811.

15. Hamilton, *The Book of Genesis: Chapters 1–17*, 179–180, and Wenham, *Genesis 1–15, Vol.1*, 70.

16. Brueggemann, "Of the same flesh and bone, Gen 2:23a," 532–542

the motif as they reorganize their understanding of the OT in the light of Jesus' life, death, and resurrection.

Peter employs the motifs of Creation, Exodus, Exile, and family to shape the letter's contours, but he is not the only NT author to draw upon the family motif originating from Creation. Familial relationships, particularly pertaining to the aspect of loyalty, no longer depend upon blood relationships. Jesus, in Matt 12:46–50 and its parallel accounts, claims that his mother and brothers are his disciples, explaining that through obedience to God familial relationships are forged. Harrington asserts that the author of Matthew's gospel drew from the Exodus narrative to formulate this theological position, but as illustrated above, the roots of the narrative originate from Creation.[17] Pairing this notion of family built upon God's covenant with his people and their obedience sheds greater light upon the Peter's choice of *accomplished* (ἐπιτελέω) in reference to the suffering experienced by his audience and their fellow Christians around the world.

5:10

And after you have suffered for a little while, the God of all grace, who has called you into his eternal glory in Christ, will himself restore, support, strengthen, and establish you.

But the God of all grace: By placing the phrase ὁ δὲ θεὸς πάσης χάριτος to the front of the sentence, Peter signals that he is moving onto a new topic. Moreover the use of *but* (δὲ) communicates that this sentence logically builds upon the sentence prior.[18] Peter assures his audience that the God to whom they belong is the cosmic fount of grace. The honor and shame motif makes a final appearance in this verse reminding the audience that in the Kingdom of God their experiences of suffering and rejection do not bring shame but lead them to honor and glory.

who called you into is eternal glory in Christ: The use of the term *called* (καλέσας) encompasses a sense of summoning and inviting.[19] Peter once again invokes the theme of calling and vocation, reminding his audience that the great impetus of their lives is Christ. Through Christ humanity regains the ability to carry on and fulfill the vocation of an image bearer of God and one who was called to serve and keep creation. In this context this phrase harkens back to many transitions Peter names: from dark to light

17. Harrington, *The Gospel of Matthew*, 192.
18. Dubis, 171.
19. BDAG, 502–03.

or from *not a people* to *God's people*. The phrase reminds the audience that their salvation did not come from their own accomplishments.

after you have suffered a short time: Peter's use of the word *a short time* (ὀλίγον) is similar to its use in 1 Pet 1:6. It should be read from an eschatological perspective. Throughout the letter Peter asserts that suffering and rejection will continue to be part of their earthly experience, but here in verse 10 he contrasts the temporal nature of their current existence against the αἰώνιον (eternity) with Christ that is to come (cf 2 Cor 4:17).

himself restore, strengthen, empower, and establish you: Four verbs with significant semantic overlap close this verse.[20] Dubis suggests that these verbs should be taken together to express a single idea, but other commentators would rather explore the function of each verb.[21] All four verbs occur in the future tense suggesting Peter intended these verbs to function as promises as opposed to possible outcomes.[22] These verbs, *restore* (καταρτίσει), *strengthen* (στηρίξει), *make strong* (σθενώσει), and *establish* (θεμελιώσει), should be read in the light of the eschatological perspective shaping this verse, expressing a description of the already present work of Christ and the future reality yet to come.[23] God through Christ and the Holy Spirit has already begun to *restore* (καταρτίσει) his creation. Peter does not make light of the brokenness experienced by his audience, but assures them that their condition is not outside the possibility of redemption. In much the same way as Peter teaches the household servants in 2:18–25 and the wives in 3:1–7, he asserts that honor can still be claimed from their lowly position in Hellenic society through the example and work of Jesus Christ. But he also makes space for the possibility that they might not find relief from their suffering on this plain of existence. The whole of First Peter works to *strengthen* his audience. Through exhortations and teachings Peter certainly intends to strengthen the faith of his fellow Christians, but the strength they require rests with the God who promises to be with them for eternity. This verb *strengthen* functions both as a promise to the marginalized and as a reminder to the well-established members of the church that their strength alone cannot provide succor through their future troubles. The verb *make strong* (σθενόω) almost completely fulfills the same promise as to *strengthen*.

---

20. Some mss read three items rather than four, but one or another may have been omitted due to similar ending. Metzger, TCGNT, 627. See also the excursus on Temple imagery, 190–200..

21. Dubis,172.

22. Achtemeier, 345–346, Dubis, 172, and Jobes, 316.

23. BDAG, 526, 945, 922.

The last verb of the four, *to establish* (θεμελιόω) fills a similar role as *strengthen*, but much more significance is freighted upon the term.[24]

Andrew Mbuvi finds it significant that Peter would include the verb *establish* (θεμελιόω) at the end of this verse as he omitted this word when quoting Isaiah 28 in 1 Pet 2:4–10 in order to emphasize the rejected stone as the actual foundation of the spiritual house the members of the church constitute.[25] The verb θεμελιόω and its noun form θεμέλιος are often used in the OT in reference to the laying of a temple›s foundation, and so Mbuvi identifies this verse10 as a reference to the temple motif.[26] The last reference to the Temple narrative coincides with a series of promises declared by Peter, and sets the context for how the earlier three verbs should be understood. Of the narratives drawn into this letter, Peter leans most on the Exile narrative, which pervades the whole of this letter, to construct a spiritual, social, cultural, and historical matrix of meaning for the suffering his audience experiences. According to Mbuvi many of the Christians living during the times of the NT and Early Church felt that the nation of Israel was still in exile.[27] In a sense Peter's audience were suffering from a triple sense of exile: exile from Israel, from their local community, and the spiritual–political exile of Israel. But the establishment, purification, and restoration of the Temple would mark the end of Israel's exile. And so the Exile narrative comes into contact with a declaration that boldly states the foundation of the Temple has been laid and God promises its restoration. In other words, Peter declares to his audience the end of Exile is both upon them and ahead of them.

Additionally, Vince Conroy posits that Peter chooses to employ four verbs in order to reference the four rivers in the Creation narrative.[28] Beale suggests that the four rivers symbolize the life giving properties of Eden; from Eden life ought to spread to the rest of the world.[29] If this is the case, Peter could be referring to an eschatological reality where the exile not only ends but the life-giving reign of God spreads to the rest of the world. Peter does not offer any concrete images of what it will look like. Instead he choose to pastorally comfort his audience in the here and now, but with an eye on the future.

---

24. BDAG, 449.
25. Mbuvi, *Temple, Exile, and Identity in 1 Peter*, 124.
26. Mbuvi, 122–24.
27. Mbuvi, 122–24. Wright, *Jesus and the Victory of God*, 268–9
28. See the excursus on Temple imagery for further details, 190–200..
29. Beale, *The Temple and the Church's Mission*, 20.

5:11

To him be the power forever and ever, amen.

The body of the letter closes with a final benediction similar to the one found at 4:11. It was once believed that the benediction at 4:11, along with the sudden change in the tenor, indicated First Peter actually comprised of two letters, but that position seems to have lost popularity.[30] This second benediction is much shorter than the first and it lacks the indicative εἰμί. Because the structure of the second benediction is similar to the first and it includes κράτος, it seems best to read the sentence as *To him the be sovereignty forever, amen*. The word κράτος refers to the ability to rule and so the word «sovereignty» seems fitting.[31] It is not clear if Peter means to insert one last challenge to the Roman Empire by using the word κράτος as the word does not function prominently within the cult of the emperor, but the term appears often in political and legal settings. Outside of the New and Old Testament, the term normally refers to legal or political supremacy, and its use in doxologies is a New Testament innovation.[32]

---

30. See introduction, 6 for another explanation of the change of tone at 4:12.
31. BDAG, 565.
32. TDNT III, 905.

1 Peter 5:12-14
by Chris Maggitti

The final verses of 1 Peter have generated much discussion, though they may appear formulaic at first glance. The material in these closing verses will be treated under four sections: on Sylvanus, on the audience and the *true grace of God*, on the elect lady and Mark, and on the kiss.

5:12

Through Sylvanus, whom I consider a faithful brother, I have written this short letter to encourage you and to testify that this is the true grace of God. Stand fast in it.

Peter begins his closing statements to the Anatolian Christians[1] in much the same way as he warmly greeted the readers/hearers at the beginning of the epistle. Having lovingly instructed them in perseverance and relational matters, he closes bestowing his heartfelt words of farewell. Recall that Peter writes to the churches in "Asia," what is today known as Asia Minor that includes present day Turkey—specifically the western most portion of the land that lies between Greece and Syria. Though Peter would have spent some time traveling among these churches at points of his ministry, visiting each briefly, his great position and his apostolic duties would necessitate that he make more regular correspondence through letters and messengers like Sylvanus. It would be important that his choice be someone trustworthy and familiar with the area, one known to the churches. With the increasing presence of Christian persecution at this time, tensions escalating toward

---

1. See Goppelt, 367–68. Goppelt addresses the view that some might feel Peter is following a Pauline-like structure with a commanding yet gracious opening and a grace-filled finish, but he theorizes the content and structure present is varied enough that Peter is not entirely reliant on Paul's method of letter writing.

the significant events of 70 CE it would not do for this important letter of encouragement and teaching to be lost or fall into the wrong hands. Whoever he may be, Peter evidently knows and trusts Sylvanus enough to mention him by name, commend him to the churches, and to depend on him to deliver the message. The primary question then is, who is Sylvanus?

Though this is the first mention of him in this epistle, it is not uncommon for the epistles to have "new" names, which were not mentioned previously, included in the closing words. Sylvanus' reason for being mentioned however is very different than simply as a greeting. Presumably, Peter determines to use Sylvanus in some way significant.[2] The text allows that Sylvanus could be Peter's scribe, taking down his dictation or making copies of his letter. More likely though he means to use Sylvanus to bring and communicate this message to these far-flung believers.[3] Sylvanus seems apt to this task, coming with a certain spiritual pedigree that is hinted at by Peter. He is obviously known to all parties, likely having traveled to these areas previously. He is a reliable person. What doubt there might be of that would be nullified by Peter's backing of his character.[4] Sylvanus is also most assuredly a man of faith, again gaining validity from the fact that he is working directly with Peter, and not bringing teaching from a second hand source. There is still more evidence of Sylvanus' character elsewhere in the New Testament, this particular version of the name appearing three other times in preceding books (1 Cor. 1:19; 1 Thes 1:1; 2 Thes 1:1). These other mentions however are in those epistles attributed to the Apostle Paul, with whom Sylvanus is often named, as well as Timothy. Except for the Gospels and Acts, Peter is hardly mentioned in the rest of the New Testament, certainly not in connection with Sylvanus or Timothy. Further investigation reveals that it is likely the name Sylvanus is simply a Greek name that the better-known Silas adopted in his missionary journeys, who accompanied Paul and also was sent out by the Apostles.[5]

There is significant evidence that Sylvanus is an alternate name for Silas. The name Silas is used far more often in the New Testament texts

---

2. Jobes does not take a side but identifies a web of at least 3 possibilities concerning Sylvanus' role regarding the epistle—he could be the messenger, he could be the scribe, he could be the original writer, or he could be some mixture of each. Jobes, 320–21.

3. See Goppelt, 369–71. Though Goppelt disagrees with the assessment of authorship here, he makes a thorough study of the possibilities of Sylvanus' role with the epistle.

4. Achtemeier, 352 identifies the use of "regard" as a passing of apostolic judgment similar to something Paul might do, measuring the worth of a person.

5. Goppelt, 371, Jobes, 321, and Witherington, 245 along with a number of scholars agree with the conclusion that Sylvanus is in fact Silas.

than Sylvanus yet only in the middle portion of chapters of Acts (chapters 15–18). Curiously Silas seems to leave off where Sylvanus seems to pick up. What makes the biggest connection to Sylvanus is that Silas is also most often mentioned with Paul and also a couple of times with Timothy. This is the very same group that Sylvanus is acquainted with! After all, it would be a great oddity for these groups of traveling ministers who work so well together to break up mid mission or separate at all except for extreme circumstances (as with the glaring example of Paul and Barnabas). It might seem far-fetched that these small connections mean Sylvanus is indeed the same Silas that Acts names. Yet, both seemed to be very involved with Paul's ministry, a ministry primarily to the Gentiles out toward what might be considered to be the Rome area. It should be remembered that Paul in particular is known for his contextualization of the Gospel message (Acts 17:22–31; 1 Cor 9:19–23). It would make sense that those traveling with him would adopt a similar philosophy of ministry. It is known that Silas was present at least once in Jerusalem, for the first Jerusalem council, and was sent from there to the northwest. Acts records that he made it at least as far as Macedonia and Greece (Corinth). Given this wide range of travel, it is not inconceivable that Silas was acquainted or at least had visited a number of the churches in Asia Minor, the same churches Peter wrote to, and with which Peter claims this Sylvanus would be acquainted. It is a very logical conclusion that Silas might adopt a more Greek-like name during his prolonged ministry.[6]

I have briefly written this to exhort you and to bear witness to you that this is the true grace of God, stand in it. As with many of the other epistles, it should be remembered that the Apostles did not always have the ability to come to a specific church or area. Their one visit might be the only visit the churches in the area could get from a direct witness of Jesus for quite some time. The Apostles were so few and the churches sprouting up so rapidly that even if there were cyclical travel routes, they might rarely get the chance to revisit a group. Letters had to stand in their place, relaying important instruction to those they ministered to.[7] As with this epistle, the subjects addressed were usually in response to things the Apostles heard were going on or critical issues they knew to be relevant to certain regions. Presumably there would periodically also be new converts among those listening to the letter's contents. While Peter might never again see a certain church, his name would at least be well known among the believers and it would be

---

6. Dubis, 173. See Introduction 3 on Sylvanus' role in the letter

7. Achtemeier, 352, identifies an interesting practice and social mechanism of the period—short letters or "briefs" were actually commonplace, any correspondence of length being seen as impolite.

important for the newer converts to hear that apostolic authority was standing behind the church's teachings.

Here Peter also makes a command as much as a heartfelt plea to his audience. What he has written *is the true grace of God* and that they must *stand in it* (ταύτην εἶναι ἀληθῆ χάριν τοῦ θεοῦ εἰς ἣν στῆτε).[8] The area of the land he writes to is one heavily influenced by the pluralistic culture of Rome. It was practically "anything goes" within the Roman boundary as long as taxes were paid and there was no insurrection. Churches were undoubtedly close-knit; still, they were far from spiritual support of any authoritative kind, outside of the most spiritually mature among them. Though Peter is a brother to them in Christ, he is first and foremost their shepherd—despite the many tempting and tempestuous things going on around them, he is admonishing them to stay on the straight and narrow path of Jesus.[9] Here in this letter are the things that concern God, that please Him, the things that God's amazing grace has provided to them, that they might put aside their old ways and natures to be faithful to Jesus.

It is interesting to note that in this section some manuscripts play with the word στῆτε (stand in) as a command by changing it to εστηκατε (standing in) to more emphasize that this is already where the believers are.[10] Most textual witnesses point to Peter using the imperative form of the word as a way of command or underlining the importance of the matter. Peter has a heart for those he ministers to and wants to see them keep to the straight and narrow path. The letter of 1 Peter is not only a reminder of the listener's new life in Jesus but also a very pointed teaching on what it means to have Christian relationships, both with God and each other.

5:13

Your sister church in Babylon, chosen together with you, sends you greetings, and so does my son Mark.

This phrase introduces some mystery into Peter's final words, almost a cryptic insertion. Several interpretations have been offered for who this "she" is. If it is actually a woman Peter is talking about, and what he means by

---

8. Ibid, 352–53. Note the preposition *into* is curiously similar to a stylistic peculiarity of Mark, see Turner, *JTS* xxvi (1925) 14–20.

9. Green, 184 sees Peter's command as a means of encouraging his audience to "courageous resistance"—a way to assert their human dignity and faith without pushing for violence or uniformity.

10. Dubis, 176.

mentioning Babylon. Note that there is no explicit mention of a female in the text, it is derived from the feminine gender of *chosen* (συνεκλεκτὴ).[11] The most common hypothesis is that the *she* is actually a church.[12] Some manuscripts do actually add the word εκκλησια (church) to συνεκλεκτὴ (chosen), most notably Codex Sinaiticus.[13] The less popular opinion, but the one that might make much more sense in this context, takes the wording at face value; as mentioned, συνεκλεκτὴ (chosen) is a singular subject of the feminine gender. This could very well mean that Peter is actually referring to a specific individual, a woman with whom he and the recipients are acquainted.[14] The wording otherwise is vague enough to allow for either solution. In this line of thought, the most probable solution is that *she* is, at the least, a well-known figure within the Christian community of the area. Taking clues from the Gospels, Acts, and other epistles, it is not unusual to see prominent female figures within the faith named for reasons of greeting or praise. Peter identifying a certain individual would certainly fall in line with the rest of his closing acknowledgement of individuals: himself, Sylvanus, and Mark.[15]

The person of Mark actually presents some difficulties of its own. There is little to identify which Mark Peter means to reference. There is, again, a trio of hypotheses. The first is that it is actually the gospel writer Mark.[16] This idea holds the least weight, however, as there is almost no evidence that both men did ministry together in such a close manner. The next and most supported idea is that the reference is to a lesser-known John Mark, simply mentioned because of his association with Peter and other apostles at the time.[17] The final hypothesis is wrapped up in the mystery of the woman of Babylon, taking the text at face value with Mark being Peter's biological son and making the woman Mark's mother.

---

11. Ibid, 176.

12. *TDNT* 1:516.

13. Achtemeier,353 uses these textual grounds along with a reference from 2 John 13 in support of the hypothesis Peter is identifying a specific church.

14. Jobes, 322, highlights the most common possibilities regarding συνεκλεκτὴ (she who was chosen). These include that Peter is referencing a church, a special woman of authority in the area, or possibly even his own wife.

15. See Introduction, 3-4.

16. Stibbs, 177, identifies this hypothesis as based heavily on tradition, which also seems to see the many mentions of Mark throughout the New Testament as a single Mark rather than the possibility of different Marks. Witherington, 247, also agrees.

17. Achtemeier, 355, discusses both this hypothesis and the following (Mark being Peter's real son), giving supportive arguments, but taking no single side in the end. Jobes, 322, also supports the John Mark hypothesis.

With regard to *Babylon*, there is almost no evidence that Peter is writing about the actual area of Old Testament Babylon. Many feel this refers instead metaphorically to Rome, but still others contend it might also mean those believers in the area of the diaspora settlements.[18] Now one textual variant does explicitly substitute Rome (Ρωμη) for Babylon (Βαβυλῶνι), an interpretive addition made by the scribe.[19] Realistically of course, biblical Babylon and biblical Rome are entirely different locations and entirely different peoples. Peter is probably using the Babylonian name metaphorically to equate Old Testament Babylonian exile with what is happening in Rome—a commanding power, a mush pot of cultures devoted to many gods, a people attempting to attain a godlike status, and so on.[20] If one looks at the evidences of Peter's journeys however, which are mostly to the south of Jerusalem and to the north and west of Jerusalem, the likely choice is to side with those who feel he is referencing the diaspora. Dealing with the specific mention of Babylon in this way makes sense as much logically as it does theologically. The Jews and believers in these settlement areas would have been descendants of those who returned from the Babylonian exile (but did not return directly to Jerusalem). These areas also encompass and are fairly close in proximity to the area of Asia Minor. Also the theological implications of one being chosen out of Babylon could be a possible clue here. Just as God delivered his people from Babylonian captivity, so Jesus has redeemed all whom He has chosen to draw to Himself.

5:14

> Greet one another with a kiss of love. Peace to all of you who are in Christ.

The act of the kiss is used several times throughout Scripture. The specific wording used here, of the kiss as an act of love and greeting, is used four other times in the New Testament (Rom. 16:16; 1 Cor 16:20; 2 Cor 13:12; 1 Thes 5:26). Paul's use does differ slightly in that he modifies it with *holy* (ἁγίῳ) instead of Peter's love (ἀγάπης). The tone of the passages however are very similar; there is a close connection between those involved, a selfless and almost righteous kind of kinship. There is nothing sexual, deviant, or

---

18. Dubis, 176.
19. Witness 1611.
20. Jobes claims that there is almost no evidence to support a secretive Rome reference as there is no suggestion in the entire epistle of other apocalyptic or subversive writings. Jobes 322.

perverted about this practice.[21] One can find a number different types of non-sexual touch highlighted throughout Scripture such as kissing, embracing, handling, resting of the head, and so on. The kiss is as of one to another who is family, such as a parent to a child or between siblings. It may also be a kiss of deference or respect. Remember that quite a bit of 1 Peter dwells on the necessity of holy and honorable relationships, not just between husband and wife. Peter is further encouraging those he is writing to the practices of redeemed, well-intended relationships under the lordship of Jesus.[22]

The kiss was, at this time, a very common greeting among believers.[23] It further enhanced the idea of followers of Jesus as a family and as equals. It also set Christians apart from other peoples and religions who might not normally practice this kind of display of familiarity, especially in a public social setting.[24] Remember that a common means of Christian living at this time was in tight-knit communities. Noting Acts 2:42–47, we see that believers essentially lived together. They shared space, ate together, worshipped together, they did life together. Divisions and infighting within communities of this type could have long-term destructive effects on their faith and ministry. This is why Paul and the other Apostles came down so hard on wolves among their flocks and warned against them, such as in the latter half of Acts 20. Unity was essential. In many ways, this act of touch and closeness mirrored Jesus' own ministry on earth. He was not distant from those he came to save; he was fully present. He was and remains immanent. Jesus' outreach examplfies the way relationships were meant to be, free from self-centered intentions.[25] It also is important to see in the kiss the sign of love. The love and acceptance mirrored in the kiss is the thing that helps bind us to Jesus and to each other as believers: God's own love and acceptance through Jesus.[26] Jesus' example is to always be before the faithful, leading and guiding to the better way, the righteous way.

21. For a very thorough examination of φιλέω see TDNT 9:115–46. Note that its use in terms of erotic sexual love is almost always secondary to its use as a type of kinship or deeply respectful type of love. Most deviations from this guideline occur much later in literature.

22. Witherington, 249.

23. Stibbs, 177, determines that the kiss was normally used in both fellowship and in worship.

24. Green, 185, notes that while the kiss was in use socially at the time, it was restricted to certain relationships and social rules. Christian use of this sign included these things but also greatly surpassed them in meaning and practice.

25. Green 186, sees this greeting as exemplifying exactly the teachings Peter is trying to help his audience understand in the epistle.

26. Goppelt, 377.

As if to emphasize the points made throughout the epistle and especially about God's grace, Peter places the end cap on his letter with a pastoral blessing.[27] God's grace and His peace go hand-in-hand. For what Peter is espousing in this epistle, the following of Jesus' commands and seeking righteous relationships, divine peace is the only possible outcome. Sinaiticus again represents the unusual reading here by adding *In Christ Jesus, Amen.* (ἐν Χριστῷ Ιησου αμην). These closing words reflect the pastoral and liturgical character of 1 Peter. Sinaiticus' scribes might have included it to possibly help create a better unity with 2 Peter's text, which ends in a similar way.

---

27. Achtemeier, 356, gives a stirring description here as to why it was fitting for Peter to use peace over Paul's use of grace—namely with the growing persecutions and growing pains encroaching upon the young Church, what better way to find strength and solace than rooted in the abundant peace of Christ.

Excursus 1
The Text of 1 Peter
By Peter R. Rodgers and Stephen Rodriguez

In the Introduction, we noted the prominent place that 1 Peter holds in recent work on the text of the New Testament, since the Catholic Epistles were the first section to be revised in Nestle 28, based on the ECM and employing the Coherence Based Genealogical Method. The following is a review and commentary on a number of text-critical questions in the letter, which we consider important for contemporary exegesis. The two main sources for our conversation besides notes in the commentaries are Metzger, *Textual Commentary,* and Comfort, *A Commentary on the Manuscripts and Text of the New Testament.*

2:3: Our three oldest mss of 1 Peter (P72 P125 CS 193) all read *Christ is Lord,* using a form of the abbreviated *nomen sacrum.* Comfort[1] is correct in judging this reading to be the original/initial text, and this has considerable consequences for the theological interpretation of the letter. (PR).

2:21: The *Christi–imitatio* ἔπαθεν should be favored here as both external evidences and internal evidences support such a reading. Only a few manuscripts attest to ἀπέθανεν here (cf. P81 Codex 01 044), whereas, P72 A B C 33 81 1175 1735 1739 *Byz*) have the preferred ἔπαθεν. (SR)

3:7: Instead of the printed text, which reads συγκληρονόμοις, some mss (ACP, etc) read συγκληρονόμοι, making the word modify husbands, and suggesting that they alone are the heirs. Both the stronger manuscript evidence and the general argument of the passage make the dative plural the original/initial text, and point to the egalitarian vision of the passage and

---

1. Comfort, *A Commentary,* 387.

letter. God's intention is to restore husband and wife as equally his image and heirs in his new temple/creation.[2](PR)

3:18: The preferred reading here should be ἀπέθανεν, as opposed to the now widely accepted ἔπαθεν, due to variety of external and internal considerations. External evidences are as follows: (1) The oldest extant witnesses, namely, P72 and CS 193 agree with this reading, (2) There are at least five uncials, wherein there are two correctors who have added an article and preposition, but maintained the ἀπέθανεν reading (cf. 012 and 042). Of these witnesses all fall within a Category I or II.[3] including Codex 01*/2 (4th), Codex 02 (5th) Codex 04*/2 (5th), Codex 044 (8th/9th), (3) the miniscule witness is also quite robust with the inclusion of "the Queen of the minuscules" in 33, as well as the 1739. Other important minuscules can be seen in 1175, 1241, 1243, and 2344. (4) The best and widest mss witnesses attest to a πάσχω—ἀποθνήσκω—πάσχω chiastic structure. Internal evidences include: (1) 3:18, 21 is part of a creedal–hymnal fragment, which accounts for the departure of suffering, (2) Internal evidences suggest a πάσχω—ἀποθνήσκω—πάσχω in 2:21, 3:18, and 4:1, where the thrust of the Petrine rhetoric is focused upon the physical death of the Messiah (3:18) and the hope found in his vindication. Moreover, there is an *imitatio—sola—imitatio* chiasm, where imitation is found in 2:21, 4:1, but not 3:18 where Christ alone dies as the righteous one for the unrighteous, (3) The foreignness of ἀπέθανεν to the context points to it being the *lectio difficilior*. Thus, due to the quality and quantity of external witnesses, as well as the internal evidences of a hymnal-creedal fragment found in the midst of a rhetorical dual chiastic structure, ἀπέθανεν should be the preferred reading. (SR).

4:1: Much like 2:21, παθόντος is the better reading over ἀποθανόντος. The only witness that deviates from the πάσχω form is the original reading of Codex 01. All other witnesses agree that Christ suffered in the flesh. (SR).

4:14: At the end of 4:14 the majority of mss add the words *among them it is blasphemed, among you it is glorified*. (κατα μεν αυτοθς βλασφημειται, κατα δε υμας δοξαζεται). Although considered a gloss by most commentators, some consider it original.[4] It is likely that the words were omitted accidentally due to *homeoteleuton* (similar line ending). The phrase corresponds to the style of 1 Peter, and likely incorporates an echo of Isa 52:5. The line

---

2. See Excursus on "Temple Imagery," 190–200.
3. Kurt Aland and Barbara Aland, *The Text of the New Testament*, 109.
4. Michaels, 265, Rodgers, "The Longer Reading, *CBQ*, 43(1981) 93–5.

refers to the blaspheming of the *name* rather than to the blasphemy against the *spirit,* as is often supposed. (PR).

4:16: Nestle 28 reads *matter* (μέρει) rather than name (ὀνόματι). This judgment follows the ECM and is based on application of the "Coherence Based Geneological Method." However, *name* occurs in the context, whereas *matter* (μέρει)is never used elsewhere in the letter. Furthermore the temple reference in the context, indeed in the whole letter, and the recurrent OT references to the temple as the place where God caused his name to dwell, points to ὀνόματι as the otiginal/initial text.[5] (PR).

5:1: Though Χριστοῦ is the preferred reading, P72 and 1735 have a peculiar variation indicating that it is not the sufferings of Christ, but the sufferings of God (θεοῦ παθημάτων). This is profound for the scribe(s) of P72 and its high Christology and Pneumatology (cf. nomen sacrum, 1:2, 11; 3:4, 3:18; 4:6, 14). (SR).

5:2: Some important manuscripts (01, B, CS193) omit the phrase *watching over them* (ἐππισκοποῦντες). Although Cranfield argued that the phrase was added under the influence of 2:25, it is more likely that the word was omitted because later church scribes feared that it gave the impression that the presbyter was to function as a bishop.[6] (PR).

---

5. See Rodgers, "The Text of 1 Peter 4:16 in Nestle 28," forthcoming.

6. Cranfield, 111, Comfort, *A Commentary,* 389–90, Metzger, *Textual Commentary,* 625–26, who places the words in brackets, and offers a {C} rating to their decision.

Excursus 2
The Old Testament in 1 Peter
By Peter R. Rodgers and Richard Rohlfing

It is often remarked that relative to its size, no New Testament document contains more references to the Old Testament than 1 Peter. However, as with all other aspects of New Testament study, the Gospels and Paul have received most of the attention with regard to the use of the Old Testament, and 1 Peter has been relatively neglected. The situation has recently been partially rectified with the publication of monographs by Benjamin Sargent and Patrick Egan, and a text-critical analysis by Katie Marcar.[1] These studies, taken together with D.A. Carson's chapter on the Old Testament in 1 Peter in the *Commentary on the New Testament use of the Old Testament*,[2] provide an essential starting place for students of this subject. We hope that this excursus will provide useful tools for students of this very promising field of research.

What we offer in this excursus is a chart and brief analysis of the use of the Old Testament in 1 Peter. The analysis draws from a larger study of eight lenses for studying the use of the Old Testament in the New.[3] Our aim is to offer the maximum information and perspective within the space limitations set by an excursus in a commentary.

---

1. Sargent, *Written to Serve*. Egan, *Ecclesiology and the Scriptural Narrative of 1 Peter*. Marcar, "The Quotations of Isaiah in 1 Peter," 1–22.
2. Carson, "1 Peter," CNTUOT, 1015–45.
3. Rodgers, *Exploring the Old Testament in the New*.

CHART OF THE OLD TESTAMENT IN 1 PETER (RR)

The chart below is an attempt to map the use of the Old Testament in 1 Peter. Such work is, by nature, conjectural and open to emendations.

NOTES ON CATEGORIZATION

OT quotes and allusions which appear in the Outer Margins of the Nestle–Aland 28 are noted with (NA). The Apparatus in the Outer Margins of NA28 uses *italics* to reference a direct quotation of the OT text. Thus, beyond this basic distinction, all categorization is our own, unless otherwise noted in the key or footnotes. The last column of explanatory notes in the table below is in no way exhaustive, providing background information for OT passages which might not be as readily understandable upon initial juxtaposition with material as found in 1 Peter.

EXPLANATORY KEY TO CLASSIFICATION

Quotations that appear in the Nestle–Aland 28: **Q (NA)**
    Allusions / Allusions cited in the Nestle–Aland 28: **A / A (NA)**
    Echoes / Echoes cited in the Nestle–Aland 28: **E / E (NA)**
    Narrative section presupposed: **N**
    Cross-References for further fruitful comparison: **CF**

Location in 1 Peter	Location in OT	Classification	Notes on "Story" / Use in 1 Peter
1 Pet. 1:2	a) Exod 24:7–8 b) Daniel 4:1, 6:26 (LXX Theod.)	a) E (NA) b) CF (NA)	a) After reading the book of the law Moses *sprinkles* upon the hearers the blood of the covenant, immediately after Moses, Aaron and the elders see God.

Location in 1 Peter	Location in OT	Classification	Notes on "Story" / Use in 1 Peter
1 Pet. 1:3	a) Isa 28:15–17 b) Sirach 16:12	a) CF b) CF (NA)	a) In context where a "covenant of death" is referred to the LXX uses ἐλπίδα to describe the rulers of God's people hoping in a lie. This is worth noting as Isaiah 28:16 is of central importance in 1 Pet. 2.
1 Pet. 1:7	a) Isa 48:10,11 b) Mal 3:3–4 c) Prov. 17:3 d) Psalm 66:10 e) Sirach 2:5; Wisdom 3:6	a) E or CF b) CF c) CF (NA) d) CF (NA) e) CF (NA)	a) Concern for the praise and glory of God's name in Isaiah 48:9 and 11; couched within this is verse 10 on refining of the house of Jacob, Israel. This theme: refinement for the sake of ultimate praise of God finds correspondence in 1 Peter 1:7
1 Pet. 1:10	1 Macc. 9:26	E	
1 Pet. 1:12	1 Enoch 1:2	CF	Note the mention of angels.
1 Pet. 1:13	Exodus 12:11	E	In Exodus the girding of loins is connected to the eating of the Passover to commemorate the hasty exit from Egypt. The echo may link Passover imagery to final revelation of Christ.
1 Pet. 1:16	Lev. 11:44–45; 19:2, 20:7	Q (NA)	Introductory formula διότι γέγραπται
1 Pet. 1:17	a) Psalm 89:26 (LXX v. 27) b) Jer. 3:19	a) E/A (NA) b) E	a) Calling out to God as father. b) Calling on God as father; reference to inheritance (cf. 1:4)
1 Pet. 1:18	Isa 52:3	A	
1 Pet. 1:19	Isaiah 53:7; Exod. 12:5	E; CF	

THE OLD TESTAMENT IN 1 PETER 171

Location in 1 Peter	Location in OT	Classification	Notes on "Story" / Use in 1 Peter
1 Pet. 1:24–25	Isa. 40:6–8	Q (NA)	Introductory formula διότι Omission similar to 1QIsaiah a
1 Pet. 2:3	Psalm 34:8 (LXX 33:9)	Q (NA)	
1 Pet. 2:4	a) Psalm 118:22 b) Isaiah 28:16 c) Zech. 3:9; Dan. 2:34–35, 44–45 d) Isaiah 42:1	a) A (NA) b) A (NA) c) CF d) CF	a/b) These allusions seem to anticipate fuller quotes in a) 3:10–12 and b) 1 Pet. 2:6. c) Important, possibly messianic, references to "stone" d) "my chosen one / delight"
1 Pet. 2:5	a) Exodus 19:6 b) Isa. 61:6	a) A b) CF	a) Anticipates fuller citation in 2:9 b) Priests of YHWH
1 Pet. 2:6	Isaiah 28:16	Q (NA)	Introductory formula διότι περιέχει ἐν γραφῇ Follows MT
1 Pet. 2:7	Psalm 118:22 (LXX 117:22)	Q (NA)	Follows MT and LXX
1 Pet. 2:8	Isaiah 8:14	Q (NA)	Follows MT
1 Pet. 2:9	a) Isa. 43:20–21 b) Exodus 19:6, c.f. 23:22 c) Malachi 3:17 d) Isa. 42:12 e) Deut. 10:15, 7:6 f) Isa. 62:12	a) Q (NA) b) Q (NA) c) A (NA) d) E e) CF f) CF	b) Follows LXX
1 Pet. 2:10	Hos. 1: 6, 9–10; Hos. 2:1, 3, 23, 25	Q (NA)	Corresponding with LXX

Location in 1 Peter	Location in OT	Classification	Notes on "Story" / Use in 1 Peter
1 Pet. 2:11	a) Gen. 23:4 b) Psalm 39:12 (LXX 38:12)	a) Q/A b) CF	a) Corresponding with LXX
1 Pet. 2:12	Isa. 10:3	A (NA)	Isaiah: ἡμέρᾳ τῆς ἐπισκοπῆς
1 Pet. 2:17	Prov. 24:21	A	
1 Pet. 2:22	Isa 53:9	Q/A (NA)	
1 Pet. 2:23	a) Isa 53:6–7, 12 b) Psalm 9:4	a) A b) CF	
1 Pet. 2:24	a) Isa. 53:4, 5, 12 b) Deut. 32:39; Psalm 103:3	a) A (NA) b) E	
1 Pet. 2:25	a) Isa. 53:6 b) Ezek. 34:5, 16 c) Job 10:12; Wisdom 1:6	a) Q (NA) b) A (NA) c) CF (NA)	a) Introductory phrase γὰρ
1 Pet. 3:3–4	Isaiah 3:18–23	E/CF	
1 Pet. 3:6	a) Gen 18:12 b) Prov. 3:25	a) N (NA) b) A	
1 Pet. 3:10–12	Psalm 34:13–17	Q (NA)	Introductory phrase γὰρ Follows MT and LXX
1 Pet. 3:13	Isaiah 50:9	E	
1 Pet. 3:14–15	Isaiah 8:12–13	Q (NA)	
1 Pet. 3:18	Isaiah 53:11	E	See LXX
1 Pet. 3:19	1 Enoch 9:10; 10:11–15	CF	
1 Pet. 3:20	Gen. 7:13, 17, 23; Gen. 6–8	N (NA)	
1 Pet. 3:22	a) Psalm 110 (LXX 109):1 b) Psalm 8:6–7	a) A b) CF	

THE OLD TESTAMENT IN 1 PETER

Location in 1 Peter	Location in OT	Classification	Notes on "Story" / Use in 1 Peter
1 Pet. 4:8	a) Proverbs 10:12 b) Tobit 12:9; Sirach 3:30 c) Psalm 32:1	a) Q (NA) b) CF (NA) c) CF	a) Introductory phrase ὅτι (seems to follow MT)
1 Pet. 4:14	a) Isaiah 11:2 b) Psalm 89:50–51 (LXX 88:51–52)	a) A/Q b) CF	a) Possible quote due to introductory phrase ὅτι
1 Pet. 4:17	a) Ezek. 9:6 b) Jer. 25:29; Amos 3:2	a) E b) CF	a) Scholars are divided on possible connection between these passages.
1 Pet. 4:18	Prov. 11:31	Q	Introduced with καὶ Follows LXX
1 Pet. 4:19	2 Macc. 1:24 etc.	CF	It is of note that the prayer is upon the lips of post-exilic Nehemiah and includes an appeal in verse 27 for God to both gather together his scattered people, help those who are rejected and despised that "the Gentiles may know that you are God." Compare with 1 Peter 1:1 and 2:12.
1 Pet. 5:3	Isaiah 44:28, Isaiah 63:11; Ezekiel 34:4 etc.	CF/E?	Isa. 63:11 is noteworthy due to mention of not only shepherd, but also the one who places his Holy Spirit (c.f. 4:14); cf. also "crown of glory" in 1 Pet. 5:4 and language in Isa. 62:3.
1 Pet. 5:5	Prov. 3:34	Q	Introductory phrase ὅτι Follows LXX

Location in 1 Peter	Location in OT	Classification	Notes on "Story" / Use in 1 Peter
1 Pet. 5:6	Ex. 3:19; 6:1; Deut. 9:26	E	Reference to God's "mighty hand" in the Exodus experience.
1 Pet. 5:7	a) Psalm 55:22 (LXX 54:23) b) Wisdom 12:13	a) A b) A	b) Correspondence and use of ὅτι
1 Pet. 5:8	a) Psalm 22:13 (LXX 21:14)	a) A	

ANALYZING THE OLD TESTAMENT IN 1 PETER. (PR)

This rich amalgam of quotations, allusions, echoes, and narratives from the Old Testament in 1 Peter may usefully be studied with the help of eight lenses.

Form: Any study of the use of the Old Testament in the new must pay careful attention to the text form of the source text and the document in which it is quoted. This will involve careful analysis of all known textual variants, whether in the Hebrew Bible, the LXX or other versions. We note that while often 1 Peter's quotations conform to the LXX, they do not always do so, and that at least twice Peter's form of text is closer to the Hebrew than to the Greek.[4] 1 Peter thus displays a pluriformity of text similar to Paul[5] and the Dead Sea Scrolls.[6] We note also the fascinating similarity of 1 Peter 1:24–25 and 1QIsaa at Isaiah 40:6–8[7] where both omit a line due to *homoeoteleuton* (similar line ending). Most LXX manuscripts omit the lines as well, but 1 Peter and Qumran are our earliest evidence of this omission. The details of this kind of textual analysis can tell us much about the textual affinities and social setting of the letter.

Introduction: The list of introductory formulae or terms listed in Marcar is instructive.[8] Only two verses are introduced with a formula as

---

4. See Marcar, "The Quotations of Isaiah in 1 Peter," 20.
5. Silva, "Old Testament in Paul," *DPL*, 631.
6. Tov, *Textual Criticism of the Hebrew Bible*, 107–112.
7. Col.XXXIII (Isa 40:2–28) where another scribe has written in the omitted words above the line and in the margin. See Tov, *Textual Criticism of the Hebrew Bible3,386* for a picture of the Isaiah scroll and its omission.
8. Marcar, "The quotations from Isaiah," 4.

such (1:16, 2:6). Several are preceded by an introductory word (οτι, διοτι). Most of the citations from the scriptures of Israel are not introduced at all. For example, phrases from Isaiah 53 are weaved into 1 Peter 2:21-25 without any recognition that they are from scripture. This implies that this text, like so many in the letter, needs no introduction, but is well-known to both writer and readers. The absence of introductory formulae can tell us as much as their presence.

Selection: The above chart reveals that several Old Testament passages were especially important for 1 Peter. Note that there are several references to Psalm 34 (LXX 33) in the letter. Citations from Isaiah 8 and Isaiah 53 also recur. The author appears to have been especially influenced by Isaiah 40–55, in a manner similar to that of Mark and Romans.[9] In seeking the motives or principles that governed the selection of these passages, we note that 4 Mac 18:10-19 cites verses from the same passages as 1 Peter (Psalm 34, Proverbs 3, Isaiah 43). These two documents, roughly similar in date, drew from scripture passages especially important for God's people in time of trial.

Application: In the New Testament scripture texts have been employed to support and explicate gospel facts and lifestyle. Isaiah 53 is an important example.

In 1 Peter 2 the initial aim of the use of phrases from this text is to encourage Christians to follow closely in the steps of Christ, in not retaliating when they are treated unjustly. But in verse 24 the application shifts to Christ's sacrificial and substitutionary death, in which he *bore our sins in his body on the tree*. This is the most extensive and thoughtful use of Isaiah 53 in early Christian literature. Note that 1 Clement, who clearly has knowledge of 1 Peter, reverts to a simple exemplary use of the text (1 Clement 16). In both documents "recourse is had to Isaiah 53 for a portrait of Jesus."[10] In the study of the application of scripture texts by early Christian writers a comparison with first century Jewish exegetical practices will prove fruitful.[11]

Combination: The practice of combining texts from different places with interpretive effect was common in ancient literature, both Jewish and Greco-Roman.[12] 1 Peter is especially rich in such combination. We note especially the collection of "stone testimonia," combined with other texts in 1 Peter 2:1-10. Similarly, the combination of phrases from Isaiah 53 with

---

9. See Watts, *Isaiah's new Exodus in Mark*, Wagner, *Heralds of Good News*.

10. Philip Carrington in a handwritten note in his copy of W.K.Lowther Clarke's *The First Epistle of Clement*, in my possession.

11. Rodgers, *Exploring the Old Testament in the New*, 40-44.

12. See Adams and Ehorn, *Composite Citations in Antiquity*, Vol 1.

the reference to Deut 21:23[13] underlines the salvific (as well as exemplary) character of Christ's death.

Combination of scripture texts in 3:10–17 and 4:12–19 deserve careful study.

History: The study of the history of biblical interpretation in the second temple period proves fruitful for the student of 1 Peter. The use of Isaiah 28:16 in the Dead Sea Scrolls (1QS VIII 5–8) and 1 Peter 2:6 allows us to note the similarities and differences in assumptions and approach between early Christianity and Qumran. And the use of Psa 110:1 in 1 Pet 3:22 invites us to set Peter's use in the context of the history of interpretation of this text. This is the most frequently-quoted Old Testament text by early Christian writers. Peter's employment of images of Exodus, Exile and Temple, and of Sarah (3:5–6) and Noah (3:20) should be studied against the rich interpretive background that we find for these images and characters in the second temple period.

Story: The narrative of God and his people is richly reflected in 1 Peter, and the scriptures of Israel have been employed to tell that story with Christ as the climax and hermeneutical key. For example the story of God as shepherd (cf Psalm 23, Ezekiel 34, ect) is reflected in 1 Pet 2:25, 5:4. Note the "high Christology" of these passages in which Old Testament texts referring to God are applied to Christ in 1 Peter (cf 3:15, citing Isa 8:13). Note, too, how the story of the Anatolian Christians' pilgrimage is seen by the author as a figural fulfillment of the wilderness wanderings of ancient Israel (cf 1 Cor 10:1–13).[14] They have already been delivered by the blood of the spotless lamb (1:19)) and God's *mighty* hand (5:6) in the new Passover/Exodus, but await the final inheritance which is assured (1:4, 3:7, 3:9). For now, the Christians are kept by God in *all their sojournings.* (2:11). God's future work is assured on the basis of God's finished work.

Function: It is sometimes assumed by commentators that the scriptures play a supportive rather than a creative role in the letter. A quotation from scripture is seen either as a proof-text or is brought in to clinch an argument.[15] On the contrary, the scripture functions much more in a creative way in 1 Peter. The author has clearly meditated on Psalm 34, to which he refers several times, and his rich use of Isaiah 53 at the end of Chapter 2 gives evidence of a searching study of the scriptures. The recurrence of quotations and allusions from Isaiah 40–55 suggests that he has thought deeply about that section of scripture, and that he has a regard for the context, the "story"

---

13. See the valuable discussion in Elliott, 533.
14. Liebengood, *Eschatology in 1 Peter,* 135–7.
15. Kelly, 137.

of the text.[16] For 1 Peter, the scripture has not been so much plundered as pondered. This deep meditation on scripture invites the reader to follow in the author's steps, and to read, mark, learn and inwardly digest the scripture.

---

16. I would argue that this is true even at 2:10 in Peter's use of Hos 1:6,9, 2:25.

Holy and Royal Priesthood
Interpretation of 1 Peter 2:5,9 in Church History

By Greg Flagg

If you ask people on the street what the role of a priest looks like today you would probably get responses ranging from blank stares to thoughts about robes, beards and possibly something about scandals. Our current church and religious environment is far removed from what the concept of a priest looked like to the first century audience of 1 Peter and definitely from the worlds of first and second temple Judaism[1]. The Bible does give us some glimpses and one might argue that priests in the Orthodox traditions are our closest link to the priests of the early Church. Yet, few verses have more impacted and divided our current view of hierarchy within the church than 1 Peter 2:5 and 9. These two verses written in a first century, second temple, Greco-Roman context would become foundational to the late middle ages, in the Protestant Reformation movement in 16th century Europe. They now influence how many modern church traditions understand the dividing line, if any, between church leadership and laity. A brief exploration of how these two verses and the concepts of the "holy priesthood" in 1 Peter 2:5 and the "royal priesthood" (also translated as a "kingdom of priests" or a "priestly kingdom") in 1 Peter 2:9 have been understood throughout the history of the church will help us understand how these verses have shaped our current church culture. This may also present challenges and questions that, depending on the answers given, will shape the future for the church in the world.

---

1. McKnight, 113.

The developments noted here are written from a Western and Protestant perspective. It would be instructive to trace the idea of "Royal Priesthood" in the Greek Orthodox, Syriac and Coptic traditions, but this is beyond the constraints of this essay.

For many of the post-apostolic fathers, these two verses seem to have had little to do with roles and responsibilities within the church. They were instead understood as a marker delineating the people of God now understood as those who were "in Christ."[2] Justin Martyr in his *Dialogue with Trypho* refers to his fellow Christians as, "the true high priestly race of God."[3] Ignatius in his epistle to the Ephesians greets his readers with the words, "Blessed then, are ye who are God-bearers, spirit-bearers, temple-bearers of holiness. . .being 'a royal priesthood, a holy nation, a peculiar people."[4] In their reference to these verses in 1 Peter, they refer to the whole Christian church. The Church at large is understood as the new Israel, the title of "royal priesthood" promised in Exodus 19:6 is now enlarged to encompass the whole of the new church, the new Exodus that follows in the footsteps of Jesus.

Another focus of the early Church fathers from the priesthood language in 1 Peter is the responsibility of the priests to offer the "spiritual sacrifices" mentioned in 1 Peter 2:5. Tertullian recalls the image of an unblemished sacrifice in the Hebrew when he writes, "We are the true adorers and the true priests, who, praying in spirit, sacrifice, in spirit, prayer. . .this victim, devoted from the whole heart, fed on faith, tended by truth, entire in innocence, pure in chastity, garlanded with love."[5] Irenaeus writes that, like the Levites of the Hebrew Scriptures, offering these spiritual sacrifices means that Christians inherit, "neither lands nor houses."[6] Along with the theme of offering a spiritual sacrifice, Origen writes, "If you want to exercise the priesthood of your soul, do not let the fire depart from your altar." Clement of Alexandria also uses the image of a priest offering sacrifices when he writes, "the offering which is made in prayers and in the teachings by which souls which are offered to God are won."[7] Again, these images and understanding "priesthood" in 1 Peter apply to the whole church community. The image of a priest sacrificing a victim on an altar was all too familiar to the church fathers living in the Roman Empire where animal sacrifices,

2. DLNT, 966.
3. ANF, 1, 257.
4. Ibid., 1, 53.
5. Ibid., 3: 690.
6. Ibid., 1: 471.
7. ACC,XI, 87.

and other sacrificial offerings, were commonplace. We take the concept of a "spiritual sacrifice" for granted in our current Church culture and would be wise to understand the revolutionary nature of the preferred sacrifice for Christians being spiritual rather than physical. The movement away from animal sacrifices was especially poignant during a time when sacrifices were used as political and cultural markers between Jews and Gentiles.[8] While there are passages from the Hebrew prophets showing that animal sacrifices were falling out of favor[9], and even the Pharisees and the Qumran community focused on deeds and obedience to the law as superior to animal sacrifices[10], the focus of these sacrifices is no longer the atonement for and cleansing of sins. Instead, a spiritual sacrifice serves as a witness to the world of the acts of God, specifically for Christians in the sacrifice and resurrection of Jesus.[11] For 1 Peter and the early Church fathers, these spiritual sacrifices demarcate the new people of God and call them to maintain their focus and worship on the one, true, God. The God who has called them, like Israel, out of the world, as Jesus leads them out of bondage, out of the trials and tribulations that surround them.[12]

The priesthood language of 1 Peter 2 would later play a "special role"[13] within the church during the period of Protestant Reformation that swept across Western Europe in the 16th century, as many in the Church began responding to not only clerical abuses but to the shifting cultural, technological and civic landscape. Luther would use this text to address the abuses of priestly and clerical power rampant in the Roman Catholic Church at the time. In his own commentary he would write, "We have had much discussion on this point, maintaining that those who are now called clergy are not priests in the sight of God; and it is founded upon this passage of Peter."[14] However, in this reaction against the priestly abuses, Luther seeks to reclaim the communal meaning and focus of the passage and that the title of priesthood mentioned here is meant to apply to, "the whole congregation, to all

---

8. Frederick James Murphy, *Early Judaism : The Exile to the Time of Jesus*, 324. Mass.: Hendrickson Publishers, 2002

9. See Micah 6:8, Isaiah 1:11, Amos 5:21–24.

10. Which probably helped them, along with Christians, to endure the destruction of the second temple in 70 CE. See Craig S. Keener , *The Ivp Bible Background Commentary : New Testament*, 666.

11. Achtemeier,157.

12. Nijay K. Gupta, "A Spiritual House of Royal Priests, Chosen and Honored: The Presence and Function of Cultic Imagery in 1 Peter," *Perspectives in Religious Studies* 36, no. 1 (2009), 71.

13. Martin and Elliott, *Augsburg Commentary on the New Testament*, 84.

14. Martin Luther and J. G. Walch, *Commentary on the Epistles of Peter and Jude*, 88.

Christians"[15] and not to the "monkey play of the Papists."[16] This focus on "the whole congregation" would come into the sharpest focus often among the Anabaptists and other radical reformer groups. Among the Anabaptists, specifically, lay members were empowered and encouraged to serve and take up responsibilities traditionally held by clergy. It was common that, "ordinary members read the Scriptures publicly and no doubt expounded them at meetings held in homes."[17]

The leaders of the Reformation also take up the theme of the "spiritual sacrifices" offered by the "holy priesthood" inaugurated in Christ. John Calvin writes that the most important spiritual sacrifice for the believer is the "offering of ourselves." It is after that initial offering and denial of self that the other sacrificial deeds may follow, "prayers, thanksgiving, almsdeeds, and all the duties of religion."[18] For Luther as well, the offering of spiritual sacrifices as the responsibility of the royal priesthood calls the believer to appear before God and offer prayers for others and to humbly teach and instruct others in scripture and "divine things."[19] So the goal of the Reformation understanding was not just to take down the abusing priests and popes, but to raise up the responsibility of the lay people in the church through the "priesthood of all believers" interpretation of this passage. It is the whole of the church that is called out and proclaimed a "holy" and "royal priesthood" and therefore all believers have a responsibility, as Christ's "brethren," to offer spiritual sacrifices.[20]

So, after this brief overview of how the "holy" and "royal priesthood" of 1 Peter has been understood over this history of the church, how then should the church understand them at the present time? As was stated in the introduction, for most people today the concept of a priest and priesthood is quite alien and something from the ancient past. If the contemporary church is to find meaning in these passages we would do well to wrestle with what the "priesthood" referenced by the author of 1 Peter might look like today. J.H. Elliott has done much to move the conversation towards the community focus of the early church fathers of the "royal priesthood" in 1 Peter. Noting Israel's calling by God to be a "royal priesthood," Elliott writes, "the terms cannot be applied to the believers as individuals, but only to

15. Ibid., 100.

16. Ibid., 92.

17. Wolfgang Schäufele, "Missionary Vision and Activity of the Anabaptist Laity," 102.

18. Calvin, 64.

19. Herman A. Preus, "Luther on the Universal Priesthood and the Office of the Ministry," 57.

20. Luther and Walch, 89.

the believing community as community."²¹ As Israel was called as a nation, so too is the Christian community called as a community to live into the calling to be a "holy" and "royal priesthood." A community of priests also has the unique role to typify, "the redeemed/restored people of God. . . that finds its supreme expression in Jesus Christ."²² A priest's role is not relegated to just offering sacrifices and performing rites, but is to be a witness to the redemption and restoration God seeks for the world. As the Church lives into this reality of witnessing to God's redemption, it also bridges the gap between the eternal and temporal. One might recall the common image of a chasm between God and man that is bridged only by the cross of Christ. When the calling of the community of believers to be a holy priesthood is understood in this way, we are called to not merely walk across the chasm and show others the way, but to live into the sacrificial nature of the cross of Christ that helps bridge the gap.²³ Among those who demonstrate the responsibilities of the royal priesthood should primarily be the ordained clergy. This does not mean that the individual believer is exempt from the following the exhortation of this passage, as both individual believers and the Christian community can be mutually appealed to in this passage²⁴. This verse often serves as a dividing line between those who support an ordained clergy and those who would rather the church serve as one, large, organic body whose only head is Christ. However, a priest, pastor or leader should be the first to live into the responsibilities of the Christian community called to be a holy priesthood. They are not so much called to guide and direct the community how to live, but to witness to the real presence of Christ, serving as mediator between God and man, and living a life as the spiritual sacrifice mentioned in 1 Peter. The priest, pastor and leader testifies to the fact that, "all human life must be offered to God."²⁵ The understanding of what is the "holy" and "royal priesthood" imagery in 1 Peter 2:5 and 9 has definitely morphed and changed over Church history as the cultural and contextual needs of the church have changed and shifted. While a priest as might have been recognized by the author of 1 Peter would be completely alien today, the Church must still seek to understand what a "holy" and "royal priesthood" looks like at this present moment. It is a challenge both

---

21. Elliott, 452.

22. Alex T. M. Cheung, "The Priest as the Redeemed Man: A Biblical-Theological Study of the Priesthood," 266.

23. John Chryssavgis, "The Royal Priesthood (Peter 2:9)," 375.

24. Peter R. Rodgers, "Review of Elliott," *Novum Testamentum* 46 (2004), 293–94.

25. Chryssavgis, 377.

for the individual believer and, most importantly, for the Church community at large to embody in the world.

The Persecutions in 1 Peter
By Jonathan Elliott

1 Peter's treatment of Christian suffering has been the subject of at least as fiery a debate as the language describing the persecution. While much of the battle focuses on how the descriptions of Christian persecution gives clues as to the time of authorship, I believe that the conversation is missing out on the powerful inclusion of all suffering of the church as the body of Christ. This inclusive vision of suffering is a move toward healing for disenfranchised Christians suffering throughout history.

Despite being ultimately short-sighted, reading 1 Peter with a view towards its date of authorship is still an important exercise. Much of the interpretation has focused on whether the persecution as described is official, i.e. led from the power of the Roman government, or unofficial, populace –led. Certain phrases such as the "fiery ordeal"[1], the Christians described as "maligned"[2] and suffering "as a Christian" (4:16) have been seized upon as proof that a late, official persecution is what is described. Since the "legal prohibition of Christianity was unknown before Trajan"[3], this late date would also preclude Petrine authorship. However, recent scholarship has re-examined the textual evidence and found consensus in that the persecution being described was of an unofficial nature.[4] Leonard Goppelt suggests 65–80 CE as the range of dates that 1 Peter was likely composed[5] Citing the mss variants which soften what would later be a politically troubling rendering of "Zealots" with the much more palatable "imitators" (3:13) Forbes points to a date of composition before or during the Jewish war but not

1. 1 Pet 4:12.
2. 1 Pet 3:16.
3. Hort, 1.
4. Williams, *Persecution in 1 Peter*, 285.
5. Goppelt, 45.

after.[6] Hillyer suggests 63 CE, citing the almost naive comment about not being harmed when doing good in 1 Pet 3:13, which would hardly be written after persecution "flared up under Nero."[7] All evidence now seems to point to a time of "discrimination, ostracism, occupational disadvantages, accusations and legal proceedings before courts."[8] Even though courts were involved this does not constitute official persecution because it requires an accuser willing to press charges.[9] With the acceptance of persecutions as experienced in 1 Peter being of a varied nature, it is also no longer necessary to suppose a late date to composition of 1 Peter. This recent growth in understanding the nature of the persecutions of 1 Peter leads us to see with new eyes our current struggles as Christians in a postmodern world.

There are indications of the nature of this persecution by the language of the text. First there is the description of the trials as ποικιλοις often translated as *varied*. Hillyer renders the word as *many colored*.[10] It is best to assume then that the use of this word describes not a monolithic, ubiquitous form of persecution, but many different forms and colors of that persecution. It appears that there was in some quarters an element of name-calling or slander. The continued repetition of the word κακοποιός may indicate that the author "was accustomed to hear either this epithet or its Latin equivalent flung at Christians in Rome."[11] The word λυπεω can refer to emotional pain and grief, as well as physical pain.[12] The use of πυρωσει suggests an ordeal by fire, a purifying in a furnace.[13] This ordeal by fire need not be taken as a literal description since later the author will pick up the idea of faith being tested and fire is certainly the means by which precious metals are tested (1:6–7). While the Christians may not be being put into an actual fire at this time, they experience both the pain and their own testedness.[14] It is not that God is testing the Christian but that through the trial the Christian has already been proved. The image of being tested by fire is far from frightening, it is an encouragement. There is no question that the Christians are suffering yet the author does not address the receivers as sufferers, but as

---

6. Forbes, 113.
7. Hillyer, For further discussion see the Introduction to this commentary, 6.
8. Goppelt, 241.
9. Ibid., 39.
10. Hillyer, 33.
11. Hort, 136.
12. Forbes, 24.
13. Hillyer, 130.
14. Forbes, 24.

foreigners.[15] This description of the Christians as foreigners begs to be read through the eyes of a people in exile and the alienation that comes with that foreignness. From these indications, we can determine that the suffering of the Christians involved "slanderous accusations."[16] There is ample indication that the populace has turned against Christianity. Already in Acts there have been riots and near-riots surrounding the ministry of the apostles, and this not long after enjoying the favor of all the people.

The Christians are suffering under this persecution for one reason: the fact that they carry the name of Jesus.[17] However, a person's identity can never really be separated from action. Therefore, though the persecution is based upon their identity as Christians, their actions as Christians will be what will be powerfully decried as well. In their ever fervent respect for the authors of Western civilization a historical fallacy has developed about how secular the foundations of our society were. The Greek and Roman empires were not lands of pure reason at the expense of religious thought. Both nations were heavily committed to a strict religious pluralism. Early attacks of Christianity weren't about the absurdity of religious belief, but about its narrowness of belief. The Roman gods offered wide paths of religious expression. These religious practices involved every level of society and all aspects of Roman life including politics, philosophy, the arts, sexuality and economics. R. L. Wilken rightly purposes that "to say that Christianity is a superstition is not a matter of simple bias or as a result of ignorance; it expresses a distinct religious sensibility."[18] Thus, the existence of the Christian worldview was a challenge to Roman assumptions about life.[19] Being a believer was "anti-social at best or treasonable at worst."[20]

Already one can see the theological imagination at work trying to make sense of the suffering of the believers. The Author speaks of awaiting the much greater eschatological joy in the age to come as hope. 1 Peter also discusses the testing that suffering brings (1:9). This testing does not make the believer more genuine, it reveals the genuineness which is already present. This image of genuine faith being revealed in the fire, if not prophetic, certainly was an image that would comfort and encourage believers going to that fate. Through 1 Peter, Christians could conceptualize themselves and foreigners and aliens (2:11). They could be exiles awaiting God's deliverance

---

15. Goppelt, 19
16. Goppelt, 39.
17. Hillyer, 131.
18. Wilken, *The Christians,* 66, cited in Feldmeier, 8.
19. Feldmeier, 9.
20. Hillyer, 131.

and in the meantime also join together as a society of sufferers whose ideal model was a Christ who suffered and was victorious.

Imagining the deepest, darkest time of Christian suffering under the oppressive Roman empire may be a glorious backdrop for understanding 1 Peter, but it is not what modern scholars would have us believe. In fact, I am glad that these scholars have challenged this theory. For far too long Christians have been playing a dangerous game with human suffering, grading it like a sporting event, validating some as sufferers and others as posers. There are dangers of only legitimizing the suffering of those under official persecution and delegitimizing those who are "only" suffering unofficial persecution as envisioned in 1 Peter. The first problem with thinking this way is that disenfranchising all but those who suffer death and torture increases the "lesser" suffering. As the Church exited that period of intense Roman persecution, they were perhaps oddly distressed by the inability to achieve martyrdom. Instead they contented themselves with suffering as "confessors."[21] Because of this crisis, the Church legitimized the "lesser" suffering in a way that validated each. This wisdom of legitimizing suffering in the community has been for the most part lost in the overly competitive culture we live in now. When we allow only those who suffer greatest to be legitimized, it turns suffering into a competition with consolation being the prize. Consolation is not a prize to crown winners; it is the promise of Scripture to all who suffer. Furthermore, there is grace to be given in a community that validates each other's sufferings instead of setting one person's suffering against another. To accept each other's suffering no matter the gradation, is Christian hospitality, inviting people into a space where they are accepted, just as Christ has done for us (Rom 15:7). The even greater problem with grading each other's suffering to decide who deserves consolation is with the image of Jesus as chief sufferer. Jesus' suffering was more than just what would be expected to be experienced on the cross, since he was also dealing with the spiritual separation and outpouring of God's wrath. Therefore, if Jesus respects and honors our suffering, though His is greater, then no believer may disenfranchise another's suffering. Instead we are invited to welcome sufferers gracefully, in imitation of Christ's acceptance.

Not only is it damaging when we delegitimize another's suffering, we miss out on the beauty of welcoming each other as sufferers. Within 1 Peter's description of Christian suffering we find an invitation to be found in the image of Christ as sufferer. It is no wonder we suffer, following a Christ who suffered. We follow in the footsteps of Apostles who have suffered according

---

21. Gonzalez, *Story of Christianity: Volume 1*, 174.

to the promise of Christ.[22] When we suffer, we are invited to take our place in the great story of the Church. To be found in the likeness of Christ is a great honor for the Christian and is the high ideal of believers. When we delegitimize another Christian's suffering we take away an aspect of their life that was found to be in conformity to the one they follow. In fact 1 Peter shows sensibilities with a view to validating the sufferings of the community. The fact that the persecutions themselves are only hinted at with language from the text and the fact that 1 Peter is a circular letter point to the purpose of the describing the sufferings in a way that allows the audience to identify with the suffering of the global Church (5:9). The author paints suffering with a broad brush describing it as *varied* (1:6). This opening to the different kinds of suffering is necessary for a circular epistle since the author would neither know when that particular letter would be read nor what the situation of the listeners would be. The author makes the choice to honor whatever suffering the community is experiencing at the time.

Embracing the sufferings of 1 Peter as *varied* is also useful in the place we find ourselves as members of a post-Christian world. Persecution is a real threat the world over. Even now, many people are being jailed, tortured and killed under official government persecution for bearing the name of Jesus. At the same time unofficial persecution of Christians is also occurring. As the currents of culture shift, some ideas are given a status that is unassailable while others are not allowed to be spoken. Christian exclusivity is one such idea that has fallen into disrepute. Those that believe in Jesus as the way of Salvation are not just thought of as quaint or foolish. The idea is now often considered dangerously fanatic. In such an environment, is it possible to proclaim Christianity in a way that is both respectful to hearers and faithful to the Gospel that has been handed down to us? Already we are being faced with this reality. In 2014 the California State University system derecognized several Christian groups with statements of faith, saying that it was discriminatory against students without a faith. While the California State University system eventually restored those groups, the danger continues to exist. We cannot really believe that certain voices must be silenced in order to protect another voice. True plurality will allow the voices to have meaningful discussion amongst themselves which will lead to greater understanding, not discrimination. The idea of sin has fallen by the wayside as well. Not that people do not believe in wrongdoing, but the chief offender of our western civilization seems to be a person who judges another to be a sinner in need of grace. The problem is that Christianity teaches that all are sinners in need of grace, irrespective of any particular action being taken.

---

22. Mark 10:29

Failures on the part of Christians may be the emphasizing certain sins over others instead of claiming the falseness of humanity is partly to blame. Yet there must be an avenue to speak of the things God has spoken about as in line with his divine self and those that He has determined are not. Finally, bullying is quickly becoming an important topic when one discusses meaningful beliefs. While I applaud the feeling behind the recent anti-bullying movement, care must be taken to make sure that these concerns do not lead to people being buffaloed into silence about their sincerely held beliefs. Bullying is at heart an act of intimidation and should not be applied categorically to sincerely held beliefs. Indeed intimidation must stop, even the intimidation that would paint people with merely a different view of the world as bullies. In our important conversation about bullying, we must not make the error that takes away the right of any person to be who they are and use speech to actualize that belief.

In conclusion, the contemporary world is fast becoming like the ancient world in its confusion about people of faith in general and Christianity in particular. As Christians, we should expect that the world will not agree with us in many important areas and that those differences will cause suffering in some way. It is important that we remember our place in the grand scheme of Christian suffering and yet, we have been invited into the great story of our suffering Savior (2:21–25). Each hurt is folded into his consolation in the *eschaton* and is breaking out even now. As culture makes that shift from favoring Christianity to finding its belief repugnant, we can draw closer to the experience of Jesus and the early Church. Living in this world makes the themes of suffering and unofficial persecution in 1 Peter even more accessible than before. Let us take what 1 Peter has to offer our community and continue to pass it along to each community of faith.

Temple Imagery in 1 Peter
by Vince Conroy

According to NT Wright, for the Jews of Peter's day, the Temple was one of four key symbols which defined their identity as the people of YHWH, anchored their everyday religious and public lives, and formed the basis of their entire worldview (the other three symbols are Land, Torah and ethnic heritage) But Wright identifies Temple as the "heart of the Jewish life."[1] Drawing on Josephus, Philo and various Talmudic sources, N.T. Wright notes that the temple combined in itself the whole life of Israel, whether religious, political, economic or social.[2]

Of course, in our pluralistic American culture, we have no single metaphor to compare this to (especially a single religious symbol), but just as "Temple" defines the totality of first-century Jewish life, we could observe that for us, "Wall Street" defines finance, "Hollywood" defines entertainment, "Silicon Valley" defines technology, and "Washington" defines government and civic life—but now imagine all of those in a single metaphor. Or, if I were to say "the Force be with you" to almost anyone today it would immediately conjure up familiar characters, scenes, sounds and mythical plotlines from the *Star Wars* films. Likewise, mentioning the words "a lamb without blemish" (1:19) to a first-century Jew would surely recall the sights, sounds and smells of a ceremonial animal sacrifice performed at the altars of the Temple, probably preceded by a financial transaction in the outer temple courts to purchase the animal, and some kind of interaction with the Priest performing the sacrificial act.

However—*and this is not commonly understood by most believers today*—this Temple "meta-narrative" is not limited to Moses' tabernacle in the wilderness, Solomon's Temple, or the "second" Temple built by Herod, the one in which Jesus and Peter worshipped. As G. K. Beale documents so

---

1. Wright, *The New Testament and the People of God*, 224.
2. Wright, *ibid*. 224–25.

thoroughly, this Temple meta-narrative actually begins with the Creation account in Genesis and the "paradisal" Garden Temple of Eden, where Adam and Eve jointly performed priestly-kingly duties, and is echoed throughout the Old Testament in various forms, including Noah's Ark and the visions of Ezekiel (Eze 40–48). In the New Testament, including here in 1 Peter, the vision includes a new *spiritual house* (2:5) built out of living stones with Jesus as the cornerstone. Later this vision finds its ultimate fulfillment in the eschatological Temple of the New Jerusalem as seen in Rev 21–22 (also a "garden" temple like Eden) where we will dwell with our Creator forever. To quote the essence of Beale's thesis: "The Garden of Eden was the first archetypal temple...the model of all subsequent temples...a microcosm of all creation.[3]

As we will see, 1 Peter reflects this Temple meta-narrative, sometimes in *quotations*, but more often in *allusions* and *echoes*.

SURVEY OF TEMPLE REFERENCES IN 1 PETER

The following table surveys the significant Temple references I have identified in 1 Peter. Please note that this list is *not* intended as comprehensive, but includes what I believe is a reasonable representation of significant themes.

Passage	Temple-related Terms/Phrases	Suggested Themes/Implications
1:2	κατὰ πρόγνωσιν θεοῦ (chosen and destined by God the Father)	(Trinitarian pattern); the blood of Jesus replaces animal sacrifice in the Temple
	ἐν ἁγιασμῷ πνεύματος (sanctified by the Spirit)	The beginnings of new, permanent home for sojourners, a new sanctuary built by God rather than by human hands
	ῥαντισμὸν αἵματος (sprinkled with [Jesus'] blood)	
1:18–19	ἐλυτρώθητε (redeemed)	Concept of manumission, which involved a payment to the treasury of a pagan temple
	ἀργυρίῳ ἢ χρυσίῳ (silver and gold)	Silver and gold as vessels of the OT Temple

---

3. Beale, *The Temple and the Church's Mission*, 27. See also Levenson, "The Temple and the World."

Passage	Temple-related Terms/Phrases	Suggested Themes/Implications
2:4–10	λίθον ζῶντα... λίθοι ζῶντες (living stone/stones) οἰκοδομεῖσθε οἶκος πνευματικὸς εἰς (built into a spiritual house) ἱεράτευμα ἅγιον (a holy priesthood) πνευματικὰς θυσίας (spiritual sacrifices) τίθημι ἐν Σιών (laying in Zion) ἀκρογωνιαῖον (cornerstone) πέτρα σκανδάλου (rock of offence) βασίλειον ἱεράτευμα (a royal priesthood) ἔθνος ἅγιον (a holy nation) ἐξαγγείλητε (proclaim, evangelize) θαυμαστὸν αὐτοῦ φῶς. (his marvelous light)	"Stone" as a common Temple metaphor; Christ as the cornerstone, source of all cosmic wisdom Jewish and Gentile believers, the new Levitical priestly order, performing priestly duties in a new Temple of which they are also a part The new Temple as a dwelling place for God's presence, but as with the original paradisal Temple of Eden, one not built by human hands, but by God Global expansion of the Temple from Creation onward (the original "great commission") God himself as the source of light in the final Temple of the New Jerusalem
3:7	συγκληρονόμοις χάριτος ζωῆς (joint heirs of the gracious gift of life)	Husband and wife as joint heirs of new life Reversal of expulsion from Garden Temple
3:18–20	ἡμέραις Νῶε (days of Noah), κιβωτοῦ (ark)	Noah's Ark as an early prototype Temple
4:14–17	δόξης καὶ τὸ τοῦ θεοῦ πνεῦμα ἐφ' ὑμᾶς ἀναπαύεται (the spirit of glory... is resting on you) κρίμα ἀπὸ τοῦ οἴκου τοῦ θεοῦ· (judgement to begin with the household of God)	Recalls the shekinah glory of God visible in Moses' tabernacle and in the first Temple Jesus overturning the tables in the Temple courts as sign of a new Temple order

Passage	Temple-related Terms/Phrases	Suggested Themes/Implications
5:10	καταρτίσει, στηρίξει, σθενώσει, θεμελιώσει (restore, support, strengthen, and establish)	Building/re-building language. Use of *four* similar verbs, echoing other Temple patterns of *four* elsewhere in Scripture

Table 1: Summary of Representative Temple References in 1 Peter

For each reference, I will briefly discuss its basis for inclusion and significance, (especially within the Temple imagery from Genesis/Creation to Revelation/eschaton). The intent here is to demonstrate the pervasiveness of Temple language and how it ultimately supports the central message and purpose of the letter. Andrew Mbuvi, who devoted a full-length monograph to this subject, notes, "while the most explicit use of temple imagery occurs in 2:4–10, temple imagery undergirds the entire letter of 1 Peter."[4] The following references deserve special comment.

1 PETER 1:2—CHOSEN, SANCTIFIED, SPRINKLED

κατὰ πρόγνωσιν θεοῦ (chosen and destined by God the Father)
ἐν ἁγιασμῷ πνεύματος (sanctified by the Spirit)
ῥαντισμὸν αἵματος (sprinkled with his [Jesus] blood)

These three phrases, which follow a pattern of three, clearly invoke the Jewish Temple (and/or tabernacle) by linking the blood of Jesus to Old Testament animal sacrifices (e.g. Exod 24:3–8, Lev 4:6–10, etc.). The middle phrase ἁγιασμῷ πνεύματος is most often interpreted as the work of the Holy Spirit in the life of the believers allowing them to appropriate holiness. It may have a nuanced meaning here, given that the readers are παρεπιδήμοις διασπορᾶς, strangers without a permanent home. Along these lines, Joel Green observes that given the audience, and the presence of ἐν (in) at the beginning of the phrase, a better reading might be "in the sanctification of the Spirit," with the conclusion following that "because of the obedience and sprinkling of the blood of Jesus Christ, Peter's audience has been relocated in a new space."[5] This permanent home is the new Temple *in Christ* (5:10), a *spiritual house* (that is, one built by the Spirit), with new *spiritual sacrifices* carried out by a new "holy priesthood" (2:5).

4. Mbuvi, *Temple, Exile and Identity in 1 Peter*, 71.
5. Green, 19–20.

This meta-theme of the "homeless finding a permanent home," which began when Adam and Eve were evicted from the paradisal Garden Temple in Genesis 3:24, comes full circle, finding its ultimate fulfillment in the last Temple, the New Jerusalem, when as it was in Eden, *the home of God is among mortals. He will dwell with them as their God; they will be his peoples, and God himself will be with them* (Rev 21:3).

1 PETER 1:18–19—REDEEMED, SILVER AND GOLD

ἐλυτρώθητε (redeemed)
ἀργυρίῳ ἢ χρυσίῳ (silver and gold)

The verb ἐλυτρώθητε translated by the NSRV as *redeemed* (and the associated cognate) were used in Greco-Roman society to refer to the "manumission" of a slave, a transaction where a slave would receive freedom after a payment was made to the slave's owner through the treasury of a pagan temple, with the idea that it was the pagan god or goddess who was buying the slave. The slave would then be considered "free" in the eyes of the former owner, but in the eyes of society, would still be considered a slave of the god or goddess, having been "redeemed" by the deity.[6] This usage also has a rich OT history in the depiction of God's acts of deliverance, particularly with the Exodus.[7]

In addition to drawing a comparison between the value of *perishable things like silver or gold,* and the *the precious blood of Christ*, this verse hints at the central truth that the old Temple order, with its vessels of silver and gold, formed by human hands (e.g. 1 Kings 7:51), is being replaced by a new Temple order. Students of Revelation will recall that the eschatological Temple, the New Jerusalem, is also described as having elements made of gold, but in this case, the walls are *of pure gold, clear as glass* (Rev 21:18) and the street of the city is also *pure gold, transparent as glass*, presumably because they have been formed by God himself, untouched by human hands.

1 PETER 2.4-10: SPIRITUAL HOUSE, CORNERSTONE, LIVING STONES, THE NEW PRIESTHOOD

οἰκοδομεῖσθε οἶκος πνευματικὸς εἰς (built into a spiritual house)
λίθον ζῶντα... λίθοι ζῶντες (living stone ... stones)

---

6. Jobes, 318–19.
7. Forbes, 43.

ἱεράτευμα ἅγιον (a holy priesthood)
πνευματικὰς θυσίας (spiritual sacrifices)
τίθημι ἐν Σιὼν (laying in Zion)
ἀκρογωνιαῖον (cornerstone)
πέτρα σκανδάλου (rock of offence)
βασίλειον ἱεράτευμα (a royal priesthood)
ἔθνος ἅγιον (a holy nation)
ἐξαγγείλητε (proclaim, evangelize)
θαυμαστὸν αὐτοῦ φῶς·(his marvelous light)

1 Peter 2:4–10 contains the clearest and most direct Temple imagery anywhere in the epistle, and most commentators make this connection quite easily.[8] For example, as Achtemeier states, "one can only with great difficulty fail to find references to the temple in these passages."[9] However, as I have been showing, these references do not stand alone in the letter, in face, two of these themes (blood sacrifice, the spiritual house) are anticipated early in 1:2, and are echoed elsewhere throughout the text. As Mbuvi argues, "these concepts draw to themselves the image of the tabernacle/temple and really only make sense within the thought frame of the epistle if seen to relate to the tabernacle/temple image."[10] I will briefly review and comment on the major themes contained in the passage.

The phrase *built into a spiritual house* (οἰκοδομεῖσθε οἶκος πνευματικὸς εἰς) speaks of a "new" Temple being formed and built up by the Holy Spirit out of "living stones" with Jesus himself as the "cornerstone." But rather than viewing this "new thing" monolithically as a replacement for the "old thing" which was defective and outdated, it is more appropriate to say that "new" was typologically foreshadowed in the "old."[11] As I have previously mentioned, Beale makes a good case that all of these Temple patterns are modeled after the archetypical, paradisal Garden Temple of Genesis 2–3, and only find their ultimate fulfillment in the eschatological Temple of Revelation 21–22, the New Jerusalem.

In regards to *living stone, living stones* (λίθον ζῶντα and λίθοι ζῶντες) in 2:4–5 it is interesting to note that this "stone" metaphor also appears in Ps 118:22–23, Isa 8:14–15 and Isa 28:16, all three of which are quoted in 1 Pet 2:6–8. As Jobes notes, when Jesus referred to himself as the *rejected stone* of Ps 118:22 (in Mark 12:10 and elsewhere), he was most likely referring

---

8. see Botner on 2:4–5, 53–58..
9. Achtemeier, 159.
10. Mbuvi, 90.
11. Mbuvi, 91.

to a well-established Jewish tradition which identifies this stone with the Messiah.[12]

In picking up this "cornerstone" theme, Beale connects this metaphor with Ancient Near Eastern myths which portray "a hillock arising amidst the chaotic seas as the bridgehead of creation," which are paralleled in the biblical narrative with the Noahic flood waters, where it is on the tip of a mountain which the Ark comes to rest. According to Jewish tradition, the stone which supports the Holy of Holies in the Temple was thought to be that upon which "all the world was based." Beale argues that it is this tradition which gave rise to the notion that Israel was the "middle (or navel) of the earth" and the place where all divine wisdom resided, wisdom which emanated from the Temple and was essential to maintaining ethical order in the world after Adam and Eve sinned and were evicted from the Garden Temple. So against this background, when Peter asserts that Christ is the *cornerstone* (ἀκρογωνιαῖον) upon which the new Temple and New Creation are based, it amplifies the idea that he is also the true source of all wisdom in the cosmos (see Col 2:2–3).[13]

The terms *royal priesthood* (βασίλειον ἱεράτευμα) and *holy nation* (ἔθνος ἅγιον) used in 2:5 and 2:9 are remarkable in that, unlike with the former Temple system, these are applied to all believers, Jewish and Gentile alike. Mbuvi correctly notes that the "imagery here becomes mind-boggling given that the believers also constitute the building blocks to the 'spiritual house' as we saw above. The terms 'spiritual house' and the 'holy/royal priesthood' are more or less identical rather than analogous, in that they both are descriptive of the same object, the believers."[14]

The eschatological implication is profound, in that *all* believers are now "spiritual Levitical priests" (in fulfilment of Is 66:21) with an ongoing task to serve God in his new Temple where we will dwell forever and of which we are also a part. As Beale imagines, these priestly tasks are the same as those of the first Adam: "to keep the order and peace of the spiritual sanctuary by learning and teaching God's word, by praying always, and by being vigilant in keeping out unclean moral and spiritual things."[15] Our priestly duties, and our new identity as a chosen, royal and holy people, will come full circle in the eschaton with the New Jerusalem Temple.

Lastly, the term *proclaim, evangelize* (ἐξαγγείλητε) in 2:9 reflects God's original desire and plan that the paradisal Temple of Genesis 2–3 would be

---

12. Jobes, 147.
13. Beale, *The Temple and the Church's Mission* 333–34.
14. Mbuvi, *Temple, Exile and Identity in 1 Peter*, 107.
15. Beale, *The Temple and the Church's Mission*, 399.

expanded by Adam and Eve to cover the entire earth (the original "great commission" according to Beale[16]). In the same verse, the term *his marvelous light* (θαυμαστὸν αὐτοῦ φῶς) is reminiscent of Rev 21:23–25 which speaks of the source of light in the final Temple: *And the city has no need of sun or moon to shine on it, for the glory of God is its light, and its lamp is the Lamb. The nations will walk by its light, and the kings of the earth will bring their glory into it. Its gates will never be shut by day—and there will be no night there."*

There is much more which can be said regarding this rich passage of 2:4–10 and its relationship to the Temple meta-narrative, but space is limited, and additional parallel and complimentary themes can be found elsewhere in the letter.

1 PETER 3:7 — HUSBAND AND WIFE AS JOINT HEIRS OF LIFE

συγκληρονόμοις χάριτος ζωῆς (joint heirs of the gracious gift of life)

1 Peter 3:1–7 contains the familiar set of instructions to wives and husbands, but as Mbuvi has noted, these are more than just moral instructions, and must be understood as having eschatological ramifications and fulfillment because of the unique nature of the husband–wife relationship, which is compared to Christ's relationship to the Church, more akin to worship than to personal or social relationships. Therefore, as Mbuvi writes, "the primary motivator in this case is *prayer* (3:7), a cultic function closely associated with the sanctuary. . . . in the early church, the prayer hours of Tamid-offering in the temple were still observed by the believers (Acts 2:46; 3:1), while the breaking of bread and sharing in the meals of fellowship was done at home (Acts 2:44)."[17]

This joint inheritance of the *gracious gift of life* (which in my view, parallels the "Tree of Life" of Eden), is promised equally to husband and wife as co-heirs, and I would posit, can be viewed as a reversal of the expulsion of Adam and Eve from the Genesis Garden Temple where they functioned *jointly* as priests and kings[18], where they were jointly given the charter by God to fill and subdue the entire earth: *God blessed them [plural—Adam and Eve], and God said to them, 'Be fruitful and multiply, and fill the earth*

---

16. Beale, 328.
17. Mbuvi, 110.
18. Beale, 81.

and subdue it; and have dominion over the fish of the sea and over the birds of the air and over every living thing that moves upon the earth.'(Gen 1:28) .

1 PETER 3:20 NOAH'S ARK AS A "PROTOTYPE" TEMPLE

ἡμέραις Νῶε (days of Noah), κιβωτοῦ (ark)

In his project to trace the development of Temple themes throughout scripture, Beale notes the many similarities between the construction of Noah's Ark, mentioned here in this verse, and other familiar Temple motifs. First, Noah "offered burnt offerings on the altar." Second, these offerings were said to be "soothing aroma" before the Lord, and the only other place where "burnt offerings" are mentioned as a "soothing aroma" are related to tabernacle sacrifices. Third, Noah offers these sacrifices on a mountain (Ararat). Fourth, the distinction between "clean and unclean" animals is made for the first time here (Gen. 7:2, 8)."[19]

Further, Mbuvi points out that readers of 1 Peter would also be familiar with various extra-Biblical, Jewish legends regarding the Ark and the Temple, further strengthening this connection.[20]

1 PETER 4:14, 17—SHEKINAH GLORY, JUDGEMENT IN THE HOUSE

δόξης καὶ τὸ τοῦ θεοῦ πνεῦμα ἐφ' ὑμᾶς ἀναπαύεται (the spirit of glory. . . is resting on you)

κρίμα ἀπὸ τοῦ οἴκου τοῦ θεοῦ (judgement to begin with the household of God)

This phrase in 4:14, *the spirit of glory and of the God* is strongly reminiscent of God's shekinah glory resting on the wilderness tabernacle as a visible sign of God's presence (Exod 33:9), and similarly, in the first Temple where a visible cloud hovered at the entrance to the sanctuary (1 Kgs 8:9–11; 2 Chr. 5:13–14). In the case of this new "spiritual house" (2:5), the Holy Spirit falls on and indwells the New Testament believer (e.g. Acts 2 and elsewhere).

Regarding verse 17 and the phrase *judgement to begin with the household of God*, Mbuvi notes that in light of "the pervasiveness of the general

---

19. Beale, 105.
20. Mbuvi, 114. Witherington, 190.

theme of judgment beginning in the 'house of God'—both in the OT and in Second Temple Jewish literature—it is likely that the author of 1 Peter did not have a specific passage in mind but rather a recurrent theme." However, he goes on to note that similar OT language in both Mal 3:1–5 and Eze 9:6 supports the assessment that this action of judgment is associated with the Temple/community rather than a plain "household."[21]

To this, I would add that Jesus' cleansing of the Temple (Matt 21:12–17; Mark 11:15–19; Luke 19:45–48; John 2:13–17), which can be seen as a "judgement" of the former Temple system, might also have been in view to Peter in writing this.

1 PETER 5:10 — RESTORE, SUPPORT, STRENGTHEN AND ESTABLISH

καταρτίσει, στηρίξει, σθενώσει, θεμελιώσει (restore, support, strengthen, and establish)

These four similar verbs, which overlap in semantic domain, are reminiscent of "building" or "rebuilding" activities, and as Dubis notes, "conjure memories of the exile of the children of Israel in Babylon" (who longed to return to Jerusalem and restore the Temple). The last verb, θεμελιώσει (derived from θεμέλιοω), speaks of the foundation of a building or a wall, or to ground something firmly.[22] This language by itself, especially the last verb, would most likely recall Temple imagery for the readers of 1 Peter, but why did the author use four, very similar verbs here? Was it just for increased emphasis, or is there another reason?

In *The Dictionary of Biblical Imagery*, Ryken suggests a possible reason: "Grouping objects or phrases in fours is a Hebrew literary technique used to picture *universality*. Just as naming the extreme points of east, west, north and south suggests everything in between, so biblical sets of four elements or poetic lines serve as an image indicating *universal participation* or including aspects not specifically mentioned."[23] Following this lead, I discovered numerous places in scripture where this *pattern of fours* is used in association with the Temple in its various representations (not including the obvious architectural fact that most buildings have four sides/walls).

Just to mention a few examples, Genesis 2:10 lists *four* branches of the river which flows out of Eden (Pishon, Gihon, Tigris and Euphrates), the

---

21. Mbuvi, 121. Pace Elliott, 799–800.
22. Achtemeier, 346.
23. Ryken, *The Dictionary of Biblical Imagery*, 307.

garden of paradise which Beale identifies as the first archetypal Temple and the model for all subsequent Temples;[24] Exodus 25–39, which contains detailed descriptions of Moses' tabernacle with its *four* rings of gold, *four* cups, *four* pillars, *four* horns, *four* bronze rings and *four* rows of precious stones; Ephesians 3:16–18, where Paul prays for believers to be root and *grounded* (τεθεμελιωμένοι) in Christ so that they could comprehend "the breadth and length and height and depth" (note *four* dimensions) of his love; and in the ubiquitous refrain of four similar nouns found throughout the book of Revelation, of *every tribe, tongue, people and nation* gathered together as God's people, where the universal theme of *four* is clearly evident.[25] This is but one new interpretive possibility in the letter opened up by the link between Temple and creation. Many more await the interpreter with eyes to see and ears to hear.[26]

---

24. Beale, *The Temple and the Church's Mission*, 74.
25. A scribe could easily have left one of the words out because of similar endings.
26. See especially the comments on 2:9 and 3:7.

Bibliography

Achtemeier, Paul J. *1 Peter*. Hermeneia. Minneapolis: Fortress, 1996.
Adams, Sean A. and Ehorn, Seth M., eds. *Composite Citations in Antiquity. Volume One: Jewish, Greco-Roman and Early Christian Uses*. LNTS 525. New York: T. & T. Clark, 2016.
Ådna, Jostein. Jesu Stellung zum Tempel: *Die Tempelaktion und das Tempelwort als Ausdruck seiner messianischen Sendung*. WUNT 2/119. Tübingen: Mohr Siebeck, 2000.
Aland, Kurt and Aland, Barbara. *The Text of the New Testament: An Introduction to the Critical Editions and to the Theory and Practice of Modern Textual Criticism*. Grand Rapids: Eerdmans, 1989.
Albl, Martin C. "And Scripture Cannot Be Broken: The Form and Function of Early Christian Testimonia Collections." *NovTSup* 96. Leiden: Brill, 1999.
Alexander, T. Desmond and David W. Baker, eds. *Dictionary of the Old Testament: Pentateuch*. Downers Grove: InterVarsity, 2003.
Applegate, Judith K. "The Co-Elect Woman in 1 Peter." *NTS* 38 (1992) 587–604.
Attridge, Harold W. *The Epistle to the Hebrews: A Commentary on the Epistle to the Hebrews*. Hermeneia. Minneapolis: Fortress, 1989.
Bailey, Kenneth E. *Finding the Lost: Cultural Keys to Luke 15*. St. Louis: Concordia, 1992.
———. *The Good Shepherd: A Thousand Year Journey from Psalm 23 to the New Testament*. Downers Grove: IVP Academic, 2014.
Barker, P.A. "Sabbath, Sabbatical Year, Jubilee," DOT, Downers Grove, InterVarsity Press, 705.
Barth, Karl. *Church Dogmatics*. Translated by G. W. Bromiley. Edinburgh: T. & T. Clark, 1974.
Bates, Matthew W. *Salvation by Allegiance Alone: Rethinking Faith, Works, and the Gospel of Jesus the King*. Grand Rapids: Baker Academic, 2017.
Bauer, Walter, Frederick W. Danker, William F. Arndt, and F. Wilbur Gingrich. *A Greek-English Lexicon of the New Testament and Other Early Christian Literature*. 3rd ed. (BDAG) Chicago: University of Chicago Press, 2000.
Beale, G. K. and D. A. Carson, eds. *Commentary on the New Testament Use of the Old Testament*. Grand Rapids: Baker Academic, 2007.
———. *The Temple and the Church's Mission*. Downers Grove: InterVarsity, 2004.
Beare, Francis Wright. *The First Epistle of Peter: The Greek Text with Introduction and Notes*. Oxford: Basil Blackwell, 1966, 1970.

Bede, The Venerable, *Commentary on First Peter*. ACC XI: James, 1–2 Peter, 1–3 John, Jude. Downers Grove: InterVarsity Press, 2000.

Bengel, Johann Albrecht. *Gnomen: Auslegung des Neuen Testamentes in fortlaufenden Anmerkungen*. Deutsch von V. F. Werner. Siebente Auflage. Band II Briefe und Offenbarung, Teil 2. Stuttgart: J. F. Steinkopf Verlag, 1876.

Best, Ernest. *1 Peter*. NCBC. Grand Rapids: Eerdmans, 1982.

———. "I Peter II 4–10—A Reconsideration." *NovT* 11 (1969): 270–293.

Bigg, C.A. *Critical and Exegetical Commentary on the Epistles of St. Peter and St. Jude*. ICC. New York: Scribner's, 1901.

Bonhoeffer, Dietrich, *Gemeinsames Leben*. Heraugegeben von Gerhard Müller und Albrecht Schönherr. Dritte Auflage München: Chr. Kaiser Verlag, 2008.

———. *Nachfolge*. München: Chr. Kaiser Verlag, 1958.

Boring, M. E. *1 Peter*. ANTC. Nashville: Abingdon, 1999.

Bornemann, W., "Der Erste Petrusbrief: Eine Taufrede des Silvanus? *ZNW* 19 (1919–20) 143–65.

Bray, Gerald Lewis, and Thomas C. Oden. *James, 1–2 Peter, 1–3 John, Jude*. ACC. XI Downers Grove: InterVarsity, 2000.

Brodd, Jeffrey and Reed, Jonathan L., eds. *Rome and Religion: a Cross-Disciplinary Dialogue on the Imperial Cult*. Writings from the Greco-Roman world supplement series 5. Atlanta: Society of Biblical Literature, 2011.

Brown, F. S. Driver and C. Briggs, eds. *The Brown-Driver-Briggs Hebrew and English Lexicon*. Peabody: Henrickson, 1994

Bruce, Frederick F. *Biblical Exegesis in the Qumran Texts,* London: Tyndale Press, 1959.

Brueggemann, "Of the same flesh and bone, Gn 2:23a." *CBQ* 32 (1970) 532–42.

Calvin, John. *Institutes of the Christian religion*. LCC 20–21. Translated by Ford Lewis Battles. Philadelphia: Westminster, 1960.

———. *The Epistle of Paul to the Hebrews* and *The First and Second Epistles of St. Peter.* Calvin's Commentaries, edited by David W. Torrance and Thomas F. Torrance. Translated by William B. Johnston. Grand Rapids: Eerdmans, 1976

Campbell, Barth. *Honor, Shame and Rhetoric in 1 Peter*. SBL Dissertation series 160. Atlanta: Scholars Press, 1998.

Carey, Holly J. *Jesus' Cry From the Cross*. LNTS 398. New York: T. & T. Clark, 2009.

Carrington, *The Primitive Christian Catechism: A Study in the Epistles*. Cambridge: Cambridge University Press, 1940.

Carson, D.A., "1 Peter." In *CNTUOT*, 1015–45.

Carter, Warren. "Roman Imperial Power: A Perspective from the New Testament." 137–151 in Brodd and Reed, *Roman Religion*.

Charlesworth, James H., ed. *The Old Testament Pseudepigrapha: Apocalpyptic Literature and Testaments*, Vol. 1. Garden City: Doubleday, 1983.

Cheung, Alex T. M. "The Priest as the Redeemed Man: A Biblical-Theological Study of the Priesthood." *JETS* 29, no. 3 (1986) 265–75.

Childs, B.S. *Isaiah*. Louisville: Westminster John Knox, 2001.

Christensen, Sean M. "Solidarity in Suffering and Glory: The Unifying role of Psalm 34 in 1 Peter 3:10–12." *JETS* 58/2 (2015) 335–52.

Chryssavgis, John. "The Royal Priesthood (1 Peter 2:9)." *The Greek Orthodox Theological Review* 32, no. 4 (1987) 373–77.

Clarke, W. K. Lowther. *The First Epistle of Clement to the Corinthians*. New York: MacMillan, 1937.

Comfort, Philip W. *A Commentary on the Manuscripts and Text of the New Testament.* Grand Rapids: Kregel Academic, 2015.
Coutts, J. "Ephesians I.3–14 and 1 Peter I.3–12." *NTS* 3 (1956–57) 115–27.
Cranfield, C. E. B. *I & II Peter and Jude: Introduction and Commentary.* London: SCM Press, 1960.
Cross, F. L. *1 Peter: A Paschal Liturgy.* London: Mowbray, 1954.
Dalton, William J. *Christ's Proclamation to the Spirits.* Analecta Biblica 23. Rome: Pontifical Biblical Institute, 1965.
Dautzenberg, P. Gerhard. "Σωτηρία ψυχῶν (1 Petr 1,9)." *BZ* 8 (1964) 262–76.
Davids, P. H. *The First Epistle of Peter.* NICNT. Grand Rapids: Eerdmans, 1990.
Deterding, P. E. "Exodus Motifs in First Peter." *Concordia Journal* 7 (1981) 58–65.
Diessmann, Gustav Adolf. *Light from the Ancient East: The New Testament Illustrated by Recently Discovered Texts of the Graeco-Roman World.* Translated by Lionel R.M. Strachan. Grand Rapids: Baker, 1965.
Dodd, C. H. *According to the Scriptures: The Sub-Structure of New Testament Theology.* New York: Scribner's Sons, 1953.
Donelson, Lewis R. *I & II Peter and Jude: A Commentary.* Louisville: Westminster John Knox, 2010.
Dubis, Mark. *Messianic Woes in First Peter: Suffering and Eschatology in 1 Peter 4:12–19.* Studies in Biblical Literature 33. New York: Peter Lang, 2002.
———. *1 Peter: A Handbook on the Greek Text,* edited by Martin M. Culy. Waco: Baylor University Press, 2010.
Egan, Patrick T. *Ecclesiology and the Scriptural Narrative of 1 Peter.* Eugene: Pickwick, 2016.
Elliott, J. H. "Disgraced Yet Graced." *Conflict, Community and Honor: 1 Peter in Social-Scientific Perspective,* 51–86. Eugene: Wiptf and Stock, 2007.
———. *The Elect and the Holy: An Exegetical Examination of I Peter 2:4–10 and the Phrase βασίλειον ἱεράτευμα.* NovTSup 12. Leiden: Brill, 1966.
———. *A Home for the Homeless: A Social-Scientific Criticism of 1 Peter, Its Situation and Strategy.* 2nd ed. Minneapolis: Fortress Press, 1990.
———. *1 Peter: A New Translation with Introduction and Commentary.* AB 37B, New York: Doubleday, 2000.
———. "Salutation and Exhortation to Christian Behavior on the Basis of God's Blessings (1:1–2:10)." *RevExp* 79 (1982) 415–25.
Feldmeier, Reinhard. *The First Letter of Peter: A Commentary on the Greek Text.* Translated by Peter. H. Davids. Waco: Baylor University Press, 2008.
Filson, Floyd. "Partakers with Christ: Suffering in First Peter." *Int* 9 (1955) 400–412.
Fitzgerald, John T, "Virtue and Vice Lists," *ABD* 6, 857–59.
Fitzmyer, Joseph A. *The Acts of the Apostles.* AB 31. New York: Doubeday, 1998.
———. *Essays on the Semitic Background of the New Testament.* London: Geoffrey Chapman, 1971.
———. *Romans: A New Translation with Introduction and Commentary.* AB 33. New York: Doubleday, 1993.
Forbes, G. W. *1 Peter.* Exegetical Guide to the Greek New Testament, edited by Andreas J. Köstenberger and Robert W. Yarbrough. Nashville: B & H Academic, 2014
Freedman, David Noel. *The Anchor Bible Dictionary.* 6 vols. New York: Doubleday, 1992.

Friesen Stephen, "Normal Religion, or, Words Fail Us: A Response to Karl Galinsky's 'The Cult of the Roman Emperor: Uniter or Divider?'" 23-26 in Brodd and Reed, *Roman Religion*.

Gärtner, Bertil. *The Temple and the Community in Qumran and the NT*. SNTSMS 1. Cambridge: Cambridge University Press, 1965.

Gonzalez, Justo L. *Story of Christianity, Vol. 1: The Early Church to the Dawn of the Reformation*. 2nd ed. New York: HarperCollins, 2010.

Goppelt, Leonhard. *A Commentary on 1 Peter*, edited by Ferdinand Hahn. Translated by John E. Alsup. Grand Rapids: Eerdmans, 1993.

Graham, Steve. "Aliens and Strangers in the World." *Reality* 69 http://www.reality.org.nz/article.php?ID=473

Green, Joel B. *1 Peter*. THNTC. Grand Rapids: Eerdmans, 2007.

Grudem, Wayne A. *The First Epistle of Peter: An Introduction and Commentary*. TNTC. Grand Rapids: Eerdmans, 1988.

Gupta, Nijay K. "A Spiritual House of Royal Priest, Chosen and Honored: The Presence and Function of Cultic Imagery in 1 Peter." *Perspectives in Religious Studies* 36 no. 1 (2009) 61–76.

Hamilton, Victor P. *The Book of Genesis: Chapters 1–17*. NICOT Grand Rapids: Eerdmans, 1990.

Harrington, Daniel J. *The Gospel of Matthew*. SP 1. Collegeville: Liturgical Press, 1991

Hawthorne, Gerald F., Paul Martin, and Daniel G. Reid, eds. *Dictionary of Paul and His Letters*. Downers Grove: InterVarsity, 1993.

Hays, Richard B., *Echoes of Scripture in the Gospels*, Waco, Tx: Baylor, 2016

———. *The Faith of Jesus Christ*. Chico: Scholars Press, 1983.

Henry, Carl F. H. *Christian Personal Ethics*. Grand Rapids: Eerdmans, 1957.

Hill, David. "On Suffering and Baptism in 1 Peter." *NovT* 18 (1976) 181–89.

Hillyer, Norman. *1 and 2 Peter, Jude*. NIBC. Peabody, MA: Henrickson, 1992.

Horrell, David G. *Becoming Christian: Essays on 1 Peter and the Making of Christian Identity*. LNTS 394. London: T. & T. Clark, 2013.

———. *1 Peter: New Testament Guides*. New York: T. & T. Clark, 2008.

Hort, F. J. A. *The First Epistle of S. Peter: I.--II.17: The Greek Text with Introductory Lecture, Commentary, and Additional Notes*. London: Macmillan, 1898.

Jacobs, M. *Gender, Power and Persuasion: The Genesis Narratives and Contemporary Portraits*. Grand Rapids: Baker Academic, 2007.

Jobes, Karen H. "'Got Milk?' A Petrine Metaphor in 1 Peter 2.1–3 Revisited," *Leaven*. Vol 20: Iss. 3, Article 5. http://digitalcommons.pepperdine.edu/leaven/vol20/iss3/5.

———. *Letters to the Church: A Survey of Hebrews and the General Epistles*. Grand Rapids: Zondervan, 2011.

———. *1 Peter*. BECNT. Grand Rapids: Baker Academic, 2005.

Joseph, Abson Prédestin. *A Narratological Reading of 1 Peter*. LNTS. London: T. & T. Clark, 2012.

Keener, Craig S. *The IVP Bible Background Commentary: New Testament*. Downers Grove: InterVarsity, 2014.

Kelly, J. N. D. *A Commentary on the Epistles of Peter and of Jude*. BNTC. London: A. and C. Black, 1969.

Kendall, David W. "1 Peter 1:3–9." *Int* 41 (1987) 66–71.

———. "The Literary and Theological Function of 1 Peter 1:3–12." In *Perspectives on First Peter,* edited by Charles H. Talbert. NABPR Special Studies Series 9. Macon, GA: Mercer Universtiy Press, 1986,. 103–20.
Kennedy, George A. *A New Testament interpretation Through Rhetorical Criticism.* Chapel Hill: University of North Carolina Press, 1984.
Kilpatrick, George D. "1 Peter 1:11 τίνα ἤ ποῖον καίρον." *NovT* 28 (1986), 91–92.
Kittle, G. and Friedrich, G., eds. *Theological Dictionary of the New Testament.* Translated by G. W. Bromiley. 10 vols. Grand Rapids: Eerdmans, 1964–1976.
Klawans, Jonathan. *Purity, Sacrifice, and the Temple: Symbolism and Supersessionism in the Study of Ancient Judaism.* Oxford: Oxford University Press, 2006.
Koehler, L., W. Baumgartner and J. J. Stamm. *The Hebrew and Aramaic Lexicon of the Old Testament.* (HALOT). Translated and edited under the supervision of M. E. J. Richardson. 4 vols. Leiden: Brill, 1994–1999.
Koenig, John, "Hospitality," *ABD* 3, 299–301.
Lange, John Peter et al. *A Commentary on the Holy Scriptures: 1 Peter.* Bellingham, WA: Logos, 2008.
Leighton, Robert. *Commentary on First Peter.* Grand Rapids: Kregel, 1972.
Levenson, Jon D. "The Temple and the World." *JR* 64 (1984) 275–298.
Lewis, C. S. "First and second Things." In *Essay Collection and Other Short Pieces,* edited by Lesley Walmsley, 653–6. London: HarperCollins, 2000.
———. *Studies in Words.* Cambridge: Cambridge University Press, 1960.
Lidell, H. G. R. Scott and H. S. Jones. *A Greek-English Lexicon.* 9th ed. with Rev. Supplement. Oxford: Clarendon, 1996.
Liebengood, Kelly D. *The Eschatology of 1 Peter: Considering the Influence of Zechariah 9–14.* SNTSMS 157. Cambridge: Cambridge University Press, 2014.
Lightfoot, Joseph B. *The Epistles of 2 Corinthians and 1 Peter: Newly Discovered Commentaries,* edited by Ben Witherington III and Todd D. Still. Downers Grove: InterVarsity, 2016.
Louw, Johannes P. and Eugene A. Nida, eds. *Greek-English Lexicon of the New Testament: Based on Semantic Domains.* 2nd ed. New York: United Bible Societies, 1999.
Lust, Johan, Erick Eynikel, and Katrin Haupie, eds. *Greek-English Lexicon of the Septuagint.* Rev. ed. Stuttgart: Duetsche Bibelgesellschaft, 2003.
Luther, Martin, and J. G. Walch. *Commentary on the Epistles of Peter and Jude.* Grand Rapids: Kregel, 1982.
Marcar, Katie. "The Quotations of Isaiah in 1 Peter: A Text-Critical Analysis." *TC* 21 (2016) 1–22.
Marshall, I. Howard. *1 Peter.* Downers Grove: InterVarsity, 1991.
Martin, Ralph P. *2 Corinthians.* WBC 40. Waco: Word, 1986.
Martin, Ralph P. and Peter H. Davids, eds. *Dictionary of the Later New Testament & Its Developments.* Downers Grove: InterVarsity, 1997.
Martin,Raymond A., and John Hall Elliott. *Augsburg Commentary on the New Testament: James, I–II Peter/Jude.* ACNT. Minneapolis: Augsburg, 1982.
Martin, Troy W. *Metaphor and Composition in 1 Peter.* SBLDS 131. Atlanta: Scholars, 1992.
Maurice, Frederick Denison. *The Unity of the New Testament.* Vol. 1. 2nd ed. London: MacMillan, 1884.
Maycock, Edward. *A Letter of Wise Counsel: Studies in the First Epistle of Peter.* London: United Society for Christian Literature, 1957.

Mays, James Luther. *Psalms: Interpretation: A Biblical Commentary for Teaching and Preaching*. Louisville: Westminster John Knox, 1994.
Mbuvi, Andrew Mūtūa. *Temple, Exile, and Identity in 1 Peter*. LNTS 345, London:T. & T. Clark, 2007
McKelvey, R. J. *The New Temple: The Church in the New Testament*. Oxford: Oxford University Press, 1969.
McKnight, Scot. *1 Peter: The NIV Application Commentary from Biblical Text. . .To Contemporary Life*. The NIV Application Commentary. Grand Rapids: Zondervan, 1996.
Metzger, Bruce M. *Apostolic Letters of faith, Hope and Love: Galatians, 1 Peter, and 1 John*. Eugene: Cascade, 2006.
———. *A Textual Commentary on the Greek New Testament*. 2nd ed. New York: United Bible Societies, 1994.
Michaels, J. Ramsey. *1 Peter*. WBC 49. Waco: Word, 1988.
Miller, Donald G. "Deliverance and Destiny: Salvation in first Peter." *Int* 9 (1955) 413-25.
Milligan, G and Moulton, James Hope. *Vocabulary of the Greek Testament (Greek Edition)*. Peabody: Hendrickson, 1997.
Mitton, C. L. "The Relationship Between 1 Peter and Ephesians." *JTS* 1 (1950) 67-73.
Moltmann, Jürgen. *Theology of Hope*. New York: Harper & Row, 1975.
Moulton, J. H. *A Grammar of New Testament Greek*. Edinburgh: T. & T. Clark, 1906.
Moyise, Steve. "Isaiah in 1 Peter." In *Isaiah in the New Testament*, edited by Steve Moyise and Maarten J. J. Menken, 175-88. The New Testament and the Scriptures of Israel. London: T. & T. Clark, 2005.
Murphy, Frederick James. *Early Judaism: The Exile to the Time of Jesus*. Peabody: Hendrickson, 2002.
Nauck, Wolfgang. "Freude im Leiden: Zum Problem einer christlichen Verfolgungstrastration." *ZNW* 46 (1955) 68-80.
Neill, Stephen C. *New Testament Interpretation, 1861-1961*. London: Oxford University Press, 1991.
Nicoll, W. Robertson, ed. *The Expositor's Greek Testament*. 5 vols. New York: Dodd, Mead and Company, 1910.
Parsons, Samuel. *We Have Been Born Anew: The New Birth of the Christian in the First Epistle of St. Peter (1 Petr. 1:3, 23)*. Dissertation. Universitas a S. Thomas Aq., Rome, 1978.
Pearson, Sharon C. "Hymns" in *DLNT*, 522-24.
Perdelwitz, Emil Richard. *Die Mysterienreligion und das Problem des 1. Petrusbriefes: Ein literarischer und religionsgeschichtlicher Versuch*. Giessen: Töpelmann, 1949.
Phillips, John. *Exploring the Epistles of Peter: An Expository Commentary*. Grand Rapids: Kregel, 2005.
Preus, Herman A. "Luther on the Universal Priesthood and the Office of the Ministry." *Concordia Journal* 5, no. 2 (1979) 55-62.
Price, S. R. F. *Rituals and Power: The Roman Imperial Cult in Asia Minor*. Revised Edition. Cambridge: Cambridge University Press, 1985.
Rahlfs, Alfred, and Robert Hanhart, eds. *Septuaginta*. Stuttgart: Deutsche Bibelgesellschaft, 1935. Rev. ed., 2007.
Reike, Bo. *The New Testament Era: The World of the Bible from 500 B.C. to A.D. 100*. Philadelphia: Fortress Press, 1974.

Roberts, Alexander, James Donaldson, A. Cleveland Coxe, and Allan Menzies. *Ante-Nicene Fathers: The Writings of the Fathers Down to A.D. 325.* 10 vols. Peabody: Hendrickson, 1994.
Robinson, J. A. T. *Redating the New Testament.* London: SCM Press, 1976.
Rodgers, Peter R. "1 Peter," in *DTIB*, 581–83.
———. *Exploring the Old Testament in the New.* Eugene: Wipf and Stock, 2012.
———. "Fear," "Fear of God." *EBR* 8, 1025.
———. "The Longer Reading." *CBQ*, 43 (1981) 93–5.
———. "Review of 1 Peter, a New Translation with Introduction and Commentary by John H. Elliott." *NovT* 46 no 3 (2004) 293–95.
———. "The Text of 1 Peter 4:16 in Nestle 28." Forthcoming.
Ryken, L, J. C. Wilhoit and T. Longman III, eds. *Dictionary of Biblical Imagery.* Grand Rapids: InterVarsity, 1998.
Sakenfeld, Katharine D, Samel E. Balentine and Brian K. Blount, eds. *The New Interpreters Dictionary of the Bible.* 5 vols. Nashville: Abingdon, 2007.
Sargent, Benjamin. *Written to Serve: The Use of Scripture in 1 Peter,* LNTS 547, New York: T. & T. Clark, 2015.
Schäufele, Wolfgang. "Missionary Vision and Activity of the Anabaptist Laity." *The Mennonite Quarterly Review* 36, no. 2 (1962) 99–115.
Schiffman, Lawrence H. "Community without Temple: The Qumran Community's Withdrawal from the Jerusalem Temple." In *Gemeinde ohne Temple (Community without Temple): Zur Substituierung und Transformation des Jerusalemer Tempels und seines Kults im Alten Testament, antiken Judentum und fruhen Christentum,* edited by Beate Ego et al., 267–84. WUNT 118. Tübingen: Mohr Siebeck, 1999.
Schreiner, Thomas R. *1, 2 Peter, Jude.* The New American Commentary 37. Nashville: B & H, 2003.
Schüssler Fiorenza, Elizabeth. *In Memory of Her, A Feminist Theological Reconstruction of Christian Origins.* New York: Crossroad, 1983.
Selwyn, E. G. *The First Epistle of St. Peter: The Greek Text with Introduction, Notes and Essays.* 2nd ed. London: Macmillan, 1946, Grand Rapids: Baker, 1981.
———. "Eschatology in 1 Peter." In *The Background of the New Testament and Its Eschatology* (C.H. Dodd Festschrift) Edited by W. D. Davies and D. Daube, 394–401. Cambridge: Cambridge, 1954.
Senior, Donald P. *1 Peter.* SP 15. Collegeville: Liturgical Press, 2003.
Shimada, Kazuhito. *The Formulary Material in First Peter: A Study According to the Method of Traditionsgeschichte.* Th.D. Dissertation. Union Theological Seminary, New York, 1966.
———. *Studies on First Peter.* Tokyo: Kyo Bun Kwan, 1998.
Silva, Moises., ed. *New International Dictionary of New Testament Theology and Exegesis.* (NIDNTTE) 5 vols. Grand Rapids: Zondervan, 2014.
———. "Old Testament in Paul," *DPL*, 630–42.
Sly, D.I. "1 Peter 3:6b in Light of Philo and Josephus." *JBL* 110 (1991) 126–29.
Snodgrass, Klyne. "I Peter II. 1–10: Its Formation and Literary Affinities." *NTS* 24 (1977) 97–106.
Spicq, Ceslas, *Les Epitres dans Saint Pierre: Sources Biblique.* Paris: Libraire Lecoffre, 1996.
Stark, Rodney. *The Rise of Christianity.* Princeton: Princeton University Press, 1976.

Stibbs, Alan M., and Andrew F. Walls. *The First Epistle General of Peter*. TNTC. London: Tyndale, 1959.
Thompson, Michael. "The Holy Internet." In *The Gospel for All Christians*, edited by Richard Bauckham. Grand Rapids: Eerdmans, 1978, 49–70.
Thurén, Lauri. *Argument and Theology in 1 Peter: the Origins of Christian Paraenesis*. JSNTSup 114. Sheffield: Sheffield Academic, 1995.
Tite, Philip L. *Compositional Transitions in 1 Peter: An Analysis of the Letter-Opening*. San Francisco: International Scholars Publications, 1997.
du Toit, A.B. "The Significance of Discourse Analysis for New Testament Interpretation and Translation: Introductory Remarks with Special Reference to 1 Peter 1:3–13." *Neot* 8 (1974) 54–79.
Tov, Emanuel. *Textual History of the Hebrew Bible*, 3rd ed. Minneapolis: Fortress, 2012.
Turner, Cuthbert H. "Notes on Markan Usage," *JTS* 26 (1925) 14–20.
Ulrich, Eugene, ed. *The Biblical Qumran Scrolls: Transcriptions and Textual Variations*. Vol. 2: *Isaiah–Twelve Minor Prophets*. Leiden: Brill, 2013.
Vanhoozer, Kevin J., ed. *Dictionary for Theological Interpretation of the Bible*. Grand Rapids, Baker, 2005.
Vermes, G. *The Dead Sea Scrolls in English* (DSSE) London: Penguin, 2004.
Volf, Miraslov. "Soft Difference: Theological Reflections on the Relation Between Church and Culture in 1 Peter." *Ex Auditu* 10 (1994) 15–30.
Von Balthasar, Hans Urs. *Heart of the World*. Translated by Erasmos Leiva. San Francisco: Ignatius Press, 1979.
Wagner, J. Ross. "Heralds of the Good News: Isaiah and Paul "in Concert" in the Letter to the Romans." *NovTSup* 101. Leiden: Brill, 2002.
Wallace, Daniel B. *Greek Grammar Beyond the Basics*. Grand Rapids: Zondervan, 1996.
Walls, David and Max Andres, *Holman New Testament Commentary, I & II Peter, I, II &3 John, Jude*. Nashville: Broadman and Holman, 2007.
Waltke, Bruce K. *The Book Of Proverbs: Chapters 1–15*. New International Commentary on the Old Testament. Grand Rapids: Eerdmans, 2004.
Wand, J.W.C., *The General Epistles of St. Peter and St. Jude*. London: SPCK, 1934.
Watson, David. *I Believe in the Church*. Grand Rapids: Eerdmans, 1978.
Watts, Rikki. *Isaiah's New Exodus in Mark*. Grand Rapids: Baker, 2000.
Weiser, Artur. *The Psalms: A Commentary*. Translated by Herbert Hartwell. Louisville: John Knox, 1962.
Wenham, Gordon J. *Genesis 1–15*. WBC 1. Waco: Word, 1997.
Wilken, Robert L. *The Christians as the Romans Saw Them*. New Haven: Yale University Press, 1984.
Wilkins, Michael J. "Brother, Brotherhood," ABD 1, 782–83.
Williams, Travis B. "Benefitting the Community Through Good Works?: The Economic Feasibility of Civic Benefaction in 1 Peter." *Journal of Greco-Roman Christianity and Judaism* 9 (2013) 147–95.
———. *Good Works in 1 Peter: Negotiating Social Conflict and Christian Identity in the Greco-Roman World*. Wissenschaftliche Untersuchungen Zum Neuen Testament 337. Tübingen: Mohr Siebeck, 2014.
———. *Persecution in 1 Peter: Differentiating and Contextualizing Early Christian Suffering*. (Novt Sup) Leiden: Brill Academic, 2012.
———. "Suffering from Critical Oversight: The Persecutions of 1 Peter Within Modern Scholarship." *CBR* 10 (2012) 271–88.

Willis, William W. "The Letter of Peter (1 Peter) in James E. Goehring (ed.), *The Crosby-Schøyen Codex MS 193 in the Schøyen Collection* Leuven: Peeters, 1990, 135–215.

Witherington, Ben, III. *Letters and Homilies for Hellenized Christians: A Socio-Rhetorical Commentary on 1–2 Peter*. Downers Grove: InterVarsity, 2007.

Woolf, Virginia. *A Room of Ones Own*. London: Hogarth Press, 1929.

Wright, N. T. *The Climax of the Covenant: Christ and the Law in Pauline Theology*. Minneapolis: Fortress Press, 1992.

——— *The Day the Revolution Began: Reconsidering the Meaning of Jesus's Crucifixion*. San Francisco: HarperOne, 2016.

——— *Jesus and the Victory of God, Vol 2*. Christian Origins and the Question of God. Minneapolis: Fortress, 1997.

——— *The New Testament and the People of God*. Christian Origins and the Question of God, Minneapolis: Fortress, 1992.

——— *Paul and the Faithfulness of God*. Christian Origins and the Question of God. Minneapolis: Fortress Press, 2013.

Index of Names

A

Achtemeier, Paul J, 2, 13, 33, 34, 35, 36, 37, 38, 40, 41, 43, 44, 45, 47, 48, 53, 54, 55, 61, 62, 64, 65, 66, 69, 72, 74, 75, 78, 80, 83, 88, 100, 106, 107, 108, 119, 124, 125, 130, 131, 133, 135, 151, 154, 158, 159, 161, 164, 180, 195, 199
Adams, Sean A. and Ehorn, Seth M;, eds., 175
Ådna, Jostein, 55
Aland, Kurt and Aland, Barbara, 7, 166, 169
Albl, Martin C., 58
Applegate, Judith K., 3
Attridge, Harold W., 56, 57

B

Bailey, Kenneth E., 9, 78, 138
Barker, P.A., 115, 116
Barth, Karl, 3
Bates, Matthew W., 40, 101
Beale, G. K. and D. A. Carson, eds., 9, 61, 155, 190, 191, 195, 197, 198, 200
Beare, Francis Wright, 3, 14, 16, 61, 153
Bede, The Venerable, 78
Best, Ernest, 49, 56, 58
Bigg, C.A., 77, 93, 159
Bonhoeffer, Dietrich, 147
Boring, M.E., 14, 56, 131, 132
Bornemann, W., 94
Brodd, Jeffrey and Reed, Jonathan L., eds., 66

Bruce, Frederick F., 26
Brueggemann, 152

C

Calvin, John, 18, 19, 114, 115, 119, 138, 139, 140, 181
Campbell, Barth., 3, 11, 73
Carey, Holly J., 77
Carrington, 7, 14, 48, 71, 175
Carson, D.A., 14, 58, 133, 134, 168
Carter, Warren, 66
Cheung, Alex T.M., 182
Childs, B.S., 14
Christensen, Sean M., 94
Chryssavgis, John., 182
Clarke, W. K. Lowther, 175
Comfort, Philip W., 7, 51, 165, 167
Coutts, J., 16, 17
Cranfield, C.E.B., 76, 92, 137, 138, 142, 143, 145, 148, 167
Cross, F.L., 7, 16

D

Dalton, William J., 107, 108, 109
Dautzenberg, P. Gerhard, 24
Davids, P.H., 4, 72, 89, 93, 114
Deterding, P.E., 8
Dodd, C.H., 58, 59
Donelson, Lewis R., 50, 53, 90, 93
du Toit, A.B., 20
Dubis, Mark., xv, 26, 27, 29, 32, 33, 34, 36, 37, 38, 39, 40, 41, 43, 45, 48, 49, 51, 71, 78, 93, 95, 107, 115, 116, 118, 119, 120, 134, 153, 154, 159, 160, 162, 199

INDEX OF NAMES

E

Egan, Patrick T., 168
Elliott, J.H., 1, 2, 3, 4, 5, 10, 11, 12, 13, 23, 53, 54, 55, 56, 57, 58, 60, 70, 73, 74, 75, 77, 81, 82, 83, 85, 86, 88, 89, 90, 91, 92, 93, 95, 123, 127, 133, 152, 176, 180, 181, 182, 184, 199

F

Feldmeier, Reinhard, 3, 21, 51, 71, 74, 113, 114, 117, 118, 120, 137, 138, 139, 143, 144, 145, 147, 150, 186
Filson, Floyd, 21
Fitzgerald, John T., 88
Fitzmyer, Joseph A., 9, 58, 71
Forbes, G. W., xv, 32, 34, 37, 38, 39, 40, 41, 42, 43, 46, 48, 49, 88, 111, 114, 119, 120, 121, 184, 185, 194
Friesen, Stephen, 66

G

Gärtner, Bertil, 56
Gonzalez, Justo L., 187
Goppelt, Leonhard, 14, 17, 19, 32, 33, 34, 35, 42, 46, 49, 50, 53, 56, 62, 64, 71, 72, 74, 80, 90, 93, 95, 118, 139, 140, 142, 144, 145, 157, 158, 163, 184, 185, 186
Graham, Steve, 63
Green, Joel B., 4, 9, 12, 24, 26, 27, 33, 34, 35, 36, 37, 38, 39, 40, 47, 48, 49, 51, 71, 75, 80, 86, 89, 91, 93, 96, 99, 101, 107, 126, 128, 129, 133, 150, 160, 163, 193
Grudem, Wayne A., 14, 19, 93, 133
Gupta, Ninjay K., 180

H

Hamilton, Victor P., 152
Harrington, Daniel J, 153
Hays, Richard B., 64, 77
Henry, Carl F.H., 88, 89
Hill, David, 21
Hillyer, Norman, 46, 48, 73, 89, 95, 185, 186
Horrell, David G., 5, 8, 12, 13, 84, 120
Hort, F. J. A., 13, 44, 46, 53, 184, 185

J

Jacobs, M., 84
Jobes, Karen H., 1, 2, 3, 4, 12, 13, 22, 26, 27, 28, 31, 32, 35, 36, 38, 43, 44, 46, 48, 49, 51, 53, 57, 58, 60, 62, 63, 70, 75, 77, 80, 82, 83, 84, 92, 93, 94, 95, 96, 97, 99, 102, 107, 108, 114, 117, 118, 119, 122, 123, 125, 126, 133, 137, 139, 140, 141, 144, 149, 150, 154, 158, 161, 162, 194, 195, 196
Joseph, Abson Prédestin, 134

K

Keener, Craig S., 180
Kelly, J. N. D. A., 15, 17, 142, 176
Kendall, David W., 16, 18, 21
Kennedy, George A., 3
Kilpatrick, George D., 26
Klawans, Jonathan, 56
Koenig, John, 125

L

Lange, John Peter et al., 101
Leighton, Robert, 11, 140, 141, 143, 145, 148
Levenson, Jon D., 191
Lewis, C.S., 72, 146
Liebengood, Kelly D., 8, 22, 37, 129, 176
Lightfoot, Joseph B., 5, 77
Louw, Johannes P. and Eugene A. Nida, eds., 142
Lust, Johan, Ericj Eynikel, and Katrin Haupie, eds., 141
Luther, Martin, and J. G. Walch, 180, 181

M

Marcar, Katie, 60, 168, 174
Marshall, I. Howard, 2, 96, 101
Martin, Ralph P., 71, 72
Martin, Raymond A., and John Hall Elliott, 180
Martin, Troy W., 17, 22
Maurice, Frederick Denison, 146, 147
Maycock, Edward, 44, 46, 48
Mays, James Luther, 63

INDEX OF NAMES

Mbuvi, Andrew Mũtũa, 9, 10, 13, 14, 45, 56, 131, 133, 155, 193, 195, 196, 197, 198, 199
McKelvey, R. J., 58
McKnight, Scot, 178
Metzger, Bruce M., 109, 154, 165, 167
Michaels, J. Ramsey, 25, 26, 27, 54, 62, 64, 72, 77, 89, 91, 95, 97, 98, 100, 102, 118, 166
Miller, Donald G., 20
Milligan, G and Moulton, James Hope, 64
Mitton, C. L., 16
Moltmann, Jürgen, 18
Moulton, J. H., 49
Moyise, Steve, 58
Murphy, Frederick James, 180

N
Nauck, Wolfgang, 21
Neill, Stephen C., 3

P
Parsons, Samuel, 16, 17, 18, 20
Pearson, Sharon C., 7
Perdelwitz, Emil Richard, 16, 17
Phillips, John, 113
Preus, Herman A., 181
Price, S. R. F., 66, 135

R
Rahlfs, Alfred, and Robert Hanhart, eds, 141
Robinson, J. A. T., 2
Rodgers, Peter R., 9, 27, 37, 44, 60, 71, 112, 166, 167, 175, 182
Ryken, L. J. C., 199

S
Sakenfeld, Katharine D., Samuel E. Balentine and Brian K. Blount, eds., 125
Sargent, Benjamin, 4, 27, 29, 168
Schaufele, Wolfgang, 181
Schiffman, Lawrence H., 56
Schreiner, Thomas R., 97, 98, 99, 100, 101, 102, 103
Schüssler Fiorenza, Elizabeth, 80, 81

Selwyn, E. G., 3, 6, 7, 10, 14, 25, 28, 33, 34, 36, 40, 41, 46, 48, 49, 50, 53, 62, 64, 67, 68, 69, 71, 80, 91, 93, 94, 108, 122, 123, 124, 127, 137, 138, 141, 142, 143
Senior, Donald P., 53, 56
Shimada, Kazuhito, 17, 105
Silva, Moises, ed., 35, 37, 49, 174
Sly, D.I., 84
Snodgrass, Klyne, 53, 54, 56, 58
Stibbs, Alan M. and Andrew F. Walls, 2, 72, 88, 93, 122, 123, 124, 161, 163

T
Thompson, Michael, 125
Thurén, Lauri, 23
Tite, Philip L., 17
Tov, Emmanuel, 174
Turner, Cuthbert H., 160

U
Ulrich, Eugene, ed., 58

V
Volf, Miraslov, 10, 71, 151

W
Wagner, J. Ross, 175
Wallace, Daniel B., 107, 111
Walls, David and Max Anders, 96
Waltke, Bruce K., 134
Wand, J.W.C., 77
Watson, David, 126
Watts, Rikki, 175
Weiser, Artur, 95
Wenham, Gordon J., 152
Wilken, Robert L., 186
Wilkins, Michael J., 90
Williams, Travis B., 5, 6, 10, 62, 64, 69, 73, 74, 184
Witherington, Ben, III., 3, 4, 6, 12, 26, 27, 29, 48, 61, 73, 158, 161, 163, 198
Wolff, Virginia, 82
Wright, N. T., xi, 8, 9, 13, 76, 104, 106, 155, 190

Index of Scripture and Other Ancient Texts

OLD TESTAMENT/ HEBREW BIBLE

Genesis

1:28	198
2	152
2–3	195, 196, 152
2:10	199
2:22	152
2:23	152
3:24	194
6	110
6–8	172
7:13	172
7:17	118
7:2–8	198
12	84
12:2	120
12:13	84, 13
16:2	83
17	172
17:5	13
18:12	83, 172
20:5	84
21:10	83
21:12	83
22:4	37
23	172
23:2	63
23:4	63, 172
47:9	37

Exodus

6:6	38
9:15	39
9:18–20	39
12:5	39, 170
12:11	31, 170
13:12–13	38
19:4	106
19:6	57, 60, 61, 171, 179
20:3–5	117
20:8	115
21:30	38
24	14, 39
24:3–8	193
24:7–8	169
25–39	200
25–40	57
30:12–16	38
31:12–17	115
32	117
33:3	50
33:9	198
34:6–8	37

Leviticus

1:3–4	57
4:6–10	193
5:9	14
7	54

Leviticus (continued)

8	54
9:5	54
11:44–45	170
16	77
16:9	104, 106
17:4	57
18	34, 54
19	34
19:2	35
21	54
21:17	54
23	54
25	38

Numbers

16:40	54

Deuteronomy

9:26	174
10:15	171
21	77
21:23	67, 77, 176
5:15	70, 115
6:21	70
15:15	70
15:17	70
16:12	70
24:18	70
24:20	70
24:22	70
25:9	152
30:19–20	95
32:5	72
32:39	172

2 Samuel

7:12–14	55

1 Kings

8:9–11	198

1 Chronicles

17:11–13	55
29:15	37

2 Chronicles

5:13–14	198

Job

5:8	71
10:12	172

Psalms

2:7	17
8:5	29
8:6–7	172
9:4	172
18:27	91
22:13	174
23	9, 78, 141, 176
23:3	78
30:6 LXX	135
32:1	124, 173
33(34)	54
33:5	53
33:6	53
33:6 LXX	53
33:9	53
33:13 LLX	94
33:13–16	53
34:13–17	172
33:18	33
33:23	53
34	77, 94, 97, 175, 176
34:8	171
34:16b	95
(LXX,34/33):6	53
38	63
39	63
39:12	37
39:13	63
85:2	124
89:50–51 34/(34/)	53
34(33 LXX)	49, 51
34:12b–16 (LXX 33:13b–17)	94
34:22	38
39:12	172
55	21
55:22	148, 174
58:11	36

66:10	170
77:8	72
78:8	38
88:27	36
(LXX 88:51-52)	173
89:26	170
103:3	172
109:103	49
110:1	112, 172, 176
(LXX 109):1	172
118	59
118:22	59, 171, 195
118,34	60
118:22-23	195
118(117):22	54, 58
130:4	37
147:11	33

Proverbs

3	175
3:19	89
3:25	172
3:34	91, 173
10:12	124, 173
11:31	134, 173
17:3	170
20:22	92
24:21	172
29:23	91

Ecclesiastes

12:14	36

Isaiah

1:11	180
3:18-23	172
8	99, 175
8:4	58
8:12	54
8:12-13	99, 172
8:13	54, 100, 176
8:14	54, 60, 171
8:14-15	195
10:3	172
10:3-4	65
11:2	131, 173
28	155
28:15-17	170
28:15	59
28:16	54, 58, 59, 170, 171, 176, 195
40-55	176
40	45, 46
40-55	175
40:2-28	174
40:6-8	171, 174
40:11	78, 141
40:28	89
42:1	171
42:12	171
43	65, 175
43:20	12
43:20-21	60, 171
44:22-23	38
44:28	173
48:9	170
48:10	170
48:11	170
49:6	13
50:9	97, 172
53	2, 14, 38, 72, 76, 77, 78 104, 170, 175
52-53	2
52:3	38, 170
52:5	166
52:12-13	75
52:13	41
52:13-15	67
53:4	172
53:5	77
53:6	78, 172
53:6-7	172
53:7	76, 170
53:8	105, 106
53:9	172
53:10	77, 104
53:11	106, 172
53:12	105, 106, 172
53:15,	14
56	65
58:5	91
61:6	171
62:3	173
62:12	171
63:11	173

Isaiah (continued)

65:2	80

Jeremiah

1:17	31
3:19	36, 170
6:15	65
10:12	89
23	141
25:29	133, 173
33:9	37

Ezekiel

34	9, 78, 141, 176
34:5	172
34:11	142
40–48	191
44:6	116
44:16	54
9:6	133, 136, 173
34:4	173
43	133

Daniel

2:34–35	171
4:1	169
6:22	67
9:3	26

Hosea

1:6	171, 177
1:9	60, 177
1:9–10	171
2:1	171
2:3	171
2:23	60, 171
2:25	171, 177
11:1	35

Amos

3:2	133, 173
5:21–24	180

Micah

6:8	180

Zechariah

3:9	171
13:7	78
13:7–9	22, 133

Malachi

3:1–5	133, 199
3:3–4	170
3:17	171

APOCRYPHA

Tobit

12:9	173

Wisdom

1:6	172
3:4–6	22
3:6	170
12:13	174

Sirach

2:1–6	22
2:5	170
3:30	173
16:12	170

1 Maccabees

9:26	170

2 Maccabees

18:15	94

PSEUDEPIGRAPHA

1 Enoch

1:2	170
9:10	172
10:2–3	110
10:11–15	172
12:4—13:2	108
13:15–16	108
20:2	109

21:10	108	12:46–50	153
54:7–10	110	13:35	40
65:1–12	110	17:26	67
66–67	110	18:27	90
67	110	18:33	90
67:3	110	20:25	144
67:4	110	21:12	199
67:7	110	22:34	67
67:13	110	24	149
69:1	110	25	149
83–84	110	25:31–46	87
89	110	28:20	13

4 Maccabees

1:10–11	66
13:23	89
18:15	94
18:10–19	175

Mark

1:8	55
1:24	35
1:41	90
6:34	90
8:2	90
8:31–145	54
8:32	76
9:22	90
10:29	188
10:42	144
10:45	38, 75, 91
11:15–19	199
11:17	56
12:10	54, 195
14:29	137
14:32–42	137
14:47	137
14:50	137
14:54	137
14:65	73
14:66–72	137
16:7	138, 142

NEW TESTAMENT

Matthew

5:5	83
5:9	95
5:10–11	98
5:16	65
5:29	102
5:38–48	65
5:43–44	92
5:43–48	90
5:44	65
5:38–48	92
5:46–48	69
5:48	69
6	83
6:25–34	148
6:34	116
6:4	83
6:9	36
8:17	78
9:36	90
10:22	151
10:25	116
10:28	69
11:29	83, 145
12:36	119

Luke

1:58	90
1:78	90
2:29	71
6:27	92
6:27–28	92
7:13	90
10:33	90, 92
12:35–36	31
15	9
15:1–7	78

Luke *(continued)*

15:20	90
19:45	199
22:24	145
22:31	137
22:37	75
22:41–44	21
22:42	36
23:46	135
22:61	137
23:46	135
24	11
24:21	38
24:26	11, 28
24:45–48	140

John

1:29	106
2:13–17	199
3	17
10	9
10:11	78
10:13	148
10:28	20
13	145
13:1–15	145
13:34–35	90
15:18–24	151
17:24	40
18:10f,	137
19:36	94
20:29	23
21	9
21:22	142
21:15–19	137, 141

Acts

1:8	12, 139
10:34	37
12:5	44
16:7	27
17:22–31	159
2	198
2:1–4	55
2:17	40
2:36	79
2:42–47	163
2:44	197
2:46	197
4:11	54
4:24	71
5:30	77
7:47	56
7:49	56
7:59	36
9:4	139
10	77
10:34	37
10:39	77
12:5	44
13:29	77
16:7	27
17:22–31	159
20	163
20:19	91
20:28	141

Romans

2:9–10	36
4:7	124
6	114
6:11	77
6:2	105
6:7	105
6:8	105
7:14	64
7:14–35	114
8	27
8:17	28
8:18	11
8:28	21
8:5–9	50
8:9	27
9:32–33	59
9:33	58
9:5	127
10:21	80
12	88
12:1	57, 58
12:10	90
12:2	34, 49
12:15	89
12:17	92
12:6–8	126
13:1–7	65

14:10	119	4:2	91
15:5	89	4:3	88
15:7	187	4:11	126
16:16	162	4:25–32	92

1 Corinthians

Philippians

1:19	158	1:19	27
1:2	36	1:21	105
1:30	38	2:1	90
1:31	22	2:2	89
3:2	48	2:3	91
9:19	146	2:5–8	91
9:19–23,	59	2:5–11	72, 74
10:1–13	176	2:6–8	145
11:17	92	2:7	145
12:26	89	2:8	67, 77
12:7–11	126	4:5	71, 72
13	88	4:6	148
13:12	20		
16:13	149	## Colossians	
16:16	145	2:2–3	196
16:20	162	2:18	91
		2:20	105

2 Corinthians

		3:8–11	92
1:3	16	3:12	91
4:5	36	23	91
4:17	11, 154		
5:14	105	## 1 Thessalonians	
8:18	3	1:1	158
10:1	71	2:10	139
10:17	22	4:11	83
13:11	89		
13:12	162	## 2 Thessalonians	
13:13	13	1:1	158

Galatians

		3:12	83
2:20	105		
3:13	67, 77	## 1 Timothy	
4–5:15	81	2	87
4:6	36	2:2	83
5:13	145	3:2	125
5:17	64	5:14	92
		6:12	139
## Ephesians		6:17	123
1:3	16		
1:4	40	## 2 Timothy	
3:16–18	200	2:2	139

221

2 Timothy (continued)

2:12	140
2:22	95

Titus

1:8	125

Philemon

14	142

Hebrews

1:2	40
3:1–6	56
4:15	89
5:12	48
9:26	40
12:1	139
12:14	95
12:23	108
13:1	90
13:15	57, 58
13:2	125

James

1:2–4	22
5:3	40
5:20	124

1 Peter

1	43, 175
1:1	4, 66, 173
1:1–2	31, 54
1:2	14, 33, 35, 39, 44, 167, 169, 191, 195
1:2—2:3	43
1:3	9, 10, 20, 22, 31, 32, 44, 53, 80, 114, 170
1:3–5	23, 55, 58
1:3–7	54
1:3–9	16
1:3–21	42
1:4	23, 31, 38, 45, 61, 80, 83, 93, 170, 176
1:5	10, 20, 25, 33, 64, 65
1:6	22, 119, 154, 188
1:6–7	185
1:6–8	31
1:7	22, 33, 41, 65, 128, 129, 144, 170
1:7bb	22
1:9	25, 31, 186
1:10	33, 170
1:10–11	27
1:10–12	10, 11, 25, 27, 29, 31, 46, 51, 59
1:11	10
1:12	28, 33, 43, 92, 170
1:13	8, 10, 33, 43, 65, 149, 170
1:13–20	8
1:11	26, 41, 50, 144, 167
1:14	4, 29, 63, 64, 80
1:15	34, 37, 43, 68, 74, 93
1:15–16	64, 69
1:16	35, 105, 120, 170
1:17	9, 37, 71, 80, 170
1:17–21	36
1:18	4, 37, 117, 170
1:18–19	68, 114, 191
1:19	8, 63, 190, 170, 176
1:20	10
1:20–21	47
1:21	32, 41, 54, 144
1:22	43, 47, 48, 89
1:22—2:3	43
1:22b–2:1	43
1:23	38, 46, 47, 80, 83
1:23–25	43, 55
1:24	35, 47, 50, 63
1:24–25	46, 171, 174
1:25	47, 49
1:25b	47
2	76, 175, 180
2:1	50, 65, 71, 95
2:1–10	175
2:2	43, 48, 63, 80
2:2–3	43
2:3	7, 53, 55, 94, 165, 171
2:4	10, 55, 109, 171
2:4–5	128, 195
2:4–10	155, 192, 193, 195, 197
2:5	8, 9, 10, 35, 43, 53, 54, 63, 64, 109, 147, 171, 179, 193, 196
2:6	35, 54, 58, 171, 175, 176

2:6-8	54, 195	3:2	71
2:7	60, 171	3:3	82
2:8	99, 171	3:4	167
2:8-9	80	3:3-4	172, 82
2:9	8, 10, 36, 54, 57, 64, 74, 80, 93, 117 171, 178, 182, 196, 200	3:5	32, 79, 112
		3:6	4, 8, 85, 93, 172
		3:7	33, 61, 80, 83, 87, 165, 176, 192, 197, 200
2:9-10	4, 13, 44, 60, 62		
2:10	171, 177	3:8	145
2:11	63, 64, 88, 127, 138, 172, 176, 186	3:8-9	74, 94
		3:9	65, 76, 80, 90, 91, 93, 176
2:12	10, 37, 63, 64, 65, 67, 69, 79, 150, 172, 173	3:9-12	95
		3:10a	94
2:13	63, 65, 79, 112	3:10-12	94, 171, 172
2:13-14	67	3:10-17	176
2:13—3:17	73, 85	3:12	97
2:14	63, 65	3:13	97, 98, 172, 184, 185
2:15	67	3:13ff	114
2:16	10, 37, 63, 81, 95, 105, 145	3:13-17	96
2:17	53, 68, 69, 71, 85, 86, 89, 152, 172	3:13-18	94
		3:14	97, 98, 99
2:18	71, 79, 112, 128	3:14-15	172
2:18-25	73, 76, 79, 154	3:15	10, 54, 99, 100, 119, 176
2:19	101	3:16	72, 92, 105, 166
2:19ff	114	3:17	102
2:19-20	33	3:18	54, 104, 105, 112, 113, 114, 167, 172
2:21	10, 11, 28, 75, 93, 105, 130, 165, 166		
		3:18-20	192
2:21-23	93, 131	3:18-22	57, 104
2:21-25	26, 53, 72, 113, 114, 175, 189	3:19	107, 109, 112, 120, 172
		3:20	8, 172
2:22	75, 172	3:21	10, 41, 72
2:23	9, 73, 76, 81, 92, 119, 172	3:21-22	41
2:23a	75	3:22	10, 54, 55, 57, 71, 79, 105, 172, 176
2:23b	75		
2:23c	75	4:1	28, 114, 118, 166
2:24	10, 66, 70, 76, 77, 105, 172, 175	4:1-2	128
		4:1-5	120
2:24a	75	4:2	64, 116, 117
2:24b	75	4:2-3	105, 121
2:24c	75	4:2-4	115
2:24d	75	4:3	116, 117, 118
2:25	9, 53, 172, 167, 176, 198	4:3-4	118
2:25a	75	4:3-42	4
3:1	71, 79, 80, 85, 112	4:4	92, 118, 119, 120, 128
3:1-2	37	4:5	118, 120
3:1-6	74, 80, 87	4:6	93, 107, 120, 121, 167
3:1-7	9, 73, 154, 197	4:7	10, 32, 119, 122, 133

1 Peter (continued)

4:8	90, 173
4:9	125
4:10	22, 33
4:11	127, 147, 156
4:11b	127
4:12	6, 10, 44, 49, 129, 130, 156
4:12–14	28
4:12–19	176
4:13	10, 21, 33, 130, 144
4:13f	144
4:13ff	114
4:13–14	41
4:14	10, 27, 28, 55, 131, 133, 166, 167, 173, 198
4:14–17	192
4:15–16	105
4:16	7, 167, 184
4:17	80, 119, 133, 135, 136, 173, 198
4:17–19	9
4:18	133, 134, 173
4:19	9, 76, 130, 147, 173
5	142
5:1	27, 33, 114, 137, 139, 144, 167
5:1–4	41
5:2	139, 141
5:3	139, 146, 173
5:4	10, 53, 78, 173, 176
5:5	33, 79, 112, 173
5:5–6	139
5:5b–6	146
5:6	8, 49, 148, 149, 174
5:6–7	74
5:7	9, 52, 174
5:8	32, 150, 174
5:9	28, 151, 188
5:10	9, 33, 41, 74, 93, 144, 154, 193
5:11	147
5:12	33, 64
5:12–13	12, 3
5:13	3

2 Peter

1:7	90
2:1	71
2:4	109
2:5	109, 110, 118
2:6	110
3:3	40

1 John

2:9–11	90
2:20	35
5:1–2	90

2 John

13	161

Jude

4	71
6	109
7	110

Revelations

1:6	61
3:3	149
6:10	71
7:9	24
7:12	22
11:3	139
13:8,	40
16:15	149
21–22	191, 195
21:3	194
21:5	20
21:18	194
21:23–25	197

QUMRAN

1 Q174 I,6,	56
1QapGen XIX–XX	84
1QIsaa 40:6–8	174
1QIsab XI	3, 58
1QS 3:6–8	14
1QS VIII	5, 56
1QS VIII 5–8	176
1QS VIII, 7–8, 4Q174, 4Q175	59
4Q174 I, 1–13	55
4QI74 I	7

11Q17 IX,4–5   57

EARLY CHRISTIAN WRITERS

Barnabas
6:2   58
6:4   58

1 Clement
16   175
22:2–8   94

Hermas
2:4   143
9   143
28   143

Irenaeus IV
33:14   179

Justin
Dialogue with Trypho   179

Origen
    179

Tertullian
    179

OTHER ANCIENT WRITERS

Josephus
J.W. 7.8.6   71

Plutarch,
Moralia, 101B (LCL II 99)   64

www.ingramcontent.com/pod-product-compliance
Lightning Source LLC
Chambersburg PA
CBHW070248230426
43664CB00014B/2450